OUTPERFORMING THE MARKETS USING RELATIVE STRENGTH AND BREADTH ANALYSIS

WITH LIVE MARKET DATA, EXAMPLES AND UNIQUE TECHNIQUES

PRASHANT SHAH

INDIA · SINGAPORE · MALAYSIA

Notion Press Media Pvt Ltd

No. 50, Chettiyar Agaram Main Road,
Vanagaram, Chennai, Tamil Nadu – 600 095

First Published by Notion Press 2021
Copyright © Prashant Shah 2021
All Rights Reserved.

ISBN
Paperback 978-1-63997-505-1
Hardcase 978-1-68538-295-7

CONTENTS

Preface and Acknowledgement *15*

1   Strength & Weakness .... .19

2   Outperformance & Underperformance .... .33

3   Ratio chart .... .37

4   Relative Strength Patterns .... .59

5   Ratio Chart Analysis .... .81

6   Relative Strength Indicators 111

7   Noiseless Relative Strength 135

8   Ranking and Trading 209

9   Pair Trading 213

10   Breadth Indicators 233

11   Asset, Sector and Stock Selection 281

12   Trading and Investment 329

Bibliography *353*

LIST OF FIGURES AND IMAGES

Image 1.1:   Person A...19
Image 1.2:   Person B...20
Image 1.3:   Group of strong men...20
Image 1.4:   Group of weak men..21
Figure 1.1:   Nifty daily line chart..22
Image 2.1:   Performance cycle...34
Figure 3.1:   Daily candlestick chart of Nifty (upper panel) and Bank Nifty (lower panel) 37
Figure 3.2:   Nifty and Bank Nifty chart comparison...............................38
Figure 3.3:   Price charts of stock A and B 39
Figure 3.4:   Price charts of stock A and B 39
Image 3.1:   Line chart 41
Image 3.2:   Ratio chart...41
Figure 3.5:   Ratio charts of Stock A and B. 42
Figure 3.6:   Nifty and Bank Nifty daily ratio chart.................................43
Figure 3.7:   Nifty FMCG Index weekly line chart....................................48
Figure 3.8:   Nifty FMCG to Nifty Index weekly ratio chart..........................49
Figure 3.9:   Nifty financial services index weekly line chart........................49
Figure 3.10: Nifty financial services index to Nifty Index weekly ratio chart. 50
Figure 3.11: Nifty Auto index weekly line chart.....................................51
Figure 3.12: Nifty Auto index to Nifty Index weekly ratio chart.....................52
Image 4.1:   Bullish flying pattern..59
Image 4.2:   Bearish drowning pattern..61
Image 4.3:   Bullish lion pattern..62
Image 4.4:   Bearish cat pattern..64
Image 4.5:   Bullish star pattern..65
Image 4.6:   Price chart making a new low, the ratio doesn't make a new low................66
Image 4.7:   Price chart at support, RS chart rising................................66
Figure 4.1:   Nifty IT index weekly line chart.......................................67
Figure 4.2:   Nifty IT index to Nifty 50 weekly ratio chart. 68
Image 4.8:   Bearish star pattern...68
Image 4.9:   Bullish eagle pattern..73
Image 4.10:   Bearish eagle pattern. 74
Figure 5.1:   Daily candlestick chart of Bharti Airtel with ratio chart of Bharti Airtel to
              Nifty 50 index..81
Figure 5.2:   Daily candlestick chart of DIVIS LAB with ratio chart of DIVIS LAB to Nifty 50
              index...82

Figure 5.3:   Daily candlestick chart of Bharti Airtel with ratio chart of Bharti Airtel to
               Nifty 50 index..83

Figure 5.4:   Daily candlestick chart of AMARAJABAT with 40-period moving average
               and ratio chart of AMARAJABAT to Nifty 50 index. 84

Figure 5.5:   Daily ratio chart of Bank Nifty to Nifty 50 index...................................85

Image 5.1:   Consolidation and triangle breakout...86

Figure 5.6:   Daily ratio chart of GRASIM to Nifty 50 index......................................87

Image 5.2:   Strong trend, retracement and follow-through breakout. 88

Figure 5.7:   Daily ratio chart of M&M to Nifty 50 index..88

Figure 5.8:   Daily ratio chart of Nifty Pharma to Nifty 50 index....................................90

Figure 5.9:   Daily ratio chart of JSWSTEEL to Nifty 50 index...................................92

Image 5.3:   Hypothetical prices of 10 candles..93

Figure 5.10:   Daily candlestick chart of Nifty with 20-period AMA and 20-period
               Efficiency Ratio Indicator. 94

Image 5.4:   Chart explaining Adaptive Moving Average calculation. 95

Figure 5.11:   Daily candlestick chart of Nifty with 20-period AMA...............................95

Figure 5.11:   Daily Ratio chart of Nifty Pharma to Nifty 50 with 40-period AMA indicator.......96

Figure 5.12:   Daily ratio chart of DABUR to Nifty 50 with 40-period AMA indicator.............97

Figure 5.13:   Daily ratio chart of Nifty PSU BANK to Nifty 50 with 200-period AMMA indicator.....98

Image 5.5:   Donchian channel new high and new low is marked. 99

Image 5.6:   Donchian channel band behaviour. 99

Figure 5.14:   Daily candlestick chart with the Donchian channel indicator.................... 100

Image 5.7:   Calculation of Donchian channel middle band. 100

Figure 5.15:   Daily candlestick chart showing Bollinger band indicator bullish and
               bearish zones... 101

Image 5.8:   Narrow range and wide range.. 101

Figure 5.16:   Daily candlestick chart showing narrow and wide Bollinger bands............. 102

Figure 5.17:   Daily ratio chart of Britannia to Nifty 50 with 40-period Donchian Channel 102

Image 5.9:   Bullish and bearish closing price... 103

Image 5.10:   Bullish and bearish closing prices.. 104

Image 5.11:   Bullish and bearish prices over the last 10 sessions. 104

Image 5.12:   Green and Red team members. 105

Figure 5.18:   Daily ratio chart of Nifty 500 to Nifty 50 with RSI indicator. 106

Image 5.13:   RSI Positive divergence from the oversold zone and negative divergence
               from the overbought zone. 107

Figure 5.19:   Daily ratio chart of TATASTEEL to Nifty 50 with 20-period RSI indicator. 107

Figure 5.20:   Daily ratio chart of Nifty Mid & Small Cap 400 Index to Nifty 50 index with
               40-period RSI indicator.. 108

Figure 6.1:   Daily candlestick chart of Nifty 500 with 50-period relative strength
               indicator to Nifty 50 index.................................... 112

Figure 6.2:   Daily Candlestick chart of JUBLFOOD with 20-period moving average and
               50-period relative strength indicator to Nifty 50 index........................ 113

Figure 6.3:   Daily candlestick chart of HINDUNILVR with a 20-period moving average
               and a 50-period relative strength indicator to Nifty 50 index................... 114

Figure 6.4:   Daily candlestick chart of MARUTI with 50-period moving average and
               50-period relative strength indicator to Nifty 50 index........................ 115

Figure 6.5:   Daily candlestick chart of AMBUJACEM with 50-period moving average and 50-period relative strength indicator to Nifty 50 index. 115

Figure 6.6:   Daily candlestick chart of ADANI PORTS with 20-period moving average and 120-period relative strength indicator to Nifty 50 index. 116

Figure 6.7:   Daily candlestick chart of Nifty 50 with 20-period moving average. 117

Figure 6.8:   Daily candlestick chart of MARUTI with 20-period moving average and relative strength indicator to Nifty 50 index from February 14, 2020.. 118

Figure 6.9:   Daily candlestick chart of BAJAJFINSV with 200-period moving average, 14-period RSI and 240-period relative strength indicator to Nifty 50 index. 119

Figure 6.10:   Daily candlestick chart of LT with 50-period moving average and 50-period relative strength indicator and ratio chart to Nifty 50 index. 120

Figure 6.11:   Daily candlestick chart of SRF and 50-period relative strength–AV indicator to Nifty 50 index. 123

Figure 6.12:   Daily candlestick chart of DABUR with 50-period relative strength and RS–AV indicator to Nifty 50 index.. 124

Figure 6.13:   Daily candlestick chart of BAJAJFINSV with 120-period relative strength and RS – AV indicator to Nifty 50 index.. 125

Figure 6.14:   Ratio chart comparison of Bank, Pharma, Metal, Auto and FMCG sectors versus Nifty 50 index from January 1, 2020, to December 2020. 127

Figure 6.15:   Daily ratio chart of ADANIENT to Nifty plotted with 50-period RS–Alpha and ratio rank indicator.. 129

Image 6.1:   Cap and shoebox. 130

Image 6.2:   Large D-Cap on a bullish candle. 130

Image 6.3:   Small D-Cap on a bullish candle. 131

Image 6.4:   Large D-Shoe on a bullish candle. 131

Image 6.5:   D-Cap and shoe on a bearish candle. 131

Figure 6.16:   Daily candlestick chart of Tata Steel plotted with 50-day moving average and D-Cap shoe indicator. 132

Figure 6.17:   Daily candlestick chart of GRASIM with D Cap-Shoe indicator. 133

Figure 6.18:   Daily candlestick chart of JSWSTEEL along with the RSI indicator calculated on the ratio chart of JSWSTEEL to Nifty 50 134

Image 7.1:   Boxes are drawn on the line chart connecting the price with the previous price. . . . 135

Image 7.2:   Fixed-size boxes on a line chart. 136

Image 7.3:   Line chart 137

Image 7.4:   Line chart divided in fixed-size 10-point box. 138

Image 7.5:   10 boxes of 10 points each. 138

Image 7.6:   Boxes brought to a single column. 139

Image 7.7:   'X' replaced boxes and price index at the left. 139

Image 7.8:   Vertical plotting.. 140

Image 7.9:   Column of 'X' and 'O'.. 140

Image 7.10:   Column of 'X' represents a bullish trend and column of 'O' represents a bearish trend. 141

Image 7.11:   3-box reversal column turning to 'O'. 142

Image 7.12:   3-box reversal column turning to 'X'.. 142

Image 7.13:   Column reversal 145

Figure 7.1:   Bank Nifty divided by Nifty daily ratio chart plotted in the P&F format 145

Image 7.14:   Double-top buy... 146
Image 7.15:   Double-bottom sell... 147
Figure 7.2:   Daily 0.25% x 3 Nifty Bank to Nifty P&F RS chart............................. 148
Image 7.16:   Bullish breakout and retracement... 149
Image 7.17:   Bearish breakout... 149
Image 7.18:   Bearish breakout & retracement... 150
Image 7.19:   Bullish breakout... 150
Image 7.20:   Anchor column.. 152
Image 7.21:   Bullish anchor column follow-through in next column of 'X'.................. 153
Image 7.22:   Bullish anchor column follow-through....................................... 154
Figure 7.3:   ASHOKLEY to Nifty 50 Daily 1% x 3 P&F RS chart.............................. 155
Image 7.23:   Bearish anchor column follow-through in next column of 'O'.................. 156
Image 7.24:   Bearish anchor column follow-through....................................... 157
Figure 7.4:   PEL to Nifty 50 Daily P&F RS chart... 158
Image 7.25:   Three-column triangle.. 159
Image 7.26:   Four-column triangle... 159
Image 7.27:   Three-column triangle breakout... 160
Image 7.28:   Four-column triangle breakout.. 160
Figure 7.5:   Nifty Bank to Nifty 50 Daily 0.25% x 3 P&F RS chart........................ 161
Figure 7.6:   GAIL to Nifty 50 Daily P&F RS chart.. 162
Image 7.29:   Breakout... 162
Image 7.30:   Bullish 20-day breakout & 10-day breakout.................................. 163
Image 7.31:   55-day bullish breakout and 20-day bearish breakout........................ 164
Image 7.32:   True range... 165
Image 7.33:   5-X turtle breakout.. 166
Figure 7.7:   Daily ASTRAL to Nifty 500 1% x 3 P&F RS chart.............................. 167
Figure 7.8:   Daily 0.25% x 3 Nifty Realty index to Nifty 50 P&F RS chart................ 168
Image 7.34:   Support at the previous base... 169
Image 7.35:   Bottom of 'O' at the same level.. 169
Image 7.36:   Bullish support patterns... 170
Image 7.37:   Bullish P&F support patterns... 170
Image 7.38:   Column reversal after support pattern...................................... 171
Image 7.39:   Bullish column reversal after support patterns............................. 172
Image 7.40:   Bearish column reversal after resistance patterns.......................... 172
Figure 7.9:   Daily 1% x 3 P&F RS chart of Nifty FMCG index to Nifty 50.................. 173
Figure 7.10: Daily 0.25% x 3 P&F RS chart of Nifty Financial Services index to Nifty 50. 174
Figure 7.11: 0.25% x 3 Daily P&F chart of Nifty Metal index to Nifty 50.................. 176
Figure 7.12: Daily 0.25% x 3 daily P&F RS chart of LT to Nifty 50....................... 177
Figure 7.13: Nifty Media index to Nifty 50 daily 2% x 3 P&F chart....................... 178
Figure 7.14: 0.25% x 3 daily P&F RS chart of Nifty IT Index to Nifty 50................. 179
Figure 7.15: Daily 0.25% x 3 Nifty Auto to Nifty 50 P&F RS chart with PMOX indicator.... 181
Figure 7.16: Daily 0.25% x 3 Nifty FMCG sector chart versus Nifty 50 P&F RS chart along
              with PMOX indicator.. 182
Image 7.41:   Bullish impulse and corrective... 184
Image 7.42:   Bearish impulse and corrective... 184

Image 7.43:   Bullish breakout. 185
Image 7.44:   Bearish breakout. 185
Image 7.45:   Bullish retracement. 186
Image 7.46:   Bearish retracement. 186
Image 7.47:   Consolidation. 186
Image 7.48:   Bullish breakout. 187
Image 7.49:   Bearish breakout. 187
Image 7.50:   Bullish retracement. 188
Image 7.51:   Bearish retracement. 188
Image 7.52:   Consolidation 189
Image 7.53:   P&F Matrix performance score calculation. 190
Image 7.54:   P&F Matrix ranking score calculation. 190
Image 7.55:   Ranking score of the bullish column. 191
Image 7.56:   Ranking score of bullish columns on different box values. 192
Image 7.57:   Ranking score of bullish columns on different box values. 193
Image 7.58:   Ratio and price bullish divergence 197
Figure 7.17:   Daily 1% x 3 P&F UBL price chart and RS chart compared to Nifty 50 index. 198
Figure 7.18:   Daily 1% x 3 BALKRISHIND P&F price chart and RS chart compared to Nifty
              50 index. 199
Image 7.59:   Bullish breakout. 200
Image 7.60:   Bullish retracement: Scenario A. 200
Image 7.61:   Bearish breakout: Scenario B. 200
Figure 7.19:   Adani Enterprises daily 3% x 3 P&F chart. 201
Figure 7.20:   Adani enterprise daily 3% x 3 P&F price chart and RS chart compared to
              Nifty 50 index. 202
Image 8.1:   Buy top slot, Sell bottom slot - Continuation. 210
Image 8.2:   Sell top slot, buy bottom slot - Reversal. 211
Image 8.3:   Trading moderate score stocks. 212
Figure 9.1:   Daily ratio chart of Nifty bank to Nifty 50 along with the 40-period simple
              moving average line. 214
Figure 9.2:   Daily 0.25% x 3 P&F RS chart of DR REDDY / SUN PHARMA with 10-column
              moving average. 218
Figure 9.3:   Daily 0.25% x 3 P&F RS chart of DR REDDY / SUN PHARMA with 10-column
              moving average. 219
Image 9.1:   Reversal pair trading on the ratio chart. 220
Image 9.2:   Average height of a group of people. 221
Image 9.2:   10 cm deviation from average height of a group of people. 221
Image 9.3:   Calculation of Upper, Middle and Lower band. 222
Figure 9.4:   Nifty 50 Daily candlestick chart with 20,2 Bollinger bands. 222
Image 9.4:   Trend of bands. 223
Image 9.5:   Gap between bands. 223
Figure 9.5:   Nifty 50 daily candlestick chart with 20, 2 Bollinger bands showing the
              pattern of Walking the Bands. 224
Figure 9.6:   Nifty 50 daily candlestick chart with 20, 2 Bollinger bands showing the
              pattern of Walking the Bands. 224

Figure 9.7:   Nifty 50 daily candlestick chart with 20, 2 Bollinger bands showing the
               reverse expansion pattern.. 225
Figure 9.8:   INFY to TCS Daily ratio chart with 20,2 Bollinger bands. 226
Figure 9.9:   AXISBANK to ICICIBANK Daily ratio chart with 20.2 Bollinger bands. 227
Image 9.6:   Z-score between 2 and -2 228
Figure 9.10:   Daily ratio chart of Nifty bank to Nifty plotted with 20-period Z-Score........... 228
Figure 9.11:   Daily ratio chart of BANK BARODA to CANBK with 20-period Z-Score indicator. 229
Figure 9.12:   Daily 1% x 3 P&F RS chart of Maruti to Tata Motors. 230
Figure 10.1:   Percentage of stocks trading above their 200-day moving average in the
               Nifty 50 index.. 235
Figure 10.2:   Daily candlestick chart of Nifty along with 50-day moving average breadth
               indicator.. 236
Figure 10.3:   200-day moving average breadth indicator on the Nifty 500 group. 238
Figure 10.4:   A 200-day moving average breadth indicator of Nifty 500 index average
               plotted below Nifty 50 index daily candlestick chart............................. 239
Figure 10.5:   Daily candlestick chart of Nifty plotted along with 20-period moving
               average breadth indicator... 240
Figure 10.6:   Nifty daily candlestick chart with advance-decline breadth indicator on
               Nifty 500 index. 241
Figure 10.7:   Breadth indicator that calculates the number of stocks trading above their
               5% ATR in the Nifty 500 index. 243
Figure 10.8:   Nifty daily candlestick chart along with 14-period ATR 5% breadth
               indicator on Nifty 500 Universe... 244
Figure 10.9:   Nifty 50 daily candlestick chart along with a 14-period ATR 5% breadth
               indicator on Nifty 500 Universe... 245
Figure 10.10: Daily candlestick chart of Nifty 50 along with 14-period RSI breadth for
               mid-level. 246
Figure 10.11: Nifty 50 candlestick chart along with the 50-period moving average. The
               breadth indicator displayed in the lower pane is the 52-week high low
               breadth indicator of the Nifty 500 index. 247
Figure 10.12: Siemens daily candlestick chart with 250-period high-low momentum
               index with 10 percent band. 249
Figure 10.13: Nifty daily candlestick chart with the percentage of stocks in a bullish zone
               using the 120-period high-low momentum index breadth indicator. 250
Figure 10.14: Nifty daily candlestick chart along with HLMI breadth indicator................. 250
Figure 10.16: Daily candlestick chart of Nifty with 1% bullish percent indicator. 256
Figure 10.17: Daily candlestick chart of Nifty plotted with 1% x 3 X-percent breadth
               indicator. 257
Figure 10.18: Daily candlestick chart of Nifty 50 index along with 1% x 3 X-percent
               breadth indicator on Nifty 500 universe... 258
Figure 10.19: Nifty 50 candlestick chart along with 1% x 3 DT% breadth indicator on
               Nifty 500 index... 259
Image 10.1:   Beamer pattern... 260
Figure 10.20: Nifty 50 daily candlestick chart along with 1% x 3 DT% breadth indicator
               on Nifty 500 index. 261
Figure 10.21: Nifty 50 daily candlestick chart along with 1% x 3 DT% breadth indicator
               on Nifty 500 index. 261

Figure 10.22: Daily candlestick chart of FMCG along with 0.25% X-Anchor column% breadth indicator. 262

Figure 10.23: Daily candlestick chart of mid-cap 50 index along with 0.25% O-anchor column% breadth indicator. 263

Image 10.2: Breadth indicator zones. 264

Image 10.3: Breadth overbought and oversold zone. 265

Image 10.4: Breadth bullish and bearish momentum zone. 266

Image 10.5: Breadth yellow zone. 267

Figure 10.24: Nifty 50 1% x 3 X-percent breadth indicator. 267

Figure 10.25: Daily candlestick chart of Nifty along with 0.25% x 3 DT% breadth indicator on all sectors of NSE. 270

Figure 10.26: Daily candlestick chart of Nifty along with 0.25% DT% breadth indicator on all sectors of NSE. 270

Image 10.6: Breadth bar chart. 272

Figure 10.27: Daily Nifty 50 candlestick chart with 50-day moving average breadth indicator on Nifty 500 index. 279

Figure 11.1: Daily 0.25% x 3 P&F RS chart of Nifty to Dow Jones Industrial Average. 284

Figure 11.2: Nifty daily line chart along with the 50-period moving average. 285

Figure 11.3: Daily Ratio chart of Gold to Nifty 50 along with the 50-period moving average. 285

Figure 11.4: Daily ratio chart of Nifty GS Composite to Nifty along with the 50-period moving average. 286

Figure 11.5: Daily Ratio chart of USDINR to Nifty along with 50-period Moving average. 287

Figure 11.6: Nifty performance chart with other asset classes. 288

Figure 11.7: Daily 0.10% x 3 P&F chart of Nifty along with 10-column moving average and a 20-column XO zone. 288

Figure 11.8: Daily 0.10% x 3 P&F chart of Nifty GS Composite to Nifty along with a 10-column moving average and a 20-column XO zone indicator. 289

Figure 11.9: daily 0.10% x 3 P&F chart of Nifty USDINR to Nifty along with a 10-column moving average and a 20-column XO zone indicator. 290

Figure 11.10: Daily 0.10% x 3 P&F chart of USDINR to Nifty along with a 10-column AMA and a 20-column XO zone. 290

Figure 11.11: Daily 0.10% x 3 P&F chart of Gold to Nifty along with 10-column moving average and 20-column XO zone indicator. 291

Figure 11.12: Daily 1% x 3 P&F chart of Nifty GS Composite to Nifty along with 10-column moving average and a 10-column XO zone indicator. 292

Figure 11.13: Daily 0.25% x 3 P&F chart of GOLD along with 10-column AMMA indicator. 293

Image 11.1: RS switch. 294

Figure 11.14: Nifty 500 to Nifty 50 0.15% x 3 daily P&F RS chart. 295

Figure 11.15: Nifty mid and small cp 400 index to Nifty 50 index 0.15% x 3 daily P&F RS chart. 296

Image 11.2: Screenshot of the tweet 298

Figure 11.16: Nifty Metal Index to Nifty 50 Daily Ratio chart plotted with 200-day moving average. 304

Figure 11.17: Tata Steel to Nifty metal index daily ratio chart plotted with a 200-day moving average. 304

Image 11.3: Top-down approach 305

Image 11.4:   Top-down approach flow chart. 306
Image 11.5:   Outperformer of outperformer. 307
Image 11.6:   Swing breakout pattern and stop-loss at swing low. 308
Image 11.7:   Stop-loss calculation for double top buy pattern. 309
Image 11.8:   Stop-loss of double top buy gets triggered. 309
Figure 11.18: Daily 0.25% x 3 P&F RS chart of Nifty IT index to Nifty 50 index along with
              10-column moving average and 10,3 PMOX indicator. 312
Image 11.9:   Correction at A, reversal at B 314
Image 11.10: Corrections during a strong trend. 314
Figure 11.19: Daily ratio chart of Nifty IT Index to Nifty 50 along with 100- period AMA. 315
Figure 11.20: Daily ratio chart of Nifty Pharma index to Nifty 50 along with 100- period
              AMA. 316
Figure 11.21: Daily candlestick chart of Nifty Metal index with High-Low Momentum index. . . . 319
Figure 11.22: SAIL to Nifty 50 index daily ratio chart plotted along with a 50-day average
              line and a 20-day RSI line. 319
Figure 11.23: SAIL to Nifty 50 index daily ratio chart plotted along with a 50-day average
              line and a 20-day RSI line. 320
Figure 11.24: Daily 0.25% x 3 Point & Figure chart of SAIL during this period. 321
Figure 11.25: Nifty Alpha 50 / Nifty daily ratio chart with a 100-period AMA. 325
Image 11.11: D-Sectors calculation. 326
Image 11.12: D-Sectors report. 327
Figure 12.1:   Daily ratio chart of the NAV of ICICI Pru Technology Fund (G) divided by the
              Nifty index. 337
Figure 12.2:   Daily HDFC mid-cap opportunities fun (G) to Nifty Index 0.25% x 3 P&F
              chart with the 20-column moving average and a 20-period XO zone. 338
Image 12.1:   Options strategy pay-off chart. 345
Figure 12.3:   15700 CE divided by 15700 PE on a five-minute timeframe plotted with a
              200-period moving average. 345
Figure 12.5:   1% x 3 P&F RS chart of 15500 CE divided by 15500 PE on a one-minute
              timeframe plotted with a 10-column moving average. 346
Figure 12.6:   TOI chart of multiple-strike prices from 15700 CE and PE plotted in a
              15-minute timeframe. 347

LIST OF TABLES

Table 1.1:   Nifty Trend and Leaders. 23
Table 1.2:   Market and Stock trend–Bullish. 25
Table 1.3:   Market and Stock trend – Bearish. 25
Table 1.4:   NSE equity segment year-wise data showing the percentage of
              outperforming stocks. 27
Table 1.5:   NSE equity segment year-wise data showing the percentage of
              outperformers from top 100 stocks. 28
Table 1.6:   NSE equity segment year-wise data showing the percentage of
              outperformers from the bottom 100 underperforming stocks. 29
Table 2.1:   Market trend and Stock trend. 34
Table 2.2:   Market trend, stock trend and outperformance. 35
Table 2.3:   Market trend, stock trend and underperformance. .35
Table 2.4:   Relative strength and net return. 36
Table 3.1:   Stock A and B price 38
Table 3.2:   Ratio of Stock A and Stock B prices shown in Table 3.1.1. 40
Table 3.3:   Index (Denominator), Stock (Numerator) and Ratio trend. 44
Table 3.4:   Denominator, Numerator, Ratio Trend and Pattern. .45
Table 3.5:   Denominator and ratio trend. 46
Table 3.6:   Numerator Price trend, Ratio trend and Performance remark. 47
Table 3.7:   Nifty Trend and Leaders. 53
Table 4.1:   Table showing multi-timeframe relative strength pattern analysis. 76
Table 4.2:   Ratio trend matrix showing relative strength pattern analysis for IT index
              stocks over 10 sessions 78
Table 6.1:   Example of list of top-performing stocks based on relative strength
              indicator of stocks compared to 50-period Nifty 500 index. 121
Table 6.2:   Example of list of stocks in Auto sector RS–AV value with denominator as
              Nifty Auto. 126
Table 6.3:   Example of list of PSE Index stocks with the denominator as the PSE Index
              over the last 120-period. 128
Table 7.1:   P&F Performance and the ranking score of Pharma index on four different
              box-values. 194
Table 7.2:   Relative strength performance and the ranking score of Pharma index
              stocks versus Nifty 50 index on four different box-values. 194
Table 7.3:   P&F Fusion matrix table showing price and relative strength performance
              and ranking score on four different box-values of Bank Index stocks versus
              Nifty 50 index. 195
Table 7.4:   Group Matrix table 203

Table 7.5:   Group matrix table with more information 204

Table 7.6:   Ultimate matrix table of six major indices...................................... 205

Table 7.7:   Ultimate matrix table of bank sector 205

Table 7.8:   Multi-timeframe ultimate matrix table of the banking sector.................. 206

Table 10.1:   High-low momentum index breadth numbers on different sectors. 252

Table 10.2:   High-low momentum breadth index on all major averages..................... 253

Table 10.3:   Price and open interest analysis.. 254

Table 10.4:   All P&F breadth indicators of all sectors 273

Table 10.5:   All P&F breadth indicators of all major NSE indices. 274

Table 10.6:   BRS principles 277

Table 11.1:   BRS principles 317

Table 12.1:   Pharma sector multi-timeframe ultimate matrix............................... 339

PREFACE AND ACKNOWLEDGEMENT

I had little idea that I would write my third book so soon. I have been actively using relative strength, breadth and sentiment analysis in my trading for several years. Though I wrote a chapter on these topics in my earlier books, I always felt that not much is written about these important aspects of market analysis. I wanted to write on these subjects from a basic level and am happy that I finally found time to pen my thoughts.

When the second Covid-19 induced lockdown was announced in India in March 2021, the situation was terrible. I decided to divert my attention and focus on something productive and positive. Sharing knowledge and experience with people is always a satisfying experience. It feels great when people share their work and the trading systems they have developed based on my earlier books. I initially had thoughts of writing a series of blog posts on the subject, but I realized that it would not do justice to the subject and it deserved a dedicated book. I gathered my notes and observations, cut down my time on everything else and focused on this book.

I have tried to cover all important aspects relating to the subject in this book. I have discussed the tools and the ways to use them. I strongly feel it is important to explain logic and concepts so that people can develop a better understanding of the subject and develop their own systems. They might implement the knowledge in a much better way and make better use of it. Focus on the principles and design a strategy that suits your requirements. I have tried to explain the concepts in an uncomplicated manner with lots of recent and real-time examples.

I have logically explained everything that I practised and learnt over the years. I urge you to read the book from the beginning and not skip chapters as the book is organised in a sequential flow. The book is a journey and both of us are together in it. I intend that you develop a better understanding of the markets by reading the book. I will consider all efforts of writing this book to be worthwhile if you have even a single takeaway from this book.

I first read about the subject of relative strength analysis in 2009 when I read Charles Kirkpatrick's work. I instantly fell in love with the subject and started exploring it. I read about ratio analysis and inter-market relationships from John J. Murphy's book titled *Intermarket Analysis: Profiting from Global Market Relationships.* Martin Pring explained the relationship between asset classes in his books. I happened to come across noiseless charts around the same time. I am a great fan of Jeremy Du Plessis and Thomas Dorsey and learnt a lot about Point & Figure from their works. Thomas Dorsey developed a method of scoring and ranking. William O' Neil has done wonderful work in this field. He has developed a propriety method of ranking the stocks based on relative strength performance. Mark Minirveni also talked about William O'Neil's ranking method and relative strength indicator to pick stocks in his wonderful books. Steve Nison talked about various charting methods in his book *Beyond Candlesticks: New Japanese Charting Techniques Revealed.*

All these people and many others whom I have studied had a great impact on my thought process and understanding of the market. I can't thank them enough for their wonderful contribution to this field.

The book would not be possible without the support of the Definedge team. They implemented my ideas and supported me in countless hours of research and testing. It was not possible to develop concepts explained in the book without their support. Sincere thanks to Rajesh Badiye, Nagin Kothari, Krishna Khanna, Raghunath Reddy, Nitin Gajbhiye and the team members who played a very important role to make it possible. My colleagues and dear friends Abhijit Phatak, Raju Ranjan, Vitthal Shinde, Vinay Shah and B. Krishnakumar who helped me in continuous brainstorming and discussion about trading and analysis that helped tremendously while writing the book. Special thanks to B. Krishnakumar who helped me with the editing process and corrected my mistakes. It was impossible to complete this work without his help and support.

All charts in this book are from TradePoint software by Definedge. Though I am a founder member of the company, the software and company are a result of the unwavering hard work of many. It is because of them that this book has become a reality today.

Thanks to my family who supported me as always. Many thanks to my precious wife and best friend, Isha for the encouragement and support she has given me. I have been fortunate to have such a companion as her.

Thanks to Mr. Biren Patel who taught me what Open-High-Low-Close was and sent me to my first ever training seminar in 2005.

Thanks to the CMT Association and International Federation of Technical Analysts (IFTA), through which I was introduced to the best of the works in the field of technical analysis. They have greatly contributed to my knowledge of trading and analysis.

My sincere thanks to all Definedge subscribers for their continued trust and support. It is because of them that we could invest more in products and research, and I can contribute more through books and software.

The list is endless. Credit for anything that you learn from this book goes to them. What you do not like is my weakness.

– Prashant Shah

Chapter 1

STRENGTH & WEAKNESS

．．

We often use the words strength and weakness in markets about stocks and instruments. We often say that a particular stock or instrument is strong. This typically indicates that the behaviour of the instrument is more bullish. There are numerous tools to arrive at this conclusion, including the simple screen or tape reading.

I believe that knowingly or unknowingly, every trader or investor performs relative strength analysis. Just that a few of them are not doing it structurally or methodologically, and they probably do not even realize that they are doing it.

During my initial years in trading, I used to spend a lot of time on screen reading or tap reading and made several observations, but I did not have an idea about relative strength analysis back then. Eventually, I could connect some dots. There are many aspects to relative strength analysis. Let us understand the subject from the basics.

Strength

Take a look at the picture below. It represents a physically strong man.

A

Image 1.1: Person A

Now, take a look at the man below. He seems weak.

Image 1.2: Person B

We can simply state that these men are strong and weak without comparing them with anyone else.

Relative Strength

Take a look at the picture below. The man in Picture A is part of the group.

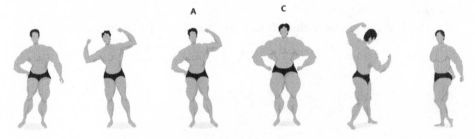

Image 1.3: Group of strong men

Person C in the above picture is the strongest. A is also strong, but C is relatively stronger.

Take a look at the picture given below.

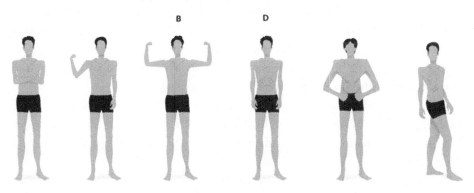

Image 1.4: Group of weak men

Person D is weaker than the others in the group including Mr. B. He is relatively weak.

Individual strengths and weaknesses matter, but when we analyze them in a group of people, we can identify who is relatively stronger and weaker. When we say strong, it is about individual strength. When we say, relatively strong, it means stronger than the others.

Now, let us extend this concept to the various stocks and sectors in the equity market.

A stock that has appreciated sharply can be considered a strong stock. Similarly, a stock falling steadily may be considered a weak stock. We can analyze the strength or weakness using the price action or any other tool. When we compare the performance of a stock with other stocks, we get to know about the relative strength and weaknesses.

Many people get confused with the relative strength (RS) and RSI (Relative Strength Index) indicators. But both are different concepts.

Relative strength is a method of identifying stocks or instruments that are relatively strong or weak while RSI is a popularly used momentum indicator.

When we discuss relative strength, the most relevant question is, relatively strong or weak when compared to what?

Let us consider the example of a group of people. For example, if the criterion for determining strength is the height of the person, then we need not necessarily look at the tallest guy; we need to look at the height of the people relative to a benchmark. We calculate the average height of the people in the group and people above the average height may be classified as relatively tall.

In the context of the stock market, the average number or the benchmark could be a stock index. We can compare the performance or returns of an instrument with a broader market index. If a stock has performed better than the market index, it is considered relatively strong or an outperformer. Bigger the outperformance, the better it is. If the stock has performed worse than the market index, it is considered relatively weak or an underperformer.

Broader market index in the Indian market context could be National Stock Exchange's Nifty 50 index or the Bombay Stock Exchange's BSE Sensex index. We can also compare the performance of a stock with sector indices or other stocks, but we shall discuss that later.

The goal of every investor would be to invest in stocks that can outperform the benchmark index. The primary purpose of trading or investment should be that. Otherwise, we will be better off investing in index ETFs.

Take a look at the historical price chart of the Nifty Index from 2003 to 2020.

Figure 1.1: Nifty daily line chart

The Nifty appreciated 6x between April 2003 to January 2008. Subsequently, there was a strong correction of about 65% in the Nifty 50 index during the 2008 global subprime correction. After forming a low in October 2008, the Nifty 50 index appreciated by about 181% by November 2010.

It corrected by about 28% from November 2010 to December 2011. Subsequently, the Index doubled from the low recorded in December 2011 to the peak of March 2015. There was a 17% correction in the index between March 2015 and February 2016, followed by a strong rally of 64% between 2016 and January 2020. The slide of about 40% in the first quarter of the calendar year

2020 was sharp but short-lived. This was followed by an impressive gain of about 105% till March 2021.

Take a look at box A in the above chart when the Index was confined to a range during the four-year period lasting from 2010 to 2014. The Nifty 50 Index was flat during these four years, representing a time correction and consolidation. As against that, the price action in circle B in the above chart represents a sharp and deep correction followed by a strong bounce.

A 40% fall in the index happened in a couple of months and was followed by a 100% rise in less than a year. They were strong trends accompanied by momentum. In contrast, the bear and bull trend in box-A were less volatile compared to the price action in circle B. So, there are strong and weak trends, and there are more volatile and less volatile phases in the markets.

There are different phases such as a strong uptrend, downtrend, slow or gradual trends and horizontal phase in the above chart. But some stocks and sectors outshine others during each of these phases. There are always unique flavours or favourites of the market in every phase. There were periods when markets fell or went sideways but that does not mean that no stock or sector was going up during that period. There will invariably be better performers in every phase.

Take a look at the table given below.

Table 1.1: Nifty Trend and Leaders

Period	Trend	Leaders
2003 - 2008	Bull	Nifty 500, Bank, IT, R-Group
2008	Bear	Bank, IT
2008 - 2010	Bull	Bank, IT, Midcap
2010 - 2011	Bear	FMCG, Pharma, Auto, IT
2011 - 2015	Bull	Pharma, Auto, Bank, IT, FMCG, Media
2015 - 2016	Bear	Consumption, Energy
2016 - 2020	Bull	Realty, Banks & Fin services, Small & Midcap
2020	Bear	Pharma, FMCG, IT
2020 - 2021	Bull	Metal, Small & Midcaps, Auto, IT, Pharma

Table 1.1 shows the leaders of each leg. Mid-cap, small-cap, Reliance group stocks, Banks and IT index did well during the 2003–2008 rally. Banks and IT fared relatively better in the fall of 2008. Banks, IT and mid-caps were the top performers during the bounce from 2008 lows to 2010 high. It was the turn of FMCG, Pharma, Auto and IT sectors to do well in the fall and consolidation

between 2010–2011. Pharma, Auto, Bank, IT, FMCG and Media stocks lead the bull market that lasted between 2011 to 2015.

The Consumption and Energy sector performed well during the fall of 2015–2016. Realty, Bank, financial services, small-cap and mid-cap stocks did well during the rally that lasted between 2016 to 2020. Pharma, FMCG, and IT did relatively better during the Covid-led fall in 2020. Metal, Auto, Pharma and small-mid-cap stocks did well in the rally till March 2021.

Our portfolio will outperform if we can identify the flavour and theme of the market.

We will come back to this table again.

Let us discuss what we mean when we say a stock is relatively strong against the market.

There are two major takeaways here:
1. There are always outperformers, no matter what the trend of the market is.
2. The market leaders change in every phase.

The first point is the good news because if we know that there will be outliers, we must develop a technique to identify them for better trading and investment opportunities. Similarly, in a bearish trend, there will always be a bunch of underperformers that will fall more than the index.

The second point is the key reason why markets may recover but portfolios may not. Investors buy the strong stocks of the previous rally and keep holding them. Other stocks having better businesses, viable ideas and favourable trends may lead the markets in the next leg of the rally. Investors often think that the stocks that performed well in the recent cycle will continue to do so and hold them. But times change, and the market typically resumes the uptrend with new leaders. Hence, the market may go up, but individual portfolios can underperform.

The bottom line is that developing a technique to identify outperformers and underperformers can help us in both, trading, and investment. There are many methods of analysing prices and developing trading systems. But the key aspects in the business of trading is the stock selection and a clear understanding of the market phase. The stocks that we select to trade, if identified using the relative strength concept, will be extremely rewarding as we would be focusing on outliers.

When we talk about relative strength, the initial assumption is that a stock is considered strong if it rises when the market is also rising. But that is not the right approach. When a stock performs better than the market or benchmark index, only then will it be considered relatively strong.

In the following instances, we can conclude that a stock is doing better than the market:

Table 1.2: Market and Stock trend–Bullish

Market trend	Stock trend
Up	Up, more than the market
Down	Up
Down	Flat
Down	Less Down
Flat	Up

On all the above occasions, the stock performed better than the market. A simple word to define this is "outperformance". So, in all the above instances, the stock outperformed the market but remember not on all occasions did the stock move up.

Similarly, it is also possible that a stock was bullish, but it did not outperform. This happens if the returns generated by the stock is lesser than the market returns. This means that other stocks in the market were more bullish and propelled the index higher.

In the previous table, we discussed the various scenarios of outperformance. The logic would be flipped upside down to determine relative weakness. Take a look at the table below.

Table 1.3: Market and Stock trend – Bearish

Market trend	Stock trend
Down	More Down
Up	Down
Up	Flat
Up	Less Down
Flat	Down

In a nutshell, when a stock is outperforming the market it can be called a relatively strong candidate and when it is underperforming the market, it is a relatively weak candidate.

The basic principle of relative strength analysis is that we should invest in outperformers and get rid of the underperformers.

Now, the question is, in what time frame is this relative strength study valid and relevant? The simple answer is that the concept is applicable and relevant in all timeframes including intra-day, daily, weekly, monthly, and yearly. We will discuss this in detail later.

Let us make a beginning with a simple concept.

We shall check the performance of any instrument in a yearly timeframe. Fifty-two weeks is a popular parameter and market participants look for a 52-week high or a 52-week low to identifying breakouts. So, when a stock is outperforming an index over 52-weeks, it is considered relatively strong. When it is underperforming over 52-weeks, it is considered relatively weak.

For example, if we wish to identify relatively strong and weak stocks of the year, we can apply the rules listed in the above table. First, we calculate the returns of the Nifty 50 index for the year and compare it with the returns of all stocks. If the Nifty index was bullish in that year, we need to check stocks that did better than the Nifty.

If the Nifty was bearish, we need to identify stocks that were either flat or did not drop as much as the index. The other possibility of course is that the stock could have gained while the index was falling. In all these instances, the stock would be considered an outperformer.

The third possibility is that the Nifty could be flat for the year. In this case, we need to look for stocks that were bullish during the year. In simple words, I need to find the stocks whose returns were better than the Nifty. These are the outperformers. The ones that delivered lesser returns than the Nifty are the underperformers.

It is a common belief that big winners can be easily identified only in hindsight. The fact is that we can identify such stocks in any timeframe well before the big move gets underway. The next logical question is if we identify an outperforming stock, should we immediately invest in them? Let us dig deeper into this.

We will typically look to invest in a stock that has outperformed recently, on the assumption that the outperformance will continue in upcoming sessions as well. If I am looking at a yearly timeframe, a stock that outperformed last year is likely to do well this year too.

Let us check if this hypothesis is valid or not. Nifty for instance gained 12% in 2019 and 15% in 2020. If we look at a few stocks that outperformed the Nifty in 2019, Adani Green Energy ranks at the top with a gain of 297% in 2019. It was also the top-performing stock from the Nifty 500 universe in 2019.

Building on the gains of 2019, the stock appreciated by 532% in 2020. Another example is Tanla Platforms. This stock went up by 131% in 2019, and a whopping 855% in 2020. In the case of AAVAS Financiers, the stock appreciated by 131% in 2020 but was down 14% in 2020.

These are some examples from the last two years. Let us dig deeper into this study. While the Nifty gained 12% in 2019, 237 stocks outperformed the Nifty in that year. I considered the stocks traded at the NSE equity segment for this analysis.

Out of the 237 stocks that outperformed in 2019, 119 stocks, representing about 50% of that universe continued to outperform in 2020. That is interesting data. How about a technique of building the portfolio of stocks outperforming the returns of the broader market average? But let us explore further before jumping to conclusions.

Let us check year-wise data from 2005.

Featured below is a table capturing year-wise data from 2005 to 2020 of NSE stocks traded in the equity segment.

Table 1.4: NSE equity segment year-wise data showing the percentage of outperforming stocks

Year	Nifty Returns	Stocks outperformed Nifty	Outperformed in prev year	Percentage of Prev year Outperformers	Outperformed next year	Percentage of Next year Outperformers
2005	36.34%	304	-	-	54	17.76%
2006	39.83%	148	54	36.49%	49	33.11%
2007	54.77%	367	49	13.35%	39	10.63%
2008	-51.79%	175	39	22.29%	86	49.14%
2009	75.76%	728	86	11.81%	289	39.70%
2010	17.95%	482	289	59.96%	156	32.37%
2011	-24.62%	349	156	44.70%	142	40.69%
2012	27.70%	571	142	24.87%	134	23.47%
2013	6.76%	269	134	49.81%	167	62.08%
2014	31.39%	793	167	21.06%	511	64.44%
2015	-4.06%	841	511	60.76%	343	40.78%
2016	3.01%	585	343	58.63%	34	5.81%
2017	28.65%	768	34	4.43%	91	11.85%
2018	3.15%	183	91	49.73%	69	37.70%
2019	12.02%	237	69	29.11%	119	50.21%
2020	14.90%	744	119	15.99%	-	-

The above table captures the total number of stocks that outperformed the benchmark index. It also captures the number and percentage of current year outperforming stocks that outperformed in the previous year and the next year as well.

The numbers of outperforming stocks are more in bullish years and less in bearish years which makes sense.

When a market is bullish, but if the number of outperforming stocks is less, it means that the heavyweight stocks lifted the index and investments in those stocks would have yielded better returns. It happened in the year 2006. The theme in that year was large caps. There were years like 2015–2016 where markets were in a sideways mode but quite a few stocks delivered good returns during this period. Almost 60% of stocks in those years also outperformed in the previous year. The theme during such phase would be an investment in mid-caps, small caps over large caps. Better returns can be generated by doing that. In years like 2008, 2013, 2014 and 2019 most of the stocks that outperformed also outperformed in the subsequent year.

But on an average, about 34% of stocks from the current year's outperformers, outperformed in the previous year also. And, close to 35% of stocks from the current outperformers list managed to outperform in the subsequent year as well.

Let us check the data if we consider the top 100 stocks that outperformed the Nifty every year.

Table 1.5: NSE equity segment year-wise data showing the percentage of outperformers from top 100 stocks

Year	Nifty Returns	Next Year Outperformers % from top 100
2005	36.34%	16.00%
2006	39.83%	32.00%
2007	54.77%	3.00%
2008	-51.79%	44.00%
2009	75.76%	29.00%
2010	17.95%	35.00%
2011	-24.62%	38.00%
2012	27.70%	22.00%
2013	6.76%	54.00%
2014	31.39%	59.00%
2015	-4.06%	32.00%
2016	3.01%	12.00%
2017	28.65%	27.00%
2018	3.15%	27.00%
2019	12.02%	49.00%

On an average about 32% of stocks of current year outperformers were previous year outperformers and outperformed in the subsequent year as well.

Before we take this discussion forward, let us consider other data points too. Let us take a look at the underperformers too. The data featured below shows the top 100 stocks that underperformed in the market each year.

Table 1.6: NSE equity segment year-wise data showing the percentage of outperformers from the bottom 100 underperforming stocks

Year	Nifty Returns	Next Year Outperformers % from bottom 100
2005	36.34%	17.00%
2006	39.83%	37.00%
2007	54.77%	10.00%
2008	-51.79%	63.00%
2009	75.76%	16.00%
2010	17.95%	16.00%
2011	-24.62%	32.00%
2012	27.70%	8.00%
2013	6.76%	32.00%
2014	31.39%	33.00%
2015	-4.06%	26.00%
2016	3.01%	8.00%
2017	28.65%	8.00%
2018	32.70%	10.00%
2019	12.02%	36.00%

On an average, about 23% of underperforming stocks were outperformers the previous year and outperformed in the next year too. 63% of stocks that were in the bottom 100 in 2008 outperformed next year.

We can compare the above returns with the larger universe of stocks like the Nifty 500 as well, but the outcome will be almost the same. We will come to that point later.

The above studies were to illustrate how stocks behave on a yearly basis. Such studies can be performed on any timeframe including half-yearly, quarterly, weekly or monthly. The objective is to understand broad concepts and principles.

Here are two key takeaways:

1. Concept of looking at outperformers can be useful, but the trend of the Nifty (underlying benchmark) is important.

2. Confirmation and more tools are required to filter the list of stocks further

3. Knowledge of the market trend and phase can help us decide the theme to focus on. The theme here could be Large-cap, Mid-caps, Small caps, ETF, Bonds or Fixed returns, or bearish opportunities for traders etc.

The patterns of outperformance and underperformance discussed above are applicable on all instruments, and for different time horizons such as short-term, medium-term and long-term.

There are footprints of outperformance and underperformance visible across all time frames. You will get an idea when you analyze the performance and behaviour of the sectors and stocks during the move.

I have studied the behaviour of top-performing stocks over different timeframes. The same principles can be applied for different periods and timeframes. Sectors in sync with market behaviour tell us something and when they are behaving otherwise, there is a reason we need to analyze them more to find opportunities. We will explore these concepts in greater detail in the following chapters.

The same behaviour can be analyzed in a variety of markets, and sectors. There are some stocks or sectors which are the flavour of the season. They are the leaders of the trend and continue to outperform during most of the uptrend. Identifying them can prove extremely rewarding.

There are numerous methods of price analysis and indicators to design a trading system for deciding the entry and exit. But what is more important is stock selection. And the identification of the market phase is also equally important.

Our approach can be tweaked, or allocation can be planned to a particular theme based on the market phase. It is important to identify and decide if one should focus on index trading or allocate more funds to mid-caps, or shift focus to some other asset class. If you are a trader, trading gold would be more favourable if it is outperforming the Nifty. If you are an investor, you will be better off by investing in fixed deposits or bonds when the Nifty is in a bearish phase.

If we develop techniques to achieve the above things, at least to an extent, we can then achieve reasonably good performance in our trading and investments activity.

The stocks that outperformed in the previous phase, may not do well in the next cycle. We have discussed earlier that leadership changes with cycles. Every instrument goes through this transition across different timeframes.

Finding outperforming stocks and running a price-based system on them is the simplest form of relative strength analysis. A stock delivering a 200% return in a year will have to cross the 100% or 50% mark first. A possible method to pick winners is to track stocks crossing 50% or 100% return during the year. But it is important to have a logical approach to identify the stocks and instruments entering the outperformance zone, remaining outperformers and when they are no longer outperformers.

So far:

- You have understood the concept of relative strength and patterns of outperformance and underperformance.

- We studied the data to understand how different sectors performed in Indian markets and who were the market leaders. Studies suggest that there are footprints of outperformance and underperformance visible across all timeframes.

- There are some stocks or sectors which are the flavour of the season. Knowledge of the market trend and the phase can help us decide the theme to focus on.

- If we develop techniques to achieve the above things, at least to an extent, we can then achieve reasonably good performance in our trading and investments activity.

- The trend of the underlying benchmark is important. The behaviour of the numerator and the denominator is important to study the relative strength patterns.

We shall discuss the performance cycle in the next chapter.

Chapter 2

OUTPERFORMANCE & UNDERPERFORMANCE

· ·

When you identify the stock that is outperforming the market, buying it is easier said than done. There is always this conflict with our thought process and belief system. Human nature is such that we always ask for discounts or we like to buy stuff at a cheaper price. A stock that is traded near historical lows is easier to buy because we often believe in buying something that has the potential of rising. We may however exit early because riding what is going up is a psychologically tough option for many. We feel that if we buy something at a lower level, it has a limited downside and a huge upside potential. So, it is typically easier to buy underperforming and relatively weak stocks rather than strong stocks.

On the contrary, it is difficult to buy what is going up because we are worried that we might get caught with stock right near the top. Even a marginal technical correction from the highs will result in a drawdown that will make us get into a panic mode. There are pros and cons to every method. Buying when the price is rising and at high looks intelligent in hindsight. But it is not psychologically comfortable at a practical level. But I believe chances of rewards are more when we are least comfortable in trading.

Outperformance does not necessarily follow outperformance. Price can consolidate or there can be temporary underperformance. There are patterns in the behaviour of these outperformers and underperformers of stocks to index.

Broadly speaking, listed below are the possibilities:
- Outperformance – followed by Outperformance.
- Outperformance – followed by Consolidation.
- Outperformance – followed by Underperformance.

Similarly,
- Underperformance – followed by Underperformance.
- Underperformance – followed by Consolidation.
- Underperformance – followed by Outperformance.

And
- Consolidation - followed by Outperformance.
- Consolidation - followed by Underperformance.

Any stock would go through this cycle of performance. It goes through this phase of performance in relation to the market index, sector index, and across different timeframes. Just like the price has different trends and phases on various timeframes, there are different phases of relative performance too.

Outperformance -> Consolidation -> Underperformance

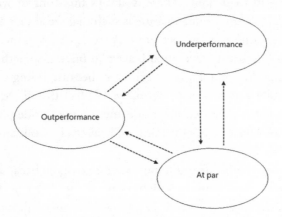

Image 2.1: Performance cycle

Identifying outperforming or underperforming stocks is the first task. The decision to trade or invest in them depends on several other factors as well. When we identify a strong stock in the universe, it is not necessary that it would continue to outperform. We can wait for a consolidation and then look for affordable trading or investment opportunity.

Take a look at the table given below; it is what we discussed in the earlier chapter:

Table 2.1: Market trend and Stock trend

Market trend	Stock trend
Up	More up
Down	Up
Down	Flat
Down	Less Down
Flat	Up

To derive patterns of the relative strength and to dig it further, let us explore this concept of outperformance and underperformance. Stocks performing better than the index is outperformance, but the nature of outperformance depends on the behaviour of the stock and the benchmark.

When the market goes up and the stock goes up more it is a strong outperformance. When the market falls, but the stock goes down a little, it is also a case of outperformance. But it is relatively weak because the market environment is bearish and even though outperforming, the stock price is falling.

So, let's enhance the above table further and focus on the nature of outperformance and underperformance.

Table 2.2: Market trend, stock trend and outperformance

Market	Stock trend	Outperformance
Up	More up	Strong
Down	Up	Strong
Down	Flat	Moderate
Down	Less Down	Weak
Flat	Up	Strong

Table 2.3: Market trend, stock trend and underperformance

Market trend	Stock trend	Underperformance
Down	More Down	Strong
Up	Down	Strong
Up	Flat	Moderate
Up	Less Up	Weak
Flat	Down	Strong

So, we have segregated the Outperformance and Underperformance into three categories: Strong, Weak and Moderate.

Now, based on the performance and the trend of the market, we can decide the stocks showing strengths and weaknesses.

If you come across a group of stocks where you see multiple stocks showing a pattern of strong outperformance, how will you decide which one is better? It is logical to say that the stocks that delivered better returns are stronger. Better the performance, the stronger it is.

See table 2.4.

Table 2.4: Relative strength and net return

Stock	Return	Index Return	Relative Strength	Net Return
A	5%	3%	Bullish	2%
B	8%	3%	Bullish	5%

The net return in the above table is the return of stock minus the return of the index.

Conceptually, both are relatively strong stocks because they are performing better than the market. Stock B is stronger than stock A. Because the net return that it is producing over the benchmark return is greater than stock A.

If that is the case, we can rank the stocks based on their performance. In the yearly data of stocks that we discussed in the earlier chapter; I studied the top 100 stocks and the bottom 100 stocks. This essentially means I ranked them based on their performance, right? The top stock in the list is the best performer.

So, we have discussed three things in this chapter:

1. There is a performance cycle that stocks go through in different timeframes versus the broader market index, sector index etc.
2. We can divide the Outperformance and Underperformance into three categories: Strong, Weak and Moderate.
3. We can rank stocks based on their performance.

Strong outperforming stocks with a high rank in terms of performance are bullish stocks and strong underperforming stocks in the bottom slot in terms of performance are bearish stocks.

We will come back to this.

Chapter 3

RATIO CHART

In the previous chapters, we discussed that the nature of outperformance and underperformance depends on the behaviour of the stock and index, or the two instruments that we are comparing and analysing.

We can plot the chart of the two instruments and analyze their behaviour.

Given below is a daily candlestick chart of Nifty 50 and Bank Nifty. The time frame considered in both charts is the same.

Figure 3.1: Daily candlestick chart of Nifty (upper panel) and Bank Nifty (lower panel)

We can analyze the charts and plot the divergences. On the left of the chart, Nifty and Bank Nifty are falling. At point A during October 2018, Nifty made a new low, but Bank Nifty did not. Nifty and Bank Nifty both went up at B, but the performance of Bank Nifty was better.

This is one of the ways to study the relative performance of two instruments. It is also a common practice to compare the performance of different instruments by plotting them on a single chart. Below is a comparative chart of Nifty and Bank Nifty over the same period.

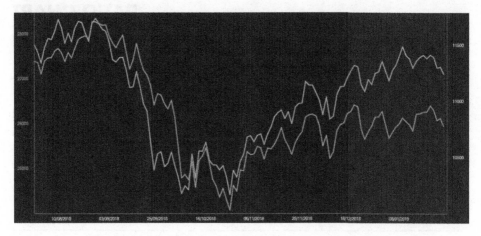

Figure 3.2: Nifty and Bank Nifty chart comparison

The above chart is another method to capture and compare the performance of two instruments.

Let us look at another example. Displayed below are the hypothetical price of two stocks, A and B.

Table 3.1: Stock A and B price

Stock A		Stock B	
Day	Price	Day	Price
0	100	0	100
1	105	1	102
2	108	2	104
3	107	3	103
4	108	4	102
5	109	5	101
6	111	6	103
7	112	7	104
8	111	8	105
9	108	9	105
10	106	10	106

Both stocks moved up from 100 to 106. We can plot both these charts and observe the trend.

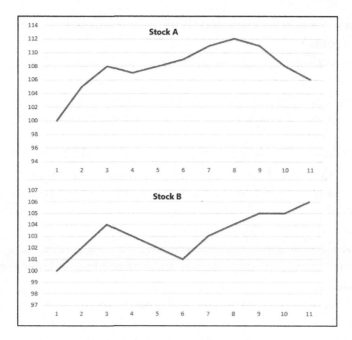

Figure 3.3: Price charts of stock A and B

What did you observe?

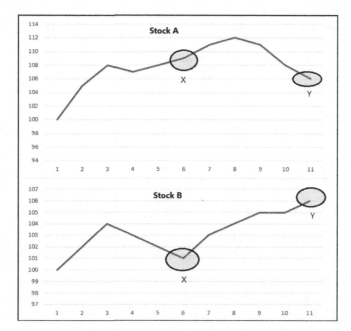

Figure 3.4: Price charts of stock A and B

Stock A was doing better than stock B till point X. Stock B outperformed from point X to point Y.

Theoretically, better returns could have been generated if our investments were in stock A till point X and in stock B from point X to Y.

A ratio chart technique will simplify the task of analysing the divergences or rate of change. We can calculate the ratio of two instruments by dividing the price of one by the other.

For example, if Bank Nifty is trading at 40,000 and Nifty at 20,000, and if we divide the price of the former by that of the latter and we get a ratio of 2. It is the ratio of one price to the other at that time. So, we need to define two instruments to plot the ratio chart. Scrip 1 is the numerator and scrip 2 is the denominator.

In the above example, the price on day 1 of stock A is 105 and stock B is 102. We can calculate the ratio of these prices by dividing both the prices for the same period.

The ratio of the price of Stock A and Stock B would be 1.03 on day 1.

1.03 = 105 / 102

Stock A is the numerator and Stock B is the denominator in this case. This way we can calculate the ratio of stock A and stock B for the remaining days.

Take a look at the table below.

Table 3.2: Ratio of Stock A and Stock B prices shown in Table 3.1.1

Ratio (A / B)	
Day	Price
0	1.00
1	1.03
2	1.04
3	1.04
4	1.06
5	1.08
6	1.08
7	1.08
8	1.06
9	1.03
10	1.00

The major advantage of calculating ratio is that the ratio of two instruments can also be derived regularly and plotted on a chart, which will look like the usual line chart plotted by connecting any price series.

A regular line chart is plotted by connecting the closing prices.

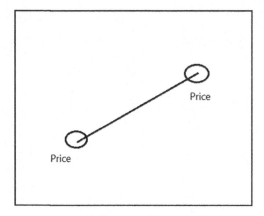

Image 3.1: Line chart

Similarly, we can also draw a ratio chart in a line chart format, by connecting two ratios.

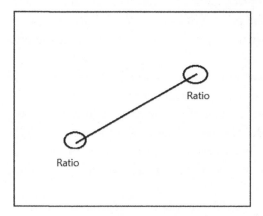

Image 3.2: Ratio chart

Here is the ratio chart of stock A and B as per the ratio calculated earlier.

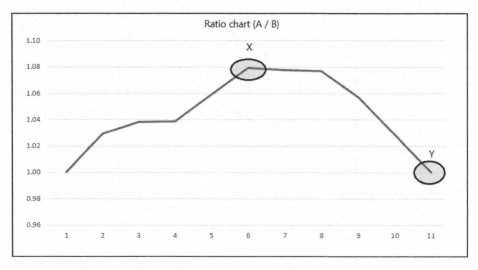

Figure 3.5: Ratio charts of Stock A and B

Observe the chart given above. It looks like a usual line chart. If the line is rising it indicates that the price is bullish while a falling line chart shows that trend is bearish. Line chart moving in a range indicates that the price is in a range and consolidating.

The ratio chart also moves up and down or sideways like a line chart but the inference here is slightly different. For the ratio line to go up, the price of the instrument used in the numerator will have to go up relatively more than that of the denominator. Hence, a rising ratio line indicates that the price of the numerator is outperforming the denominator, while a falling ratio line indicates that the price of the numerator is underperforming the denominator instrument.

In the chart given above, the outperformance of stock A till point X and underperformance from point X to Y can be analyzed by studying the trend in the ratio chart. Remember, stock A is a numerator hence the rising line shows the outperformance of stock A compared to B. The same chart also shows the underperformance of stock B till point X and outperformance from X to Y.

Below is a daily ratio chart of Bank Nifty to Nifty for the same time period captured in figure 3.1.1.

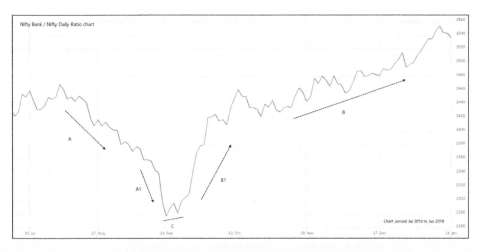

Figure 3.6: Nifty and Bank Nifty daily ratio chart

Since the numerator is Bank Nifty, Point A shows underperformance and B shows the outperformance of the Bank Nifty. The trend at A1 and B1 are relatively steep, hence A1 shows strong outperformance and B1 shows a strong trend of underperformance. The higher low at C indicates the strength of the Nifty bank when Nifty made a new low during October 2018.

Using the ratio chart, we can easily analyze the performance of the numerator compared to the denominator.

We can plot the ratio chart in any timeframe. We can use the daily prices of two instruments or the weekly, monthly, yearly, or even intraday timeframes to plot the ratio chart.

While plotting the ratio chart, some software multiplies the ratio by 100 or 1000 for better visibility and scaling. For example, if we divide the price of instrument trading at Rs. 100 with a major index that is trading at 20,000, we will get a ratio that would be in mere decimals. We have to therefore multiply the ratio by a factor of say 100 or an even higher number for better visibility while plotting the ratio chart. Multiplying the ratio by any number does not matter because it will not make any impact on the trend. It is important to realise that the absolute levels are not important in ratio charts. It is the trend in the ratio chart which is more important.

Recall the pattern of outperformance and underperformance that we discussed earlier. Outperformance does not necessarily mean that the numerator instrument is rising while the denominator instrument is falling. Outperformance simply means that the former is either rising more than the latter or falling less than it.

It should be clear by now that a rising ratio line indicates that the numerator is outperforming the denominator. A falling ratio line suggests that the numerator is an underperforming denominator instrument. The question now is, what does it mean when the ratio chart is confined to a range or moving sideways?

A ratio chart that is confined to a range indicates that the performance of the numerator and denominator is on par. This captures the scenario when there is no clear outperformance or underperformance between the two candidates.

Please read the above paragraph carefully. This concept is important for a better understanding of the ratio and relative strength. Relative strength can be a great tool for stock picking if you know what to look for. Using a ratio chart, we can easily analyze the performance of one instrument with that of another. The concept is just fascinating.

John Murphy has beautifully explained the relationship between asset classes in his book *Intermarket Analysis Explained*. He has explained some variables like interest rate and inflation that plays a role in influencing the relationship between different asset classes. He has also used ratio charts in the book to explain the relationship between different asset classes. It is a very sensible method and applicable to all types of market instruments.

Relative strength and ratio charts are mostly used interchangeably. Relative strength is a subject, while the ratio chart is a tool. There are other tools also which we will discuss in the book. Relative weakness is a bearish pattern in relative strength analysis.

We discussed the concept of outperformance and underperformance and how it depends on the behaviour of the instruments. Let us explore this further with the help of ratio charts. The trend of the ratio line that we see on the chart also tells us about the behaviour of numerator and denominator instruments. Let us try to understand that.

We will revisit the table that we discussed in the earlier chapter. See how the ratio chart will behave in the following scenarios.

Table 3.3: Index (Denominator), Stock (Numerator) and Ratio trend

Index (Denominator)	Stock (Numerator)	Ratio
Up	More up	Rising
Down	Up	Rising
Down	Flat	Rising
Down	Less Down	Rising
Flat	Up	Rising

Index (Denominator)	Stock (Numerator)	Ratio
Down	More Down	Falling
Up	Less up	Falling
Up	Down	Falling
Up	Flat	Falling
Flat	Down	Falling

The table given above explains the behaviour of the ratio chart. We can plot the ratio chart on any timeframe and study the trend across multiple time frames. This provides an interesting dimension to the subject of relative strength analysis. Plotting relative performance in a line chart format opens up a different paradigm in terms of offering us the ability to use a variety of other tools such as trendlines, indicators and pattern analysis. We will discuss more about this later.

But understanding the above table and the behaviour of the ratio chart is of utmost importance for the effective study of relative strength. When a ratio chart of a particular sector versus an index is rising, it shows the sector is outperforming the market. If we stick to the groups, sectors, or stocks that are leading the trend, we will in essence stick to the winners.

We discussed different patterns of outperformance and underperformance. Given below is a table that adds an extra dimension in the form of adding a qualifier. Take a look at the column with the heading pattern.

Table 3.4: Denominator, Numerator, Ratio Trend and Pattern

Denominator	Numerator	Ratio	Pattern
Up	More up	Rising	Outperformance - Strong
Down	Up	Rising	Outperformance - Strong
Down	Flat	Rising	Outperformance - Moderate
Down	Less Down	Rising	Outperformance - Weak
Flat	Up	Rising	Outperformance - Strong
Down	More Down	Falling	Underperformance - Strong
Up	Less up	Falling	Underperformance - Strong
Up	Down	Falling	Underperformance - Moderate
Up	Flat	Falling	Underperformance - Weak
Flat	Down	Falling	Underperformance - Strong

In the table shown above, you have all the information related to the behaviour of the numerator and denominator. How both instruments behaved, and the description of the pattern.

So now, we know how the ratio chart behaves based on the behaviour of the numerator vis-à-vis denominator.

Using the denominator and ratio columns from the above table, we can easily conclude how the numerator would have behaved and what the resulting pattern would be.

Table 3.5: Denominator and ratio trend

Denominator	Ratio
Up	Rising
Down	Rising
Down	Rising
Down	Rising
Flat	Rising
Down	Falling
Up	Falling
Up	Falling
Up	Falling
Flat	Falling

When the denominator is bullish and the ratio chart is rising, it indicates that the numerator is outperforming. You can now easily interpret the other scenarios mentioned in the above table.

Hence, the trend of the denominator is important for effective relative strength analysis. If the denominator is a benchmark index, all that we need to know is the trend of that index.

For example, if we can identify the trend in the Nifty 50 index, we can then effectively analyze the behaviour of the numerator stocks in relation to Nifty. Hence, the relative strength analysis of stocks begins by understanding the trend of the benchmark index. The assessment of the numerator or the stock depends on that.

The table we discussed earlier can be designed with the numerator as well. The numerator column is a price chart of a chosen numerator stock or instrument. Let us also use the common trading terminology by using the phrase bullish to indicate a rising trend and bearish to indicate a falling trend. We can reproduce the earlier table and bring it down to simple formations of bullish and bearish behaviour of price and ratio charts.

If the numerator is rising, we will term it as a bullish trend. Similarly, a rising ratio chart means the ratio chart is bullish. On the other hand, a falling price or ratio chart means they are bearish.

Take a look at the same table with our revised lingo.

Table 3.6: Numerator Price trend, Ratio trend and Performance remark

Numerator Price chart	Ratio chart	Remark
Bullish	Bullish	Bullish and outperformer
Bullish	Bearish	Bullish, something else is doing better
Bullish	Flat	Bullish, at par with denominator
Bearish	Bearish	Bearish and underperformer
Bearish	Bullish	Bearish, something else is falling more
Bearish	Flat	Bearish, at par with denominator

When the price and ratio chart is bullish, it means that there is a strong breakout in the price chart. In other words, the price action is bullish, and the stock is also an outperformer. When the price chart is bullish, but the ratio chart is not, it suggests that some other stock in the index is doing better. When the price chart is bullish, but the ratio chart is flat or moving in a range, it means that the price chart is bullish but the performance with index or denominator is at par with the denominator. The instrument is just an average performer.

Similarly, when the price and ratio chart is bearish, the numerator is bearish on the price chart and the stock is also an underperformer. When the price chart is bearish, but the ratio chart is not, it suggests other stocks are weaker in the index. When the price is bearish, but the ratio is flat, it indicates the stock is falling in line with the index.

So, if we understand the trend of the denominator, then analysing the price chart and ratio chart would be more effective. A price breakout that occurs in combination with relative strength in a bullish environment (bullish denominator), presents interesting trading or investment opportunities. Decision making and winning probability will improve significantly by picking the stocks that are leaders in the trend.

We have discussed earlier that when a price chart of the stock is bullish, but the ratio chart is not, an investor can still benefit by investing in the stock. But a falling ratio chart in such a scenario means that something else in the index is performing better. Investing in the leaders will do a world of good to your portfolio. When it comes to sector selection, it is important to identify which sectors are propelling the index. Looking for an opportunity in those sectors can prove extremely rewarding.

When we say that the numerator is up or down, we can also define the quantum of the rise or fall. That will help us filter the list further. But more about that later.

The goal of an investor is to outperform the benchmark. There are many methods to analyze the price of the stock. We can create trading systems based on price and associated indicators or by understanding the business and performing fundamental analysis of the stock and the sector it belongs to. But if we perform the fundamental research and or technical research and then invest only in those stocks where the price chart is bullish and they also belong to the outperforming category, our portfolio can then outperform the benchmark.

The equation is like this:

When the price chart is bullish = Instrument can go up.

When the ratio chart is bullish = Instrument can outperform.

When both are bullish = Instrument can go up significantly and outperform.

We will discuss various aspects related to identifying the winning stocks using this method. Ratio charts and relative strength analysis is a must-have tool in your arsenal irrespective of whether you are a trader or an investor.

The concept of ratio chart and relative strength analysis is applicable in all timeframes. We can also plot weekly ratio charts to understand the broader picture.

Below is an FMCG index weekly price chart.

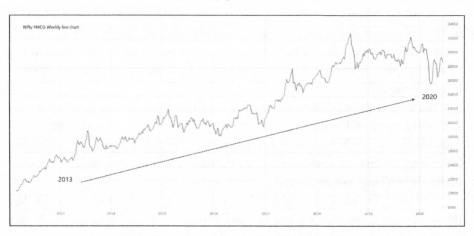

Figure 3.7: Nifty FMCG Index weekly line chart

FMCG index was in a strong uptrend between 2013 - 2020. The FMCG sector index was up by about 97% during this period.

Below is a ratio chart of the FMCG index versus Nifty 50 during this period.

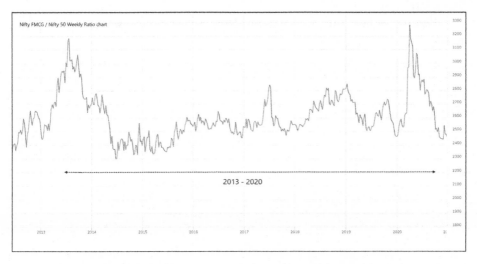

Figure 3.8: Nifty FMCG to Nifty Index weekly ratio chart

The ratio chart was range-bound even though the FMCG sector was in an uptrend because its performance was at par with the Nifty index. While there was a 97% rise in the FMCG index, the Nifty appreciated by 103% which is why the ratio chart was rangebound.

Take a look at the weekly chart of the financial services index between 2014 and 2019.

Figure 3.9: Nifty financial services index weekly line chart

The above price chart was bullish, and the index recorded a 200% gain during 2014-2019.

Featured below is the weekly ratio chart of the financial services index versus Nifty 50 for the same period.

Figure 3.10: Nifty financial services index to Nifty Index weekly ratio chart

The ratio chart was also bullish during the period. This indicates that the financial services sector outperformed the Nifty 50 index. Nifty returns were about 93% during the period while the financial services index appreciated by 200%. Investing in such sectors can help us outperform the benchmark.

Below is a weekly price chart of the Auto index from January 2017 to March 2020.

Figure 3.11: Nifty Auto index weekly line chart

Price went up during period A, followed by a sharp correction during period B.

Below is a weekly ratio chart of the Nifty Auto sector versus Nifty 50 during this period.

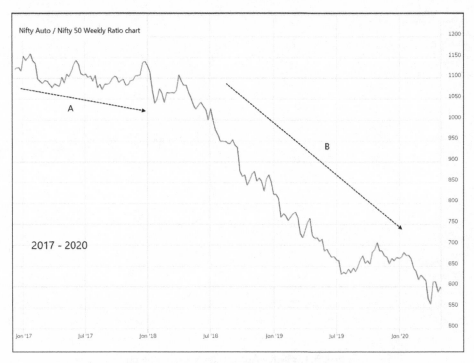

Figure 3.12: Nifty Auto index to Nifty Index weekly ratio chart

The Auto sector underperformed during period A even though the price chart was bullish. It turned out to be a significant underperformer in period B when the price and ratio chart both turned bearish.

The ratio chart can often provide an early hint and can act as a leading indicator.

If you recall, we discussed the table featured below in the first chapter.

Table 3.7: Nifty Trend and Leaders

Period	Trend	Leaders
2003 - 2008	Bull	Nifty 500, Bank, IT, R-Group
2008	Bear	Bank, IT
2008 - 2010	Bull	Bank, IT, Midcap
2010 - 2011	Bear	FMCG, Pharma, Auto, IT
2011 - 2015	Bull	Pharma, Auto, Bank, IT, FMCG, Media
2015 - 2016	Bear	Consumption, Energy
2016 - 2020	Bull	Realty, Banks & Fin services, Small & Midcap
2020	Bear	Pharma, FMCG, IT
2020 - 2021	Bull	Metal, Small & Midcaps, Auto, IT, Pharma

Some interesting observations about the table. IT and Banks fell in 2008 but the fall was relatively lower than the Nifty index. Even the Nifty mid-cap and Nifty 500 index fell by around 55% and 50% respectively in the 2008 fall whereas Nifty fell by around 65%. The leading sectors or outperformers during the fall managed to deliver better returns when the Nifty 50 turned bullish after the 2008 crash. The outperformers during the fall–Nifty Banks went up by about 164% and IT by about 150% in the 2008–2010 rally. The underperformers during the Nifty fall namely the Nifty mid-cap and Nifty 500 index recorded a lower return of 133% and 115% respectively.

The realty index underperformed and fell by around 15% during this bullish period in the Nifty 50 index. It was not surprising to note that the realty index was a big underperformer when the Nifty dropped during 2010–2011. During this fall, the realty index dropped by 50%. In that period, the FMCG index went up by about 19%. Pharma and Auto were down by 2% and 4% respectively. IT index was down by around 8%, whereas Nifty was down by 29% in this period.

Pharma and Auto were up by 180% and 154% respectively during the 2011–2015 bull trend. FMCG and IT were up by more than 95% during the same period. Metals were down during the bullish trend as well. PSU banks and Realty were not very bullish during that period. During 2015–2016 when the index fell by around 17%, Metals were down 30%. PSU banks and the realty index were down by more than 40% and underperformed the market.

In a nutshell, the footprints of outperformance and underperformance will be always visible. The relative strength study will act as a lead indicator and provide an early indication about the sectors and stocks to focus on and also the ones to avoid.

There will be a price breakout in many stocks when the Nifty, or the overall market trend is bullish. But you would also have come across instances where the stock you bought based on a price breakout failed to move up significantly while the stocks you did not buy gained handsomely. Or, what we bought might have delivered returns far lower than the ones we missed. This happens if we focus on relative underperformers.

Focusing on a breakout in RS charts can be immensely helpful in avoiding the above-mentioned scenarios. Always focus on the relative outperformers, both among sectors and stocks. Sticking to strength will help you prevent getting trapped on the wrong side of the market or make your portfolio underperform.

It is always advisable to get rid of underperformers from the portfolio and ride the strength. Strong stocks tend to get stronger as the uptrend progresses and they also tend to resume the trend quickly after corrections. Weak counters will be beaten hard during corrective phases, making the portfolio bleed and underperform the overall market. A strength centric portfolio would deliver better returns over a period.

Price breakouts can suggest that stocks could go up. Relative strength breakouts indicate which stocks can outperform. The combination of the two factors can do wonders for your portfolio.

A trader should therefore make it a point to check the relative strength chart of the stock against Nifty before buying it. Ignoring the bullish formations of a stock chart during its period of underperformance and focusing on them when it is outperforming the broader market is a logical and effective approach. Always take trades in the individual charts in the direction of the relative strength chart. Price breakouts coupled with relative strength breakouts are the key to identifying potential outperformers.

Weakness can also be analyzed and traded in the same way. Shorting the weak counters is a more profitable option when the broader market corrects. This will offer better risk-reward trades than shorting the stronger counters. Pattern studies of individual stocks certainly play an important role. Remember, trades are placed based on a study of the individual price charts. Relative strength helps in finding where to fish or to identify the trading universe.

Leaders

Leadership changes with the phase of the market. But stocks and sectors leading the rally, continue to do so in that phase. Phenomenal returns can be generated by trading those stocks in that leg. But it is easier said than done. These stocks would provide multiple opportunities to participate in them during shallow corrections and short-term consolidation. But those short-term corrections are treated as an early sign of reversals. Weak longs easily get out in such corrections and some traders, who feel that the stocks went up too much, may consider short trades too.

But it is important to understand that such stocks are in strong hands and the short-term corrections act as fuel to propel prices even higher. The short covering of weak shorts helps too. Most of the traders keep watching prices going up and they will never be able to muster the courage to buy them.

Remember, *aur kitna jayega* (how much more will it go), up or down, is a major issue with most of the traders. I have a funny anecdote to share here. My son was studying and my wife gave him some assignments which he found boring. He asked mother, *aur kitna*? She said, "I will decide it, not you." That is how the market behaves too. We get punished when we ask *aur kitna*.

William J. O'Neil said, "It is one of the paradoxes of the stock market that what seems too high usually goes higher and what seems too low usually goes lower." Jesse Livermore wrote, "Remember that stocks are never too high for you to begin buying or too low to begin selling."

If you have been in markets for a few years, try to remember a stock that kept going up in front of your eyes, but you could not buy. Surely, you can recall many names. This happens to everyone.

Newton's first law of motion states: If a body is at rest or moving at a constant speed in a straight line, it will remain at rest or keep moving in a straight line at constant speed unless it is acted upon by a force.

Newton's First Law of Motion

A body at rest remains at rest, or, if in motion, remains in motion at a constant velocity unless acted on by a net external force.

In the same way, we can define the law of relative strength analysis.

An instrument that is outperforming the denominator will continue to outperform on that timeframe until there is a reversal. Similarly, an instrument that is underperforming the denominator will continue to do so on that timeframe until there is a reversal.

> **Law of Relative Strength analysis**
>
> An instrument which is outperforming the denominator will continue to outperform on that timeframe until there is a reversal.
>
> An instrument which is underperforming the denominator will continue to underperform on that timeframe until there is a reversal.

We need to believe in this concept to be able to continue to trade winning stocks in an uptrend and losing stocks in a downtrend. It will continue to outperform in that timeframe unless there is a reversal and that is important in the above statement.

We need to develop this belief system to be able to buy winning stocks and sell losing stocks. Remember, a stock that rises by 5x would have been up 2x at some point and it might have seemed too high to buy even then. We stop looking at such candidates because we fear we will be caught on the wrong foot.

Let us address this fear. The fear we are addressing is:

1. The stock has already moved up a lot. I might get trapped at the top of the cycle.
2. What if it falls from here? The downside is huge.

A stop-loss is an important tool in trading. You can buy a stock at any price level based on any method but with a stop-loss. Once you have a stop-loss in place, winning stock is relatively a better choice, and it has a better risk-reward dimension. The downside is more in falling stock. Always remember that the market knows better than us, don't challenge it–that's the basic philosophy we need to believe in to successfully execute the principles of relative strength–buy strong, sell weak.

Like any other system, there would be periods where this approach might not yield positive results, but over time, rewards will be more favourable. It is important to develop a belief that will help us stick to the trading approach even when there is a drawdown phase.

Trading the leaders

There are broadly two types of price patterns: reversal and continuation. Reversal is an approach to identify candidates turning from a bullish to a bearish phase or a bearish to a bullish phase. Continuation patterns are signals that indicate the price and will continue to move in the direction of the prior trend. Pullback patterns are all about identifying bullish patterns in short-term correction while the long-term trend is up.

Trading continuation or pullback patterns can be extremely effective in relatively strong stocks.

I have seen stocks continue to remain on the top list of relative strength performers for several months. And they also continue to lead the market. Corrections in such leaders are typically short-lived; rather, they act as a trap to shake out the weak hands. Trading continuation and pullback patterns in such leaders are one of the best trading approaches and one that has stood the test of time for me.

To be able to ride the trend and remain invested or keep trading winning stocks, it is important that you do not try to predict reversals every now and then. People are often unable to ride the trend due to the external noise, over-analysis, or unnecessarily looking at some arbitrary support or resistance levels. It is important to follow the price chart and not to trade based on imaginary reversals.

In this chapter we discussed:

- What is the ratio chart? How does it get plotted and how is it analyzed?
- Ratio lines can help us analyze the behaviour of the numerator and denominator instruments that we studied in different table formats.
- The patterns of outperformance and underperformance can be defined and made objective using the ratio chart.
- The relative strength study will act as a lead indicator and provide an early indication about the sectors and the stocks to focus on and also the ones to avoid.
- What is the RS Law? What are the different aspects of trading the leaders?

We will discuss more about price patterns and RS later. The next chapter talks about relative strength patterns.

Chapter 4

RELATIVE STRENGTH PATTERNS

Before we discuss more about relative strength and ratio charts, it is important to define relative strength patterns clearly. I am collating the observations and the concepts that we have discussed thus far to define relative strength patterns. The patterns are defined based on the concepts and understanding the behaviour of the numerator vis a vis denominator.

We discussed different scenarios such as ratio line rising, and the numerator is outperforming. Or, when the ratio line will be rising while the price is falling, still indicating the outperformance of the numerator. We have defined various patterns based on outperformance and underperformance. Let us move ahead and define patterns using this knowledge.

Broadly there are three types of patterns for outperformance and underperformance explained below. Collectively let us call them relative strength patterns.

Flying Pattern (Bullish)
When both the numerator and denominator are rising and if the numerator is outperforming, it is a continuation relative strength pattern. We shall call this a flying pattern.

Bullish Flying Pattern: Rising denominator, the rising numerator and a rising ratio line.

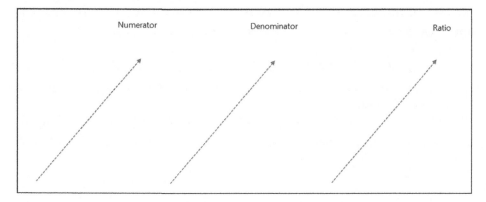

Image 4.1: Bullish flying pattern

Assuming that numerator is stock, and the denominator is an index when both are rising, it shows that the environment is bullish. The rising ratio line suggests that a numerator is outperforming the denominator in the bullish market environment. When the market trend is bullish, good business and quality company, with a high valuation, continue to perform well and generate handsome returns. Trying to invest in what might perform in the future or looking for a cheap valuation can prove costly in such times. Investing in stocks that are already displaying strength during such times is a better idea because such stocks would continue to do well and enjoy the market premium. These stocks are basically in strong hands.

So, in a bullish market trend when the denominator is rising, investing in outperforming stocks on a continuation outperforming pattern would be an effective strategy.

This concept is applicable even for trading in the short-term timeframe. When you come across a strong bullish day, trading the stocks outperforming the market will be more rewarding. Many traders would instead find reversals and look for shorting opportunities because they think that the price is overbought and run up too far. If the market continues to go up, they will get trapped and they will have to rush to cover their short positions which in turn will make the prices even higher.

Hence, the concept of relative strength is relevant in all timeframes. Normally, people are not comfortable buying outperforming stocks because they have already moved up a lot. In fact, some may even try to find the reversal to exit or initiate short positions in it. This shifts these stocks from the weaker to stronger hands.

Remember, the essence of the pattern is that the environment is bullish, and the numerator is outperforming the market. Sentiments are positive, macro and micro indicators are healthy, and the market is recognizing this resulting in the strength of the stock. Demand is more than the supply for the stock, helping the stock to outperform the benchmark. Strong stocks in a positive environment keep producing better returns.

A study of the trend of the denominator is a key aspect of this pattern. If you know that the market is bullish, then find the stocks where the ratio line and the stock price is bullish.

The key concept here is that the trend in the ratio line should be bullish. Ideally, a higher low pattern can be used as a simple definition of the bullish trend, be it in the ratio chart or the price chart. We will dig this further in the later chapters. Understanding the concept is important at this juncture.

Drowning Pattern (Bearish)

The exact opposite of the flying pattern is a drowning pattern.

Bearish Drowning Pattern: Falling denominator, falling numerator and falling ratio line.

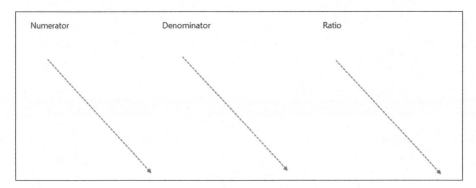

Image 4.2: Bearish drowning pattern

When both the numerator and denominator are falling and the numerator is underperforming, it is a bearish drowning relative strength pattern.

When the market is falling, and the stock or the numerator is falling more the environment is also bearish. When the sentiments are bearish, the stock price of even good companies tends to correct significantly. The ones underperforming the market might have more fundamental issues or concerns triggering the underperformance. If you are looking for shorting opportunities, the drowning pattern stocks could be ideal ones. Those who buy at supports, thinking that price has fallen a lot, get trapped and these stocks continue to fall more because the environment is bearish.

If you are not a trader and looking for investment opportunities in a falling market, you should then stay away from the drowning pattern stocks. There are other patterns that you should be looking for.

Lion Pattern (Bullish)

When the denominator is falling but the numerator is rising, resulting in an uptrend in the ratio chart is the lion pattern.

Bullish Lion Pattern: Falling denominator, rising numerator and rising ratio line.

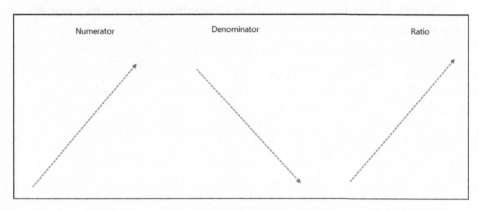

Image 4.3: Bullish lion pattern

The lion pattern represents the immense strength of the numerator which has not only stood strong but had also moved up while the market was falling. This is a strong pattern of outperformance.

However, the problem here is that the trend in the denominator is not bullish. If the market environment is not bullish, there is a possibility that even the bullish trend in the stocks may not last long.

Investing right away in outperforming stocks in a bearish market is not such a good idea. The falling index might have catastrophic impacts. If the market continues to fall and bulls give up, the strong stocks can also reverse and might contribute to the subsequent fall in the market.

Hence, this pattern needs confirmation. Wait for the market to reverse before buying bullish lion stocks.

You need to consider the following factors while dealing with the lion pattern.

1. **Inverse relationship:**
   At times, stocks and sectors have an inverse relationship with the denominator because of several underlying fundamental factors. Some sectors also tend to go through this phase often. For example, the IT index usually has an inverse relationship with markets if the currency is weak or if the dollar is strong.

There can be other factors that make a particular sector behave contrary to the market trend.

2. **Nature of correction of the denominator**

   The nature of the correction of the denominator is important to analyze. If the view is that the fall in the index price is more of a short-term correction and the overall environment is bullish, then buying stocks showing a lion divergence pattern would prove rewarding. If the nature of market correction is strong and sharp, looking for bullish stocks can prove counter-productive. Look for bearish patterns in such cases.

3. **Short-term pullback**

   There is also a possibility that the rise in the numerator is just a short-term pullback in a bearish trend. Be wary of buying bullish lion pattern stocks that are in a long-term bearish trend.

The best strategy to trade this pattern is to keep a list of stocks that qualify as a lion pattern when the markets are falling. If the market stabilizes, and if the lion pattern stocks continue to display strength, then the bullish patterns in these stocks may be traded. There is a strong possibility that they will lead the next leg of the market rally because they displayed strength when markets were correcting. The bulls of those stocks are like lions, they are dominant.

The lion pattern stocks are potential flying pattern stocks when the trend in the denominator turns bullish.

From a trading perspective, here is an interesting way to trade this pattern. If you think that the Nifty is in support or there are chances of a reversal, then buying the lion stocks instead of the index could be more rewarding. There is a possibility that the index will not have a significant reversal, but your stocks can perform.

To reiterate, a higher low pattern would be bullish, and a lower high pattern would be bearish. We will discuss interesting observations to identify a potential turnaround in sentiments in chapter 10 on breadth indicators.

Cat Pattern (Bearish)

The opposite of a bullish lion pattern is a bearish cat pattern.

Bearish Cat Pattern: Rising denominator, falling numerator, falling ratio line.

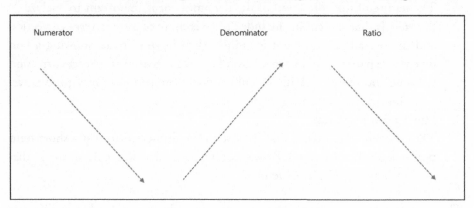

Image 4.4: Bearish cat pattern

The market is rising but stock is falling leading to a fall in the ratio line. This means that the stock is weak, and the selling pressure is strong. Stock could not hold ground even in the bullish market, which is a matter of concern.

We should keep in mind the considerations we discussed for the bullish lion pattern while analysing the cat pattern as well. They are:

1. Inverse relationship
2. Nature of correction of the denominator
3. Short-term pullback

When there is a bearish cat relative strength pattern, we need to analyze if the nature of the sector or stock is not inversely proportionate with the market trend. The nature of the bullish action in the denominator should also be studied. The distinction must be made between a strong uptrend in the denominator versus a short-term bounce within a bearish trend. It may well be the case of the stock being in an overall bullish trend and the pattern of underperformance is just a temporary correction.

If you are looking for shorting candidates, then make a list of instruments displaying the cat pattern characteristics. If they continue to remain bearish, they are good shorting candidates.

From a trading perspective, if you anticipate major downside reversal in the market, then shorting Cat pattern stocks at market resistance could be a rewarding strategy. When the market is bullish, and where most of the stocks are bullish, breakout traders would be perplexed if the market reverses suddenly. Bearish cat stocks are the ones we should be looking to short in such cases.

Bullish Star Pattern

When the market is falling, and the stock is not falling as much as the numerator, it is a sign of strength. There can also be instances where the stock could be relatively stable in a falling market environment. Both these instances would qualify as a bullish star pattern.

Bullish Star Pattern: Falling denominator, falling numerator, rising ratio line.

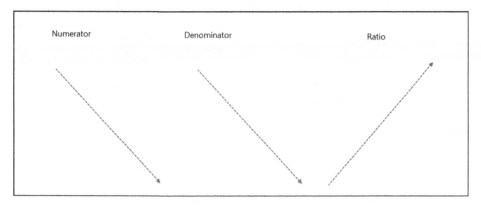

Image 4.5: Bullish star pattern

If the market is falling, and stock is not falling as much, it is possible that the selling is getting exhausted. The bears shorting the stock looking at overall weak markets could not generate enough returns even when markets fell. Bulls who bought these stocks are stuck but they have managed to hold fort even during market weakness. The buyers have lost less compared to the market.

The bullish star pattern is a variation of the lion pattern. While the lion pattern is strong, the bullish star is a comparatively weak pattern of outperformance. It is like a morning star that can turn out to be an early sign of strength.

This is a silent pattern because unlike the pattern of divergence, these stocks will not be highlighted or discussed by the media. If markets are strong, there is a possibility that these stocks will do well, lead by smart money that bought the stocks and weak shorts that will run for the cover.

The strategy should be to wait for the denominator trend to stabilize or turn bullish. If the stocks in the bullish star category complete a bullish reversal pattern such as a technical base or a higher low pattern, then the recent low could be considered a strong bottom. That bottom is an important reference point from a trading perspective. They are bullish candidates until that bottom is breached.

A star pattern is a pattern of divergence. When the price of the numerator is falling but the ratio line is not falling it shows that the overall index is in a strong downtrend and others are falling more. Especially, when the price makes new bottom and ratio does not, it is a bullish sign.

Take a look at the image below.

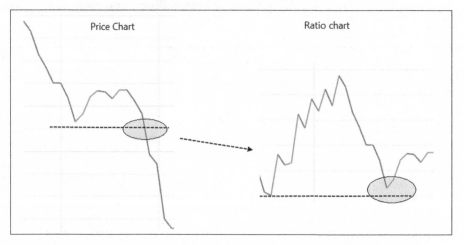

Image 4.6: Price chart making a new low, the ratio doesn't make a new low

Price is making a new bottom, but the ratio chart is sustaining above the previous low. This indicates that the price is falling but it is not relatively weak. This is the essence of the bullish star pattern.

See image 4.7.

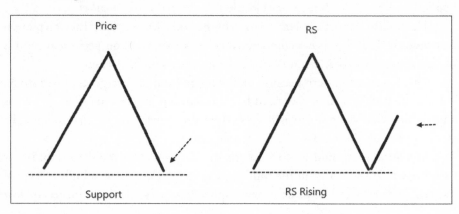

Image 4.7: Price chart at support, RS chart rising

Let us address a scenario where the price is at support and the ratio chart is rising. What does it indicate?

Let us try to decipher this scenario.
- Price is falling but is currently at support.
- The ratio chart is rising, indicating that the denominator is falling more. Hence the numerator is outperforming.
- In essence, the price is falling, the ratio line is rising, and the denominator is falling. This completes the bullish star pattern.

The support pattern that we see on the price chart is strong in that case. Taking a long trade at such a support zone offers a low-risk opportunity. The stop-loss may be placed below the recent swing low.

Hope you can now connect the dots if I tell you that relative strength analysis helps to improve the price analysis. In this context, let us take a quick look at the Nifty IT index as a case study.

Here is the weekly price chart of the Nifty IT index during 2008–2009.

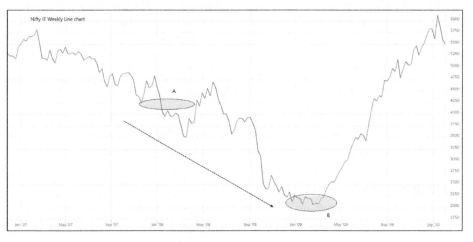

Figure 4.1: Nifty IT index weekly line chart

The index made a new bottom during January 2008 at point A and made lower lows until point B in March 2009.

Below is a weekly ratio chart of the Nifty IT index in relation to the Nifty 50, for the same period.

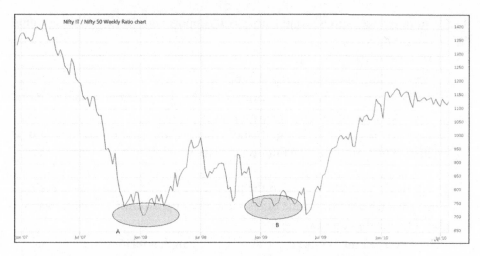

Figure 4.2: Nifty IT index to Nifty 50 weekly ratio chart

The ratio chart was also falling up to Point A in January 2008 indicating that the sector was falling and underperforming. While price dropped to a lower low at point B, the ratio chart held above the corresponding bottom formed at point A. Though the Nifty 50 and Nifty IT Index were falling the ratio chart was bullish. This is a classic example of a bullish star pattern.

When the market is bearish and the Index and other stocks are breaking their supports, the sector or stocks that are falling less are the relatively strong ones.

Star stocks are silent performers. These companies would typically have relatively better business and earnings and hence do not participate in the bear market. They could be down, but not as much as the broad markets.

Bearish Star Pattern

The opposite of the morning star is the evening star pattern.

Bearish Star Pattern: Rising denominator, rising numerator but falling ratio line.

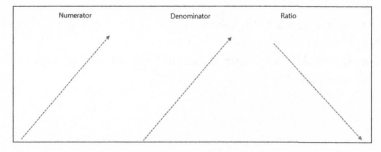

Image 4.8: Bearish star pattern

The market is rising, the stock is also rising, but the returns generated by the stock is lesser than the market. Though the trend is bullish, the relative underperformance of the stock indicates the weakness of bulls. Due to the underperformance, the investors in these stocks will not be happy. If this trend of underperformance continues, the bulls in such stocks would likely shift to the better performing candidates.

Like a bearish cat pattern, these are the candidates for shorting if you anticipate a reversal in the market. But a better strategy would be to wait for the trend in the denominator to reverse and the price of the numerator confirms weakness.

So, there are three major bullish and bearish relative strength patterns you need to look for:

- Flying and Drowning
- Lion and Cat
- Bullish Star and Bearish Star

Flying and drowning are continuation patterns. Lion, cat and star are patterns based on divergence.

Trend Reversal

When a stock is rising and outperforming the index, there is a possibility that the trend might get exhausted, and it can be followed by underperformance or consolidation. There are also occasions when there can be a sudden reversal in the markets. Usually, when the market is weak, a good strategy is to short the weak stocks. But at times, more than the weak stocks falling, the erstwhile strong stocks may reverse sharply and fall more. The complacency of the bulls is the key factor that triggers such sharp reversals.

These phases are inevitable in any instrument and timeframe. In a way, this is the price to pay for following the relative strength principles that we have discussed so far. The patterns of outperformance or underperformance will fail during such times and the price-based stop-loss will be triggered.

Hence, trading the continuation patterns does come at a cost. You must realise that there is a possibility of sudden reversal, and you might have to lose a portion of your profits when sharp reversals occur. It is essential to understand that you cannot always trade continuation, exit on a reversal, and buy again at the next low. This is desirable but never practically possible. Accept the cost involved and stick to your process. Ignore the threat of a potential reversal if you want to successfully trade the continuation pattern.

To sum up, it is essential to be aware of the following aspects:

1. It is important to know the weakness of the strategy that we follow. We need to accept that and keep the risk in control to address the weakness of the strategy.

2. There are phases when underperformers may outperform, and outperformers may underperform.

3. Signs of the weakness of the trend can help in deciding the hedging strategy.

The concept of hedging in a portfolio is normally resorted to for protection. For example, if we buy a futures contract, we can buy Put Option or write Call Option to limit the loss in the case of an unexpected sharp reversal.

Options have time value associated with them while futures can be rolled over. In a derivative portfolio, a long-short strategy can also be adopted but it would not be a hedging strategy. It is just a long-short position based on the prevailing direction. Of course, it is a sensible approach, but it should not be construed as a hedging strategy because at times the strong stocks can get hammered, causing significant drawdown.

Finding an opportunity to trade reversals in strong stocks would be an appropriate hedging strategy. If you think that the market is at resistance, then shorting bearish star stocks even to hedge the portfolio can be an effective strategy. Lion, cat and star patterns are a pattern of reversals and useful tools for hedging.

The strong stocks of the rally and the stocks making new highs tend to fall equally sharply when the market reverses suddenly. What happens during such times is that people hold on to these stocks as they have seen these stocks recover after a correction in earlier instances. So, they keep holding these stocks anticipating a recovery. But if the reversal is significant, the price might break supports and any bounce off supports would be weak and short-lived.

It is important to understand and accept this aspect of relative strength analysis. Hence, there will be a time when all strong stocks will reverse suddenly. We must remain disciplined and focus on risk management and exit strategy. We should exit upon the reversal sign or when the exits criteria get triggered.

The fear of a potential reversal mustn't inhibit you from trading or investing in strong stocks. Remember everyone will die someday, but we cannot live the whole life with the fear of eventual death. We need to accept it and move on.

The message here is that we should be aware of the weakness of the subject or strategy. Leaders tend to give up gains rapidly, and in that sense, the leaders of the rally give us enough hints about impending reversal.

An interesting anecdote in this context is the performance of stocks such as Sesa Goa, Educomp Solutions, Reliance Communications, RNRL and RPL. These stocks were the darlings of the market during the 2006-2007 bull run. RNRL for instance gained more than 700% in 2007. Most of these stocks do not even exist today. There are many such examples and stock market history will throw up lots more of such examples.

The investors who either do not have an appropriate exit strategy or if they fail to adhere to the exit strategy, end up holding such duds as a long-term investment. The stock, which was once a large-cap, ends up in the junk category. Leaders change in the next leg of the rally; Markets would recover but the portfolios of duds will not!

This brings us to the important aspect of the exit strategy. Perfect exit is not possible but selling in profit and a strategy of booking profit periodically is not a bad idea. If there is evidence of exhaustion, and sector rotation, booking profits in strong stocks and moving to the next emerging strong sectors would be a sensible approach. Studying the relative strength chart of Nifty with other asset classes, mid-cap with Nifty, small-cap to Nifty, sectoral index with Nifty are extremely important tools to plan the exit strategy. We will discuss more about this in Chapter 11.

Let me point out something interesting. Even without being aware of relative strength analysis, if I ask a trader which sector is the leader of a particular move, that person will be in a position to immediately identify it. It is that simple and evident at times. But interestingly, he may not be able to participate in that. Simple things are not always easy to implement!

I remember when the Yes Bank stock was falling in 2018–2019, many traders were asking for the support levels and buying in anticipation of a sharp reversal. HDFC Bank on the other hand in the private bank space was making new highs, but it was exceedingly difficult for many investors to buy it because what was rising and it came across as an expensive stock. It is important to realise that what is going up is relatively strong and what is falling is weak.

Though we have taken stocks as numerators to explain the concept, the above patterns are also applicable to sectors or any other instrument pair.

It is important to remember that there will always be at least one sector that is outperforming the market.

Rising and falling ratio lines are useful concepts but they must be studied in the overall context. It is practically impossible to judge a pattern or trend based on the price action in a single session. You need to study the behaviour in multiple sessions to decide the pattern and trend. The patterns discussed until now are relevant to understand the basic principles of relative strength study.

Let us consider another important topic which is multi time frame relative strength analysis.

Multi-timeframe relative strength pattern analysis

We discussed the cycle of outperformance and underperformance that stock goes through. Outperformance is typically followed by either consolidation or underperformance and then an outperformance. Refer to image 2.1.

It is therefore important to understand what is happening in the stock over multiple timeframes. We have divided relative strength patterns into three categories. They depend on the behaviour of the numerator, denominator, and their ratio. There will be different patterns on different timeframes. We can study the patterns across multiple timeframes before concluding the relative strength.

Listed below are some multi-timeframe patterns that can help analyze RS patterns over different timeframes.

All Bullish – All Bearish

If the pattern is bullish across multiple timeframes, it would be an extremely bullish scenario. A flying pattern in daily, weekly, and monthly timeframes for a stock indicates that the numerator is outperforming in all timeframes and the environment is bullish. Similarly, the drowning pattern in all timeframes captures those stocks that are weak in multiple timeframes in a bearish environment.

If the pattern is a lion in the shorter timeframe and flying on the higher timeframe, it is considered an extremely bullish scenario. Bearish star in a shorter timeframe and drowning on the higher timeframe is an extremely bearish scenario.

In a nutshell, we can define bullish patterns on all timeframes as all bullish multi-timeframe RS patterns. Bearish patterns on all timeframes can be termed as all bearish multi-timeframe RS patterns.

All Bullish RS: Bullish RS patterns on all timeframes
All Bearish RS: Bearish RS patterns on all timeframes
There are a few other possibilities too.

Bullish Eagle Pattern

When a stock is underperforming the denominator or consolidating in the short term, it is a pattern of underperformance. But it does not necessarily mean bearishness. If a stock is in a strong uptrend and bullish, the price chart will not necessarily produce a linear trend. There will be some corrections in between.

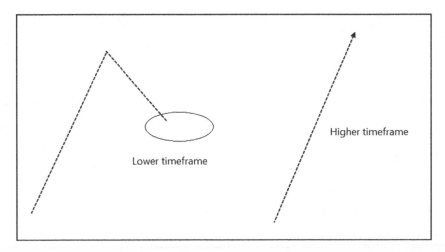

Image 4.9: Bullish eagle pattern

Those short-term corrections might result in a temporary underperformance in the ratio chart. Any strong uptrend in the relative strength charts will always have periods of underperformance or consolidation in between. It does not necessarily mean a reversal of the outperformance and we should not be looking for shorting opportunities in such stocks. Rather, such consolidation may turn out to be an opportunity to buy strong stocks that are in a pullback.

Short-term correction in an overall bullish relative strength chart is what I call an eagle pattern. If a stock is a leader on a higher timeframe, and correcting in a short-term timeframe, it is forming an eagle pattern and it is an opportunity to buy. The stock remains bullish if it remains in the uptrend on multiple higher timeframes.

Bullish Eagle Pattern: Bullish RS pattern on the higher timeframe, bearish RS pattern on a shorter timeframe

Waiting for this consolidation after the outperformance and buying on resumption of the prior trend can offer attractive risk-reward trades. It is like an eagle waiting patiently for the right time to pounce on its prey. Hence the name eagle pattern. The risk would be affordable because the price is correcting in the short term. Pivot levels or swing levels can be a logical stop-loss level for such trades. We will discuss more about entry, exit and stop-loss patterns in Chapter 7.

Bearish Eagle Pattern

The opposite of the bullish eagle is the bearish eagle pattern.

Bearish Eagle Pattern: Bearish RS pattern on a higher timeframe, bullish RS pattern on a shorter timeframe.

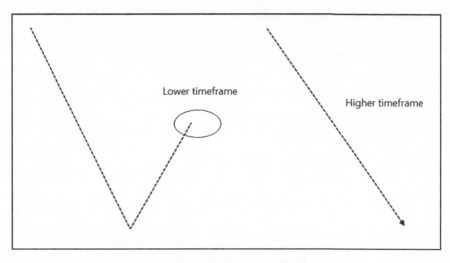

Image 4.10: Bearish eagle pattern

When a stock is outperforming in the short-term, but underperforming in bigger timeframes, It qualifies as a bearish eagle pattern.

The stock or sector that are consistently underperforming would have a temporary bout of outperformance. At times, the outperformance could be so sharp that they are too difficult to ignore. But such bounce invariably ends up as a trap. Many traders get trapped in eagle patterns because the typical urge of the majority of traders is to trade reversal patterns. The bearish eagle pattern gives a perception of an early reversal and ends up being a trap.

If you carefully examine the relative performance in multiple timeframes, you will realise that the bearish eagle is an opportunity to short because the overall trend is down or indicates underperformance.

Investors should ignore bearish eagle stocks. From a trading perspective, the pattern is more useful for short-term traders. Book profits early and exits your holdings in such instances.

The long-term reversal does start as a reversal in the short-term timeframe. Hence, there is a possibility that a bullish eagle could end up being an all-bearish pattern, and a bearish eagle ends up being an all-bullish pattern. But we should remain sceptical unless there is evidence to this effect. The only problem with waiting for confirmation is that you end up taking the trade much later and at a higher level.

There are two aspects that we must understand in this context. First, in my experience, we would get enough opportunities to participate if the reversal in the short-term timeframe spills over to bigger time frames.

Second, the desire to identify a reversal and participate early and ahead of others is the biggest problem with most traders. Remember, there is a cost associated with adopting the early entry approach. The failure ratio is generally high in such early entries. Our profitability and portfolio performance does not depend on how early we bought and how timely our exit was. The returns are a function of your exit and entry price.

Learn to focus on practical aspects such as execution and sticking to the process. What matters is your returns. It is not about the entry at lows and exiting at highs. Learn to get rid of noise between the ears which is—easier said than done.

Bearish eagle formation is an interesting pattern based on my experience. Such patterns can trap many traders and it is difficult to avoid that temptation to get in early. Particularly traders who do not have disciplined exit methods get trapped in such stocks. By the way, very few traders would have a clearly defined exit method and stick to it. Though most traders read about the importance of exits in social media, books, and podcasts, they may fail to adhere to it in real life. This was the case for several decades and will perhaps remain so for several decades going forward too.

Even in the present day of algorithmic trading, it is difficult to let your algorithms run without interruption for a long period. People will intervene and keep finding new algorithms when their strategy is not working. Machines might replace dealers, but the ratio of profitability and successful traders will not change.

Change in regime!

When you look at multiple timeframes, when a pattern is bearish on higher timeframes and bullish on more than a single lower timeframe, it indicates a regime change. For example, if you are looking at say four timeframes—daily, weekly, monthly and quarterly—and if there is a bearish pattern on a monthly and quarterly timeframe, but bullish on the daily and weekly timeframe, it indicates a possibility that stock could see a reversal from a bearish to a bullish regime.

Similarly, if the monthly and quarterly patterns are bullish, but daily and weekly patterns turn bearish, it may indicate the possibility of a trend reversal from bullish to bearish.

A table that can help analyze ratio patterns on multi-timeframe is shown below.

Table 4.1: Table showing multi-timeframe relative strength pattern analysis

Scrip	LCP	▼ Total Score	Daily	Ratio %Change	Weekly	Ratio %Change	Monthly	Ratio %Change	Quarterly	Ratio %Change
FEDERALBNK	89.00	4	Flying	0.00%	Flying	2.05%	Flying	3.69%	Flying	10.96%
IDFCFIRSTB	59.15	4	Flying	1.82%	Flying	1.82%	Flying	0.60%	Flying	0.60%
INDUSINDBK	1019.35	3	Flying	1.12%	Bearish Star	-1.19%	Flying	1.72%	Flying	1.22%
PNB	42.25	3	Bearish Star	0.00%	Flying	9.09%	Flying	13.21%	Flying	9.09%
RBLBANK	216.25	3	Flying	2.33%	Flying	2.50%	Flying	8.47%	Bearish Star	-1.29%
SBIN	422.05	3	Cat	-0.91%	Flying	3.62%	Flying	11.41%	Flying	9.78%
KOTAKBANK	1800.75	2	Flying	1.18%	Flying	0.89%	Bearish Star	-3.96%	Bearish Star	-2.66%
AUBANK	995.45	1	Flying	1.21%	Bearish Star	0.00%	Cat	-7.54%	Cat	-23.16%
AXISBANK	739.85	1	Cat	-1.54%	Bearish Star	-0.33%	Bearish Star	-3.48%	Flying	0.53%
BANDHANBNK	303.50	1	Flying	2.61%	Bearish Star	-0.23%	Cat	-14.12%	Cat	-15.13%
HDFCBANK	1503.45	1	Flying	1.25%	Bearish Star	-1.13%	Bearish Star	-0.70%	Bearish Star	-4.62%
ICICIBANK	643.05	1	Cat	-1.56%	Bearish Star	-1.40%	Bearish Star	-0.11%	Flying	4.69%

The pattern is calculated on the stocks from the Bank Index as the numerator and the Nifty Bank Index as the denominator. This pattern is identified in the daily, weekly, monthly, and quarterly timeframes. Along with the patterns, the percentage change in the ratio chart is also displayed in the table to get a broader perspective.

If the pattern is bullish the score assigned is one and the score would be 0 for a bearish pattern. Using this scoring logic, the score for different timeframes is assigned and the user can sort the stocks accordingly. This can help in stock selection.

In the above table, it is apparent that FEDERALBNK and IDFCFIRSTB are all bullish. PNB and SBI are bullish eagle patterns whereas AUBANK, BANDHANBNK and HDFCBANK are bearish eagle patterns. KOTAKBANK indicates a bullish change in regime because monthly and quarterly patterns are bearish but daily and weekly have turned bullish.

Relative strength helps in better price analysis:

When we do price analysis on the chart, the status of the ratio chart and the relative strength patterns that we have discussed earlier can help us in taking better decisions.

When there is a significant price breakout in the chart, or if the stock is trading at an important support zone, then a rising ratio line provides an important clue about the strength and sustenance of the breakout. It is indicative of accumulation and strong demand for the stock.

When a stock is trading at important support levels in a downtrend, stocks having relative strength patterns such as star or lion are good opportunities to trade.

Similarly, in a strong market downtrend, if a stock is trading at important support levels, but if its ratio line is falling, it indicates potential weakness of support. If the support is broken or if there is a bearish pattern breakout and the ratio chart is falling, they are good shorting candidates.

When a stock is trading near its previous high or at an important resistance level. A bearish star relative strength pattern could be a confirmation to initiate shorts in such stocks.

Doing price analysis after identifying the patterns in the relative strength chart can help to filter and shortlist stocks that can be traded. While there are numerous trading systems based on price and indicators, there are very few using relative strength or breadth as an integral part of the trading system. This is because not enough work or research has been done on this subject so far. There is a lack of depth. The purpose of this book is to address all important aspects related to this subject. If you can develop a system using this method, you will have an edge. Relative strength and sentiment analysis can do wonders for your price-based trading and investment systems. It can help reduce the drawdown of price-based systems.

Trading Relative Strength Patterns

Remember, understanding the market trend or the trend of the denominator is the primary step for relative strength analysis. The interpretation of the relative strength patterns depends on that.

Given below are pointers to shortlist the candidates to look for trading or investment based on the broad market trend.

- When the market is bullish, look for flying and bullish eagle patterns for long.
- When the market is falling and your view is bullish, look for a bullish star or lion pattern for long trades.
- When the market is bearish, look for drowning and bearish eagle pattern for short.
- When the market is rising but your view is bearish, look for a bearish star or cat pattern for short trades.
- For hedging perspective in a derivative portfolio, look for lion, cat and star patterns.

In the above patterns, we have taken the price chart also into account which makes it more practical and sensible. The entry, exit and stop-loss levels are always determined based on the individual price chart.

The trend in the denominator is important because if the market is falling and if the downtrend is strong, it is better to look for shorting opportunities in the drowning pattern stocks instead of identifying a lion or star divergence pattern stocks. We will discuss how to objectively define forming the overall market view or direction as well.

If the market is bullish and sentiments are strong, buying flying patterns and outperformers could be more rewarding. Nonetheless, we can have stocks with different patterns in the portfolio.

Ratio Trend Matrix

I will introduce an interesting concept here. We discussed that the rising ratio line indicates outperformance and the falling ratio line indicates underperformance. We segregated relative strength patterns into three bullish and bearish categories. These patterns provide a clear idea about the trend in the ratio chart, the numerator, and the denominator.

From a trading perspective, focusing on the pattern of the latest trading day would not be sufficient. Similarly, from an investment perspective, focusing on the patterns of the latest week or month would not be sufficient or appropriate. We must perform multi-timeframe ratio analysis to understand the behaviour across different timeframes.

It will be interesting and important to study the trend ratio over multiple sessions. For instance, If we check the relative strength performance of the last 10 sessions, we can analyze how stock, the overall market and the ratio chart behaved in the 10 sessions. If there were more bullish patterns than bearish ones. the stock would qualify as a strong outperformer.

Similarly, if there were more bearish patterns than bullish ones, the relative strength is weak. We can also assign scores to the patterns. If the ratio chart is bullish, the score of 1 would be assigned and the score would be -1 for a bearish pattern. We can thus calculate the total score for the previous sessions and arrive at a total score.

Take a look at the table given below. It is extracted from the TradePoint software.

Table 4.2: Ratio trend matrix showing relative strength pattern analysis for IT index stocks over 10 sessions

Scrip	LCP	%Change	▼ Total	Bar0	Bar1	Bar2	Bar3	Bar4	Bar5	Bar6	Bar7	Bar8	Bar9
LTI	3930.45	0.16%	7	Lion	Flying	Flying	Flying	Flying	Cat	Crowning	Flying	Flying	Cat
MPHASIS	1936.10	-1.66%	7	Crowning	Flying	Flying	Flying	Flying	Flying	Bullish Star	Flying	Bearish Star	Cat
COFORGE	3543.05	1.35%	6	Lion	Bearish Star	Flying	Flying	Cat	Bearish Star	Lion	Cat	Flying	Flying
INFY	1405.05	0.20%	6	Lion	Bearish Star	Flying	Flying	Cat	Flying	Lion	Cat	Bearish Star	Flying
MINDTREE	2355.60	1.96%	6	Lion	Flying	Bearish Star	Flying	Flying	Flying	Flying	Cat	Bearish Star	Cat
WIPRO	538.70	-0.41%	6	Crowning	Flying	Flying	Bearish Star	Flying	Flying	Crowning	Flying	Flying	Bearish Star
TECHM	1026.25	0.63%	5	Lion	Flying	Bearish Star	Bearish Star	Flying	Bearish Star	Crowning	Flying	Flying	Bearish Star
HCLTECH	942.55	0.02%	4	Lion	Cat	Bearish Star	Bearish Star	Flying	Bearish Star	Crowning	Cat	Flying	Flying
QFSS	3525.30	1.06%	4	Lion	Cat	Cat	Flying	Flying	Flying	Lion	Cat	Bearish Star	Flying
TCS	3143.60	-1.14%	2	Crowning	Bearish Star	Bearish Star	Flying	Bearish Star	Bearish Star	Crowning	Cat	Bearish Star	Flying

The relative strength pattern for IT index stocks are over the last 10 sessions is captured in the above table. The denominator is the Nifty IT index. LTI and

MPHASIS have the most bullish patterns over the last 10 sessions whereas TCS had the most bearish pattern in the ratio chart.

This can also be used for intraday and short-term trading. The last 15 bars on a 15-minute or five-minute timeframe are the recommended settings in this scenario. Stocks trading in the top slots are the ones having more bullish ratio chart patterns and those at the bottom slots are relatively weak ones. Stocks crossing the mid-level score in the above table are stocks changing the regime where there is a transition from bullish to bearish or vice versa. They are interesting candidates to analyze further for potential trade opportunities.

Let us do an exercise before we conclude this chapter. I have plotted the Sector index to Nifty 50 on the ratio chart.

See if you can understand these terms. Write down your answers on a piece of paper and verify the correct answers.

Which pattern am I referring to when I say:

A. I am buying a stock that has given a fresh bullish breakout in the RS chart when the denominator market is bearish.

B. I am selling a sector that has given a fresh bearish breakout in the RS chart even when the denominator market is bearish.

C. I feel a sector is showing strength. The RS chart of a sector is bullish. But sector and denominator markets are bearish.

D. I am buying a stock that has given a fresh bullish breakout in RS charts when the stock, its sector and denominator market, all are falling.

E. Last week, I saw that the Auto sector went up but much less than the denominator Nifty. But Nifty was very bullish.

F. I saw the Pharma sector performed well, over the last five sessions compared to the denominator Nifty. Though Nifty was bearish and went down, the sector was positive and gave much better returns.

G. Wipro gave a multi-year breakout on a price chart. The IT sector is outperforming the Nifty. The RS chart of Wipro compared to the denominator Nifty index and IT index are bullish. Interestingly, Nifty is also bullish on charts.

H. IT and Pharma were doing very well in the markets. Someone told me the Power sector will do well. I bought it. The denominator Nifty went up but the ratio chart of the power sector and price chart, both fell. Markets went up, and the sector underperformed.

I. Nifty was falling. I thought it is better to buy something that has limited risk. I saw Yes Bank available at low. I bought it. Denominator Nifty fell, RS chart of Yes Bank fell more and the stock was crashed from the 'low' price at which I bought and gave much more negative returns.

J.   I saw Reliance underperforming denominator Nifty in the short term. But the higher timeframe ratio chart is bullish and the Nifty trend is also bullish. I am looking for a bullish price pattern to trade.

These are hypothetical examples to ensure that you understand the concepts.

Answers:
A.   Lion pattern.
B.   Drowning pattern.
C.   Bullish star.
D.   Bullish star.
E.   Bearish star.
F.   Lion Pattern.
G.   Flying Pattern.
H.   Cat Pattern.
I.   Drowning pattern.
J.   Bullish Eagle pattern.

If you have answered these questions correctly, it indicates that your understanding of the relative strength concepts is clear. The idea is simple. The rising ratio line is bullish and the falling ratio line is bearish. But this pattern of classification and identification is an attempt to dig deeper and understand the behaviour of the numerator and denominator.

In this chapter:
•   We defined relative strength patterns based on the behaviour of numerator, denominator and their ratio.
•   We discussed that Flying, Lion and Bullish Star are bullish relative strength patterns. Drowning, Cat and Bearish Star are bearish relative strength patterns. We also discussed multi-timeframe relative strength patterns.
•   We discussed how to trade these relative strength patterns. Ratio trend matrix and regime change are interesting concepts.

Before moving to the next chapter, try to observe these patterns in real life. Try to recall, you must have experienced these patterns in the past. Spend some time on these concepts.

Chapter 5

RATIO CHART ANALYSIS

· ·

The concept of plotting a ratio chart of two instruments is hugely underrated. It can help achieve objectivity in analyzing the relative strength and also play a key role in developing trading systems or screeners for stocks in different market environments.

In any chart, we can analyze and study the trend and pattern. We can therefore do a similar exercise of defining the patterns in a ratio chart too. For relative strength patterns that we discussed until now, we need to study the numerator, denominator, and ratio charts. But a ratio chart can be analyzed independently and corroborated with the pattern and performance of the numerator instrument to get better insights about relative performance. This analysis can be performed in any timeframe.

We can plot the ratio chart in the lower pane and the price chart of the numerator in the upper pane and study them together. When the price and ratio charts are rising, the trend is strong. We need to be careful when there is a divergence between the price and ratio chart.

Let us study an example here. Take a look at the daily candlestick chart of Bharti Airtel. The ratio chart of Bharti Airtel to Nifty 50 is plotted in the lower pane.

Figure 5.1: Daily candlestick chart of Bharti Airtel with ratio chart of Bharti Airtel to Nifty 50 index

The Bharti Airtel stock was in a downtrend in period A and the ratio chart was also falling. A look at the top and bottom panes suggest that the stock was underperforming and the price was also in a downtrend. The price went up during period B but the ratio line was confined in a range. This suggests that though the price is rising it is not outperforming the benchmark. Breakout in the price chart and the ratio chart occurred in period C, indicating outperformance and bullish price trend.

So, when we analyze the ratio chart with the price charts, the important aspects to observe are:

1. Is the price and ratio line rising? If so, it is a bullish configuration.
2. Is the price and ratio line falling? If so, it is a bearish configuration.
3. When the price and the ratio charts are not in sync, we must look for other candidates for investment or trading.
4. When there is a breakout in the price and ratio line, they are the candidates to focus on.
5. When the price breaks a prior low, but the ratio chart does not, it is a bullish divergence.
6. When the price makes a prior high, but the ratio chart does not, it is a bearish divergence.

Given below is a daily candlestick chart of DIVIS LAB along with a ratio chart against Nifty 50.

Figure 5.2: Daily candlestick chart of DIVIS LAB with ratio chart of DIVIS LAB to Nifty 50 index

Price made a new low at A, but the ratio chart was rising, it is a bullish divergence pattern that shows outperformance. It indicates the relative strength of the bullish camp. There was a breakout in the price and ratio chart at B. Both charts were rising at C, suggesting a bullish trend and outperformance.

When the ratio chart is not in sync with price, we get a hint of what is in store.

The bullish trend at C in the above chart of Divis Labs was during January–February 2020. Pharma stocks performed well at that time because of the COVID-19 outbreak.

The chart given below shows an interesting formation in the same chart of Divis Labs during March 2020.

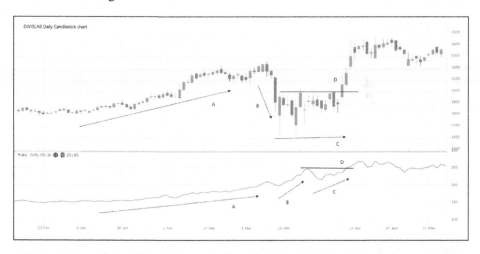

Figure 5.3: Daily candlestick chart of Bharti Airtel with ratio chart of Bharti Airtel to Nifty 50 index

The price and ratio charts were bullish at A. The price fell at point B, but the ratio chart was rising. The Nifty 50 index and Divis Lab were falling but the ratio chart was rising, suggesting Divis was not falling as much as Nifty 50.

The price went into a sideways mode at C but the ratio chart was still bullish. This shows strength in the stock and hints at the possibility of strong outperformance. There was a breakout in the price and ratio chart at D.

The stock appreciated by 100% in the next 12 months. When the price is falling but the stock is an outperformer, it is expected to do well when the denominator stabilizes and recovers. These observations during divergence between price and indicator can help you identify candidates to focus on during the next leg of the rally. When you spot a divergence, always wait for the price and ratio to be in sync before taking trades.

Instead of the Nifty 50 index as our benchmark, we can also compare the performance of a stock to its sector index as well. In our example, we can plot the chart of Divis Labs and compare it with the Pharma index. But we will discuss this later.

Can you recollect the patterns discussed in the previous chapter and identify the pattern completed at point B in the chart shown above? The stock and index were falling but the ratio line was rising. So, this would qualify as a bullish star pattern.

We can also plot other indicators on the price chart and use it along with the ratio chart. Take a look at the daily candlestick chart of AMARAJABAT plotted along with the 40-period moving average on the chart.

Figure 5.4: Daily candlestick chart of AMARAJABAT with 40-period moving average and ratio chart of AMARAJABAT to Nifty 50 index

The price moved above the moving average at point A. The price and ratio line was rising during period B. The price made a new high and was trading above the moving average at C but the ratio chart was falling. This indicated that though the stock was rising, it was underperforming the benchmark index. Eventually, the stock dropped below the moving average and the price and ratio line turned down at point D.

Notice at point C, the stock was rising but underperforming. This means that the denominator or the index is rising more rapidly than the stock. Hence this would qualify as a bearish star pattern.

We can take the analysis of the ratio chart even further. Since the ratio chart is plotted in a line chart format, we can analyze it the way we do a price chart. We can also use all other tools that are relevant and applicable in the line charts. While analyzing the price chart, the focus is on the trend and patterns. The objective is to identify the trend and the price potential. Since the ratio chart captures relative performance, we can make conclusions about the possibility of outperformance and underperformance by studying the ratio chart.

An uptrend in the ratio chart indicates outperformance by the numerator and a downtrend shows underperformance. Bullish breakout in the ratio chart captures the possibility of further outperformance, and bearish breakout shows the possibility of further underperformance. Consolidation patterns in the ratio chart indicate that the numerator and denominator are moving at par.

Other tools like trend lines, channel lines and chart patterns are applicable and relevant in the ratio chart as well. Below is a weekly ratio chart of Bank Nifty versus Nifty 50.

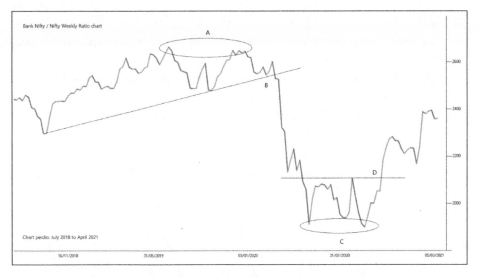

Figure 5.5: Daily ratio chart of Bank Nifty to Nifty 50 index

Point A shows area of multiple resistances. There was a breach of a bullish upsloping trendline at Point B. The breach of the trend line occurred after the resistance indicated by the previous double top pattern. The resistance and the trend line breach indicated that Bank Nifty may underperform Nifty. Point C shows the pattern of support which was followed by a breakout above the resistance from the horizontal trendline at point D.

If the overall scenario was bearish at point B, then shorting Bank Nifty or the stocks from this sector would be beneficial because the index is underperforming. At point C, we get to know that the sector is not bearish. It confirms the pattern of outperformance at point D. Buying Bank Nifty or the stocks from the sector would have been profitable at or after point D.

The patterns in the ratio chart can prove to be interesting. Popular price patterns such as cup and handle, head and shoulders and range breakout are equally relevant and important in ratio charts too. But, as the ratio chart captures relative performance, we must be aware that we are analysing the relative performance while studying those patterns in the ratio chart.

If your eye is trained to identify these popular patterns, it would not be too difficult to spot them in the ratio chart. A consolidation pattern breakout in the price chart would suggest that the price has broken out of a range. A similar pattern in the ratio chart would indicate that the numerator has commenced outperformance after a period of at par performance with the denominator.

The important takeaway is that patterns and tools are the same, irrespective of whether you use them in the price or the ratio chart. But remember that the interpretation based on these patterns and tools might be different in the ratio chart.

The relative strength chart coming out of a prolonged consolidation, or period of underperformance can be an extremely interesting observation. Such candidates should be in focus and the trend and pattern in the price chart may be studied to decide further course of action.

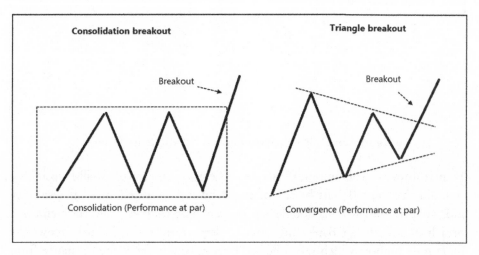

Image 5.1: Consolidation and triangle breakout

Shown below is a daily ratio chart of Grasim against Nifty 50.

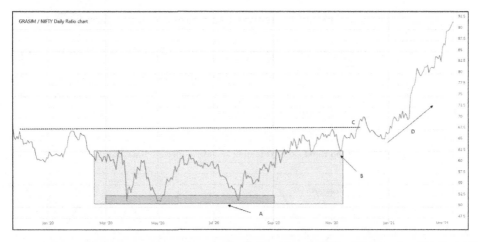

Figure 5.6: Daily ratio chart of GRASIM to Nifty 50 index

The price formed multiple bottoms at point A. The ratio chart was in the range between February and September 2020. The breakout from this range during September 2020 indicated the possibility of outperformance by Grasim. There was a test of the previous breakout at point B. The concept of breakout-retest or change of polarity principle that is popular in price charts is relevant in the ratio chart as well. At C, the ratio chart came out of an even larger range consolidation.

This suggested that the stock, that was performing in line with the index, has gotten into an outperformance cycle now by breaking out of the range. This was followed by a strong uptrend in the ratio chart during phase D. This was also a period that turned to be a favourable one for the cement sector. This stock outperformed the sector and the Nifty index significantly during this period.

It is important to understand that the concept of support and resistance that is associated with price charts are not directly applicable to ratio charts. We typically look at multiple lows in the price chart to identify support or demand zone and multiple highs to identify resistance zones. Those concepts are however approached and interpreted slightly differently in ratio charts.

The interaction of demand and supply dictates the formation of support and resistance patterns in the price chart. But the support pattern in the ratio chart indicates that irrespective of the price trend, the relative performance is improving in relation to the numerator. A ratio chart not making a fresh low or hovering around previous lows tells us that even though the stock is falling the underperformance is not as severe as the denominator. Similarly, the resistance pattern shows us that performance is weakening at that level.

Hence those patterns can be analyzed in a ratio chart, but this distinction in interpretation is important.

A strong trend followed by a shallow correction or retracement, followed by another breakout is a typical sign of strong momentum breakout in price charts. Patterns like the flag and pennant are examples of such continuation breakouts. These patterns are relevant in the ratio chart as well.

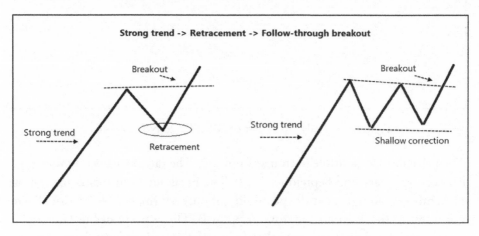

Image 5.2: Strong trend, retracement and follow-through breakout

Below is a daily ratio chart of M&M to Nifty 50.

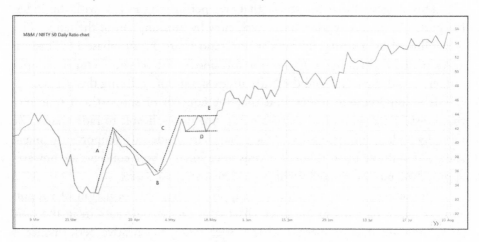

Figure 5.7: Daily ratio chart of M&M to Nifty 50 index

A strong rise in ratio chart at A indicated strong momentum and outperformance of the stock. It also indicates the possibility of a major bottom being put in place at the low of A. Though there was a correction at B, the ratio chart stayed above the prior low. The strong rise at C followed a shallow retracement and consolidation at D and a subsequent breakout at E indicated that the momentum is strong, and stock can outperform the benchmark.

A strong rising line is an important pattern in the ratio chart.

Ratio charts at previous important levels (support–resistance) and breakout are important observations of the ratio chart.

Some people think trade mean reversion strategies using the ratio chart. If you check the history of the ratio of two instruments, for example, Bank Nifty and Nifty, you will find that most of the time the ratio remains in a particular zone. For instance, if you notice that a ratio chart turns down from 10 and moves back up from 5, one can therefore sell the pair when the ratio is at 10 and buy it back at 5. You may wonder what the selling ratio is. The selling ratio is shorting the numerator and buying the denominator. Buying the ratio is nothing but buying the numerator and selling the denominator. We will discuss this in Chapter 9 on pair trading.

We discussed in an earlier chapter that there can be multiple tools to define the ratio chart as bullish or bearish. It is like price analysis. The price going up is bullish, but there are many other ways to define bullish or bearish trends. Trend lines or channel lines can be used as a tool to identify the trend.

It is also a common practice to use indicators in the price chart to identify the trend. We can use these in the ratio charts too. Applying indicators on a ratio chart can help us objectively analyze the charts. The use of indicators would also help create trading systems and build scanners for the stock selection using relative strength analysis as the primary filter. By using indicators in the ratio chart, we can make our job of multi-timeframe analysis relatively easy.

Let us discuss the use of a few popular indicators that apply to ratio charts.

Moving average

Moving average is an extremely popular indicator that can be used in the ratio charts too. The formula for moving average calculation in the ratio chart is the same as the price chart. We calculate the average of the last n periods and plot it as an overlay on the price chart.

When we plot a 20-day moving average on a line chart, it calculates an average of the last 20 closing prices. If we plot the moving average on a ratio chart, it will calculate the average price of the last 20 ratios. If the ratio is above the average of the last 20 ratios, the current ratio line will be above the moving average line. The formula and the interpretation are the same, but the calculation in the ratio chart is on the behaviour of two prices or the ratio.

A 40-period moving average is recommended as a default setting on the ratio chart. If the ratio line is above its moving average, the trend is bullish, or the numerator is considered as outperforming the denominator. If the ratio line is below its moving average, then it is a bearish scenario or underperformance of the numerator. The rising moving average is more bullish and the falling moving average is more bearish.

Take a look at the ratio chart below of Nifty Pharma v/s Nifty 50 with a 40-period moving average.

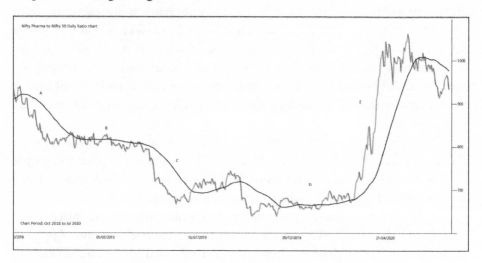

Figure 5.8: Daily ratio chart of Nifty Pharma to Nifty 50 index

The ratio line fell below the moving average at point A indicating underperformance of Nifty Pharma versus Nifty 50. The ratio was hovering around the moving average line at point B, suggesting that the performance of both indices was at par. The trend of underperformance continued at point C. Point D is a trend of consolidation again when both indices were moving on a par, followed by a strong trend of outperformance by Nifty Pharma at E.

Using moving average as a trend filter can also help in multi-timeframe analysis. For example, if the ratio is above its 40-period average on the daily, weekly and monthly chart, the numerator can then be considered extremely bullish or a strong outperformer. A list of such candidates would be the ones that are outperforming the index on multiple timeframes.

Consider a scenario where the ratio is above its moving average on higher timeframes and the ratio of the short-term chart is falling. This is an eagle pattern offering an affordable opportunity to participate in an instrument that is a long-term outperformer. By defining the bullish and bearish trend using moving average, the patterns that we discussed in the earlier chapter becomes relatively objective and easier to identify.

We described a variety of patterns such as flying, drowning, star, lion using relative strength charts. We can also define and identify these patterns using the moving average line too.

Flying Pattern
Denominator above the moving average, numerator above the moving average, ratio line above the moving average.

Drowning Pattern
Denominator below the moving average, numerator below the moving average, ratio line below the moving average.

Lion Pattern
Denominator below the moving average, numerator above the moving average, ratio line above the moving average.

Cat Pattern
Denominator above the moving average, numerator below the moving average, ratio line below the moving average.

Bullish Star Pattern
Denominator below the moving average, numerator below the moving average, ratio line above the moving average.

Bearish Star Pattern
Denominator above the moving average, numerator above the moving average, ratio line below the moving average.

I mentioned in the previous chapter that the relative strength patterns that we discussed are concepts that can be defined in multiple ways. The rules discussed above using the moving average is just an example of how you can identify the relative strength patterns in a more objective manner using different tools and indicators.

We can use different moving average periods to identify candidates for short-term, medium-term and long-term timeframes. For example, we can use a 20-period for the short-term, a 50-period or 100-period for the medium-term and a 200-period average for the long-term.

The 200-day moving average is a popular indicator used as a long-term trend filter. The advantage of using popular parameters is that you get to know what most people are looking at. There is no merit in using a Fibonacci number as a moving average parameter. It does not make sense to use a particular parameter of your indicator just because it is a Fib number.

Like moving average, any other indicator or tool can be used as a trend filter and identify the patterns.

When we use indicators like moving average on ratio charts, we can scan for stocks where there is a moving average crossover in the ratio chart. This would be an effective way to identify potential outperforming and underperforming candidates.

A higher period moving average can be used for long-term trends. Featured below is the chart of the JSWSTEL versus Nifty Daily ratio chart with a 100-period moving average.

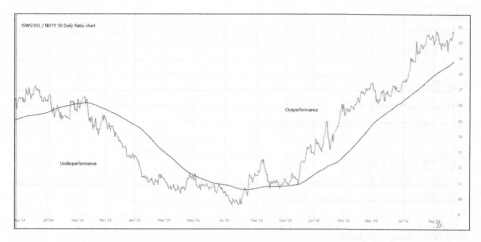

Figure 5.9: Daily ratio chart of JSWSTEEL to Nifty 50 index

Ratio trading below the moving average captures a period of underperformance. The ratio line trading above its moving average captures a period of outperformance. We should look for bearish price patterns during the period of underperformance and bullish price patterns during the period of outperformance to initiate trades.

Stocks or their ratio charts sustaining above the major moving averages even during bear markets are strong stocks. They are bullish star stocks.

We can also use a dual moving average or even a triple moving average in the ratio chart to analyze the outperformance or underperformance.

Adaptive Moving Average (AMA)

Adaptive Moving Average (AMA) is an indicator developed by Perry J. Kaufman. He explained this indicator in his book *Trading System and Methods*. It is also known as Kaufman's Adaptive Moving Average (KAMA).

Let me explain the concept of the indicator before we discuss the interpretation.

There are two important triggers on the price chart: Trend and Volatility.

Take a look at the following scenarios:

If the price moved up or down by 10 points = trend.

If the price moved by 10 points = volatility

So, a price move that shows us a trend also captures the range. If we calculate it as the rate of change or returns over a period, it represents the trend. When we make it an absolute number to calculate the range, it becomes a measure of volatility. When the price is trending, and the range is high it reflects a strong trend and momentum. When the price is not moving in a direction, but the range is high, the volatility or the noise component is high.

See the image given below. It captures the daily fluctuation of a stock over the last 10 sessions.

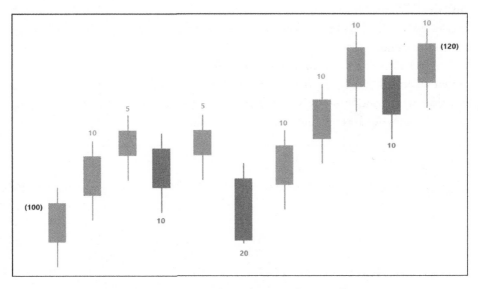

Image 5.3: Hypothetical prices of 10 candles

In image 5.3, the total daily movement of the stock is 100 points.

100 = (10+5+10+5+20+10+10+10+10+10)

So, in the last 10 sessions, the total daily movement is 100 points. That captures the volatility. Let us call it Noise.

While the total price movement was 100 points, the actual price change was 20-points from 100 to 120. The rate of change over 10 sessions is 20 points. So, the trend during the period was 20 points.

While the total moves up and down were 100 points what was the outcome? The price moved up by just 20 points. The study of these two aspects is known as the Efficiency Ratio.

Efficiency Ratio (ER) = Trend / Noise

ER in the above example is 0.20. It took a range of 100 points to gain 20 points.

For ER, the trend is also calculated in absolute terms. Meaning, if the price moves up by 20 points during the period or down by 20 points, the trend for the calculation of ER would be 20. This way, the Efficiency Ratio becomes a good volatility indicator.

If price is rising and ER is rising = strong uptrend

If price is falling and ER is rising = strong downtrend

When ER is rising, it means there is more of a trend in daily fluctuation. If ER is falling, noise is more.

Adaptive Moving Average (AMA) is a combination of the moving average and the Efficiency Ratio. Hence, it is a moving average that considers the volatility element as well. AMA moves when the trend is strong, and it does not move much when the trend is weak.

AMA rises at a rapid pace when the ER is rising (Trend > Noise) and slows down when ER is falling (Noise > Trend). So, AMA moves relatively slow during the sideways period but moves swiftly or relatively faster when the price is trending. So, it is a moving average that adapts to the volatility.

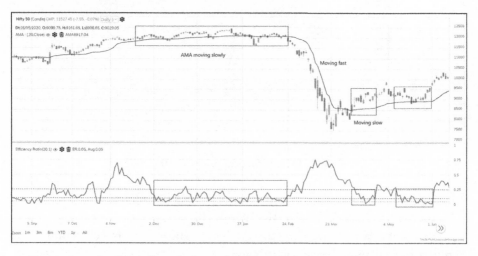

Figure 5.10: Daily candlestick chart of Nifty with 20-period AMA and 20-period Efficiency Ratio Indicator

Kaufman used Fast (FSC = 2) and Slow Smoothing Constant (SSC = 30) to make the average line adapt to ER. It gives less weightage to change in price if ER is falling and more weight if ER is increasing.

Image 5.4 explains the concept of the AMA indicator.

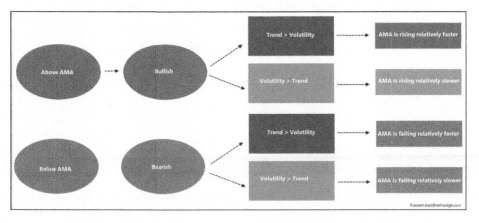

Image 5.4: Chart explaining Adaptive Moving Average calculation

From image 5.4, it should be apparent that a rising AMA line and falling AMA line are excellent signals to focus on.

- Price above AMA = Bullish
- Price below AMA = Bearish
- AMA trending = Trend is strong
- AMA is relatively flat = Noise is more

All other logic or interpretation of moving averages apply to AMA too.

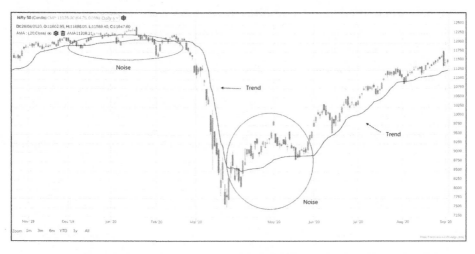

Figure 5.11: Daily candlestick chart of Nifty with 20-period AMA

The distinct feature of AMA is that it reduces the number of trades in a volatile environment because it remains relatively flat. This is an important aspect of this indicator. It might be a slightly lagging indicator but effective all the same.

We can apply AMA in the ratio charts too.

Below is the 40-period AMA applied on the ratio chart of the Nifty Pharma index to Nifty 50.

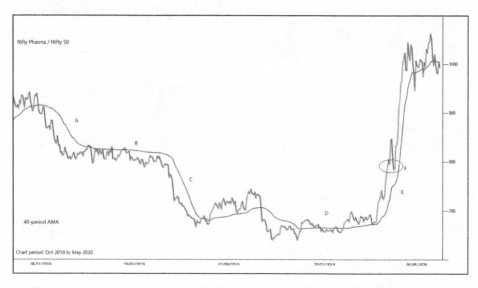

Figure 5.11: Daily Ratio chart of Nifty Pharma to Nifty 50 with 40-period AMA indicator

At Pattern A and C, the AMA line and ratio line were falling. It indicates strong underperformance. Pattern B and D is when the AMA line was relatively flat. It is a phase where the Pharma and Nifty performance was almost at par. Pattern E is where AMA and ratio line both were rising. When AMA and the ratio line are rising, it indicates strong outperformance of the numerator. When the ratio line is falling but remaining above the AMA line, we can treat it like an eagle pattern. Pattern F is a buying opportunity in the numerator. Moving average at this juncture was telling us that overall performance is bullish and that the falling ratio line can be a temporary pullback.

Given below is a daily ratio chart of Dabur to Nifty with a 40-period Adaptive Moving Average.

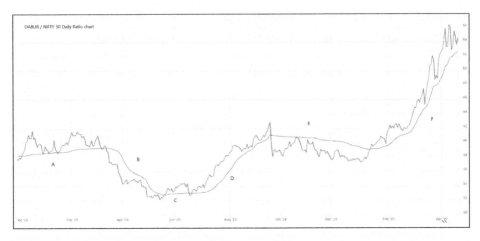

Figure 5.12: Daily ratio chart of DABUR to Nifty 50 with 40-period AMA indicator

Observe how the moving average went flat during periods A, C and E when the trend was not strong, and there was more range-bound price action. This moving average becomes more aggressive and moves when the trend is strong like in periods B and F in the above chart.

Any interpretation applicable to moving average is also applicable to the adaptive moving average.

- A ratio above the average indicates outperformance.
- A ratio below average indicates underperformance.
- This average can be used in multiple timeframes too.
- Multiple moving averages can also be plotted in a single ratio chart for confirmation.

Trading systems can be created using the ratio line behaviour and the moving average. The rising ratio line above the moving average is bullish. A falling ratio line above the moving average might be a temporary correction. The falling ratio line below the moving average is bearish. A rising ratio line below the moving average could be a temporary bounce.

AMMA

We can also plot dual moving averages on the chart to identify the crossover of averages. Typically, we need to choose a short-term period average and a long-term period average while plotting a dual moving average. But, instead of using two moving averages, we can use a combination of a regular moving average and the Adaptive Moving Average on the chart to capture the bullish and bearish crossovers. Let us call it the AMMA indicator. It is a combination of AMA (Adaptive Moving Average) and the regular MA (Moving Average).

When the price is above both averages, it is very bullish. If it is above one average line, it is semi-bullish. If the price is below both averages, it is very bearish. If it is below one average line, it is semi-bearish. Below is an example of a 200-day period AMMA indicator.

Below is the Nifty PSU bank to Nifty 50 daily ratio chart plotted with 200-period AMMA.

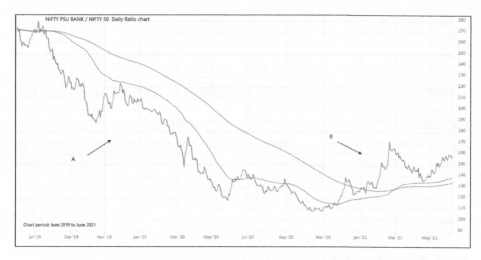

Figure 5.13: Daily ratio chart of Nifty PSU BANK to Nifty 50 with 200-period AMMA indicator

PSU Bank index was falling and underperforming Nifty at A during July–May 2020. Notice how the ratio line was below both the averages. The PSU Bank index was outperforming Nifty 50 during March-May 2021 at B when the ratio chart went above both the average lines.

Donchian channel

While moving averages can be handy to identify the trend and crossovers in the ratio chart, the channel-based indicators can also be of great help when we wish to identify range breakouts or a breakout above say the high of N days. The simplest and powerful channel indicator is the Donchian channel indicator.

Donchian channel was invented by Richard Donchian. He is known as the father of trend following trading. He was the founder of the world's first managed fund in 1949. Donchian focussed on developing a rule-based and systematic approach to trading the markets that would soon become his trend-following approach.

Three lines form part of the Donchian channel indicator. They are popularly called the upper band, middle band, and lower band. The default look-back period is 20.

- The upper band captures the highest high of the last 20 bars.
- The lower band represents the lowest low of the last 20 bars.
- The average of these two bands is the middle band.

So, if today's high is a new 20-day high, you will see the upper band rising. If today's low is a new 20-day low, you will see the lower band is falling.

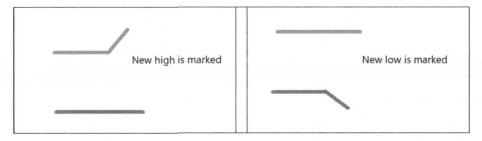

Image 5.5: Donchian channel new high and new low is marked

When the lower band is rising, that means the lowest low was the first bar in the last 20 and that bar is dropped from the calculation now. In simple words, the range has shifted and there is a new 20-day low which is higher than the previous one. The same logic is applicable when the upper band is falling.

So, on a given bar there are the possibilities mentioned below, for both the bands:

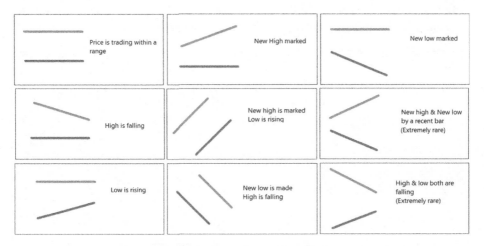

Image 5.6: Donchian channel band behaviour

One can easily identify the current state of the market using just by looking at the upper and lower bands Donchian bands.

After dropping below the lower band if the price goes above the upper band, it is a fresh bullish breakout. Otherwise, it is a continuation of a bullish breakout. Vice versa for a bearish breakout.

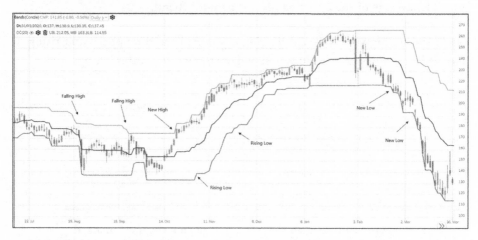

Figure 5.14: Daily candlestick chart with the Donchian channel indicator

Take a look at the image displayed below. If I merge all the 20 candles and make them a single candle, the high of that merged candle will be the highest high of the 20-bars. This will also be the upper band of the Donchian Channel. Similarly, the low of the merged candles will be the lowest low of the 20-bars and it will also be the lower band of the Donchian Channel. The average price of this candle (High + Low) /2) is the middle band. A rising middle band indicates that the average price of the last 20-days is rising and vice versa.

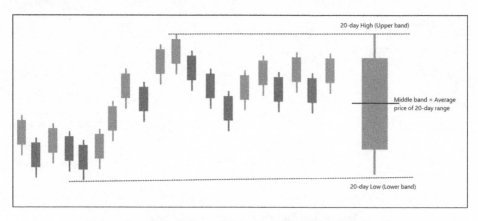

Image 5.7: Calculation of Donchian channel middle band

The middle band is a helpful indicator as well. We can define bullish and bearish zone using the middle band of the Donchian channel. To keep it simple,

- Price above the Middle band = Bullish zone
- Price below the Middle band = Bearish zone

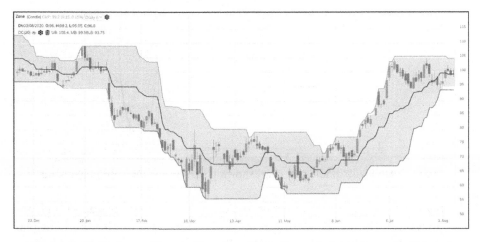

Figure 5.15: Daily candlestick chart showing Bollinger band indicator bullish and bearish zones

The distance between the upper and lower Donchian bands captures the price volatility. When the volatility is high, the distance between the bands gets wider. When the distance between the bands contracts, it is a sign of narrow range price action.

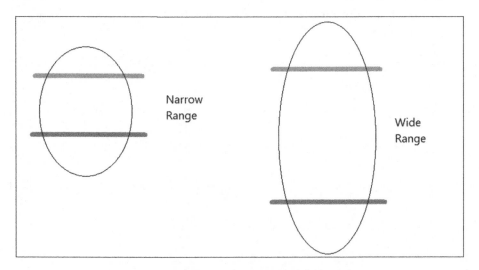

Image 5.8: Narrow range and wide range

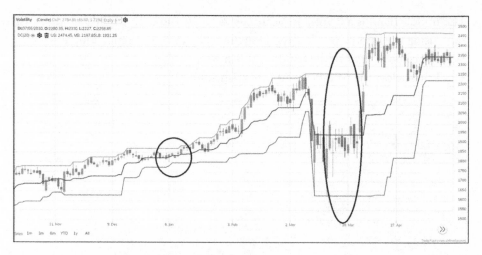

Figure 5.16: Daily candlestick chart showing narrow and wide Bollinger bands

We can use the Donchian channel on the ratio chart as well. Instead of high and low prices, we will use the closing price in the ratio chart to plot the Donchian channels. The middle band in the Donchian channel acts as a trend filter like moving average.

A 40-day Donchian channel is recommended in the ratio charts. If the ratio line is above the middle band, it indicates bullishness or outperformance. A ratio below the middle band indicates bearishness or underperformance. A ratio above the upper band is a bullish continuation breakout, a ratio below the lower band is a bearish continuation breakout.

Below is a daily ratio chart of Britannia to Nifty 50 with a 40-period Donchian channel.

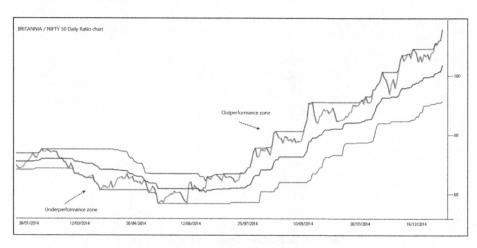

Figure 5.17: Daily ratio chart of Britannia to Nifty 50 with 40-period Donchian Channel

Using the Donchian channels, we can demarcate the ratio chart into bullish and bearish zones. If the ratio is in the bullish zone, look for bullish patterns in the stock to initiate trades. The rising upper band shows fresh breakout and indicates further outperformance. If the ratio line drops below the middle band, then it enters the underperformance zone. A falling lower band indicates that the ratio is making fresh lows. In other words, fresh lows indicate sustained underperformance.

Rising bands are bullish, and falling bands are bearish. Flat bands show that the ratio is in range and hence the numerator's performance is at par with the denominator.

If you analyze sectors using Donchian channels in the ratio chart, you can divide all sectors into bullish and bearish zones. Bullish strategies may be adopted in the outperforming sectors and bearish strategies in the underperforming sectors.

RSI

We can plot oscillator and momentum indicators on the ratio chart as well. Devised by J. Welles Wilder, RSI or the Relative Strength Index is one the most popular indicators used in technical analysis.

Let us try to understand the underlying formula and logic behind this indicator.

The RSI indicator is calculated on closing prices. We can define bullish and bearish price on a closing basis (Line chart) chart as follows:

• If the current price is higher than the previous price = Bullish bar
• If the current price is lower than the previous price = Bearish bar

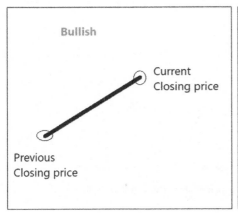
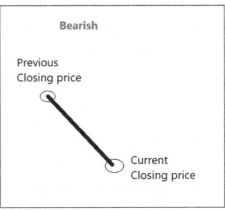

Image 5.9: Bullish and bearish closing price

Now that we have defined what is bullish and bearish, it is important to find the extent of bullishness and bearishness. If the price rises by 10 points and falls by 15 points, it indicates net bearishness.

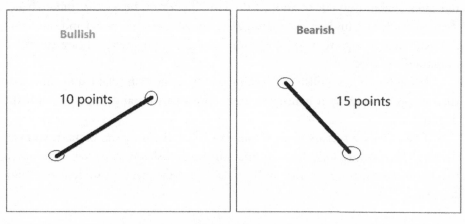

Image 5.10: Bullish and bearish closing prices

So, now we know the price trend and the amount of gain or loss.

Below is a line chart connecting 10 closing prices. Let us calculate gains and losses in this chart.

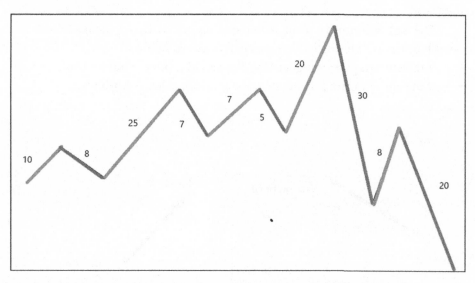

Image 5.11: Bullish and bearish prices over the last 10 sessions

In the above chart,

Bullish readings (Gain) are = 10, 25, 7, 20 & 8

Bearish reading (Loss) are = 8, 7, 5, 30 & 20

Let us calculate the simple average price of the gains & losses:

Bullish average = 14 ((10+25+7+20+8)/5)

Bearish average =14 ((8+7+5+30+20)/5)

What does the above information mean?

It means, over the last 10 days, average gains were 14 points and average losses 14 points.

These are absolute points. How do we assess the strength of the bullish camp?

Imagine there are 10 people from green and red teams sitting in a hall. Seven of them are from the Green team and the remaining three are from the Red team.

Image 5.12: Green and Red team members

What is the strength of the Green team? 70%, right?

That is what RSI represents. In the earlier chart example–the average of losing bars plus the average of winning bars was 14+14 = 28. Average gain was14. So, RSI will be ((14/28) x 100) = 50%

So, when RSI is at 50, it means the average gain is equal to the average loss.

If total points are 30 and the average gain is 18, the RSI would be at 60.

If total points are 30 and the average gain is 9, the RSI would be at 30.

A 14-day period is a recommended parameter by Wilder and you will find it as a default parameter in most of the software. Wilder used his averaging method to calculate the average in the RSI indicator.

Because of the averaging method, 75–25 can be considered a normal range. It needs a very strong trend without significant correction for the indicator to move below 10 or above 90.

When the price makes a new low, but the RSI doesn't, it is known as a bullish divergence. It means there were gains in between while the price made new lows but the gains prevented the RSI from making a corresponding lower low. The logic is reversed for the bearish divergence.

If the RSI is at 70, average gains are 70% of total gains and losses. If RSI is at 20, average gains are 20% of total gains and losses over a selected period. The average RSI is known as a signal line. It helps in smoothing the RSI data.

When we plot RSI on the ratio chart, we are essentially studying the behaviour of the two chosen instruments. Bullish RSI indicates outperformance by the numerator and bearish RSI underperformance.

Given below is the daily ratio chart of the Nifty 500 index versus Nifty 50 plotted along with the RSI indicator:

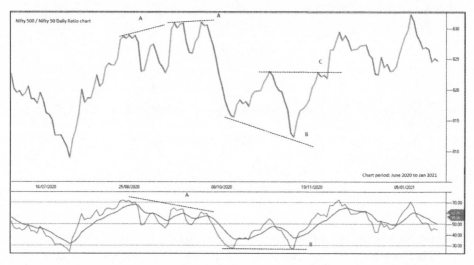

Figure 5.18: Daily ratio chart of Nifty 500 to Nifty 50 with RSI indicator

Point A is where the ratio chart made a new high, but RSI was falling showing negative divergence. It means that the numerator is outperforming but momentum is declining. The ratio made a new low at point B but the RSI did not fall below its previous bottom indicating a positive divergence. This was followed by a breakout in the ratio chart at C.

Rising RSI suggests more bullishness in the ratio chart. This in turn indicates the outperformance of the numerator. The RSI is an interesting indicator on ratio charts and the techniques to interpret RSI in a price chart is equally applicable in ratio charts as well.

Below are major observations:

- Higher the RSI reading, the stronger the performance of the numerator.
- RSI above 50 indicates ratio chart is in the bullish zone.
- RSI below 50 indicates ratio chart is in the bearish zone.
- Bullish divergence below the oversold zone and bearish divergence above the overbought zone can be useful to identify potential short-term reversals.

For a valid bullish divergence in the oversold region, the first RSI low must be below 30. Similarly, for a valid bearish divergence in an overbought zone, the first high in RSI should be above 70. Image 5.13 explains this concept.

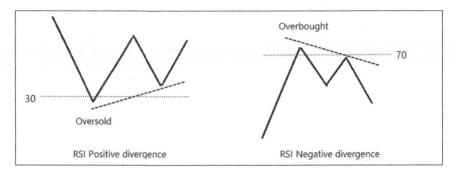

Image 5.13: RSI Positive divergence from the oversold zone and negative divergence from the overbought zone

A 20 or 40-period RSI is also useful for ratio chart analysis using the RSI indicator.

Below is a daily ratio chart of Tata steel versus Nifty 50 plotted with a 20-period RSI.

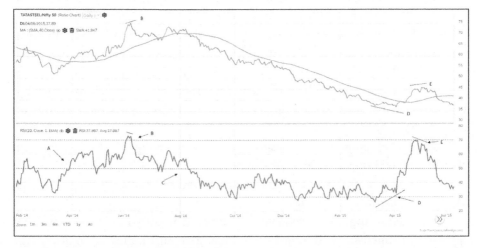

Figure 5.19: Daily ratio chart of TATASTEEL to Nifty 50 with 20-period RSI indicator

Point A is when the price is above the moving average and the RSI crossed above the 50 level. Point B is when the ratio chart is bullish and there is a negative divergence above 70 RSI levels. Point C is when RSI fell below 50 and the ratio chart is also below the moving average indicating further underperformance. Point D is bullish divergence below 30 levels in RSI that was followed by ratio line going above 50 RSI levels. Point E is bearish divergence above 70.

Below is a daily ratio chart of the Nifty Mid and Small-cap 400 index to Nifty 50.

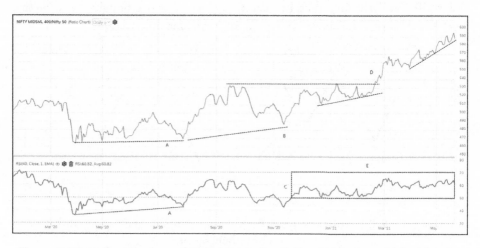

Figure 5.20: Daily ratio chart of Nifty Mid & Small Cap 400 Index to Nifty 50 index with 40-period RSI indicator

The ratio was at the same levels in period A, but the RSI indicator made a higher low suggesting strength. RSI went above 50 at C. Ratio chart triggered a breakout post-consolidation at D and the RSI was already bullish all along. The ratio chart continued to move up which marked a strong outperformance by the mid-cap small-cap index compared to the Nifty 50 index. The breakout in the ratio chart along with bullish RSI was an important lead indicator of the impending outperformance.

RSI indicator can also help in identifying short-term reversals on the chart. Like price charts, systems can be created using a combination of indicators on ratio charts as well.

Using a combination of indicators like moving average, AMA or Donchian channel and RSI on the ratio chart can be an effective trading system. When the ratio chart goes into a period of consolidation, indicators like RSI would be the ideal tool to use in such scenarios.

Trend following plus divergence can be used when you combine different types of instruments. I used some important and popular indicators to discuss the concept. I picked major indicators based on average, channels, and oscillators to explain their interpretation on the ratio chart. Ratio charts can be analyzed using other indicators too.

Any other indicator that is used in the price chart can be used in the ratio charts too. When you apply it to the ratio chart, it is calculated on the behaviour of two instruments. You can also combine price and indicator reading along with the ratio chart for trading systems.

The idea behind analyzing the ratio chart is to identify candidates with strong momentum in the ratio chart. We should trade or invest in such stocks displaying strong momentum in ratio charts.

Instead of picking stocks simply based on price returns, we can use the tools and identify the momentum of ratio charts. When the ratio line crosses an important moving average, or there is a Donchian channel breakout or prolonged consolidation breakout—we can identify stocks entering a strong outperformance zone.

All methods of analysis like Gann angles, Harmonic patterns, and other indicators are applicable on the ratio chart as well. Any approach or combination of approaches that help you identify price reversals may be effectively used in ratio charts too to identify such reversals.

Though I have shared a few indicators with recommended parameters, you should experiment with the prescribed settings and try other indicators to gain more conviction and clarity.

You have learnt about the implementation of tools and indicators on the ratio chart in this chapter. We discussed relative strength patterns in the earlier chapter. You can combine both and define the patterns using concepts discussed in this chapter.

These indicators are applicable on price, and ratio charts as well. You can define the trend in the price and the ratio chart using these indicators. You can then clearly segregate them into a bullish and bearish zone as discussed earlier. If you can identify the trend of the denominator, you can then use the indicators to define relative strength patterns. You can create objective trading systems using price and RS charts with this knowledge.

For example, if the denominator is Nifty, and you plot the indicator on the price of a stock and its ratio chart with denominator:

If Nifty is bullish:
- If the price and ratio chart is bullish, it is a flying pattern.
- If the price and ratio chart is bearish, it is a cat pattern.
- If the price is bullish but the ratio chart is bearish, it is a bearish star pattern.

If Nifty is bearish:

- If the price and ratio chart is bearish, it is a drowning pattern.
- If the price and ratio chart is bullish, it is a lion pattern.
- If the price is bearish but the ratio chart is bullish, it is a bullish star pattern.

The patterns shown above are a summary of the price and ratio chart relationship. There are endless ways to define them using different techniques, but once defined, they can transform into effective trading systems.

In this chapter, we discussed:

- We can use the ratio as an indicator on the price chart. We can analyze the pattern, apply tools and different indicators on the ratio chart.
- Patterns like momentum, horizontal, convergence which are applicable on the price chart are also applicable and useful on the ratio chart.
- Different types of indicators like momentum, trend following, oscillators, channel indicators can be plotted on the ratio chart as well.
- We can create trading systems on the ratio chart on multiple timeframes. We can make a relative strength analysis objective using the ratio chart.
  Let's discuss RS indicators in the next chapter.

Chapter 6

RELATIVE STRENGTH INDICATORS

. . . .

The ratio chart that we discussed is a tool to perform relative strength analysis. Some other techniques may also be used to plot the relationship between two instruments.

Relative Strength – Alpha

The relative strength indicator (not RSI) is another widely followed indicator to study relative strength. Unlike ratio charts, we need to define the look-back period to plot the RS indicator.

The calculation of the relative strength indicator is slightly different from the ratio chart, but the behaviour is almost the same. To calculate the RS indicator, instead of dividing the price of numerator stock by the denominator, the return or rate of change of both the stocks are calculated over the chosen look-back period. Returns of the numerator are deducted from the returns of the denominator to plot the relative strength indicator.

Here is the formula:

RS Indicator = (ROC of Numerator – ROC of Denominator)

We need to define the look-back period to plot this indicator. Popular look-back periods to plot this indicator are the 50-day, 100-day, and 52-weeks.

The calculation of the indicator is such that it will be above zero if the numerator is outperforming the denominator, and it will be below zero if the numerator is underperforming the denominator.

The crossover of the zero line indicates that the returns of the numerator have crossed the returns of the denominator. For example, if returns of numerator stock A and denominator stock B are 5% each. RS indicator reading of both will be at zero. RS reading will cross the zero line if the return of stock A increases to say 6%.

Hence, the stocks above zero line in this indicator are the bullish stocks and the ones below the zero line are bearish stocks. Higher the RS indicator reading, the stronger the outperformance.

People also call it Relative Strength Comparative (RSC) or Relative Price Strength (RPS) indicator. We can also divide the trend of the numerator by the denominator instead of subtracting it. It will however capture similar information.

If you check the logic of the indicator, it is a calculation of Alpha. The basic calculation of Alpha is deducting the total return of the stock from the benchmark. Hence, I call the above indicator Relative Strength–Alpha.

Deciding the look-back period is an important aspect of using this indicator.

An indicator above zero line shows the outperformance of the numerator and an indicator below zero line shows the underperformance of the numerator. The rising indicator line above zero lines is more bullish and the falling indicator line below zero lines is more bearish.

Given below is a chart of Nifty 500 to Nifty 50 along with a 50-period relative strength indicator.

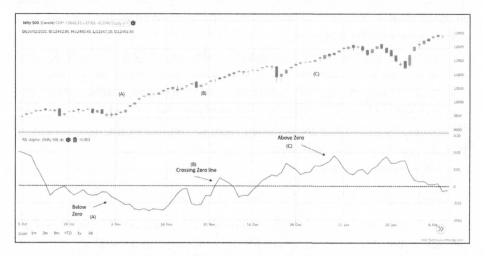

Figure 6.1: Daily candlestick chart of Nifty 500 with 50-period relative strength indicator to Nifty 50 index

The indicator displayed in the lower pane is divided between the above zero and below zero zones. The zone marked A captures the scenario where the indicator was below the zero line and falling. It shows that though the Nifty 500 index price was rising, the Nifty was outperforming the Nifty 500 during that period. This indicates that we would do better by investing in large caps than the ones from the Nifty 500 universe.

The RS-Alpha indicator crossed the zero line at B which indicates that the Nifty 500 had started outperforming the Nifty 50. The indicator was rising and was positioned above the zero line at C indicating the bullish trend and outperformance of the Nifty 500.

Like the ratio chart, we can also use the relative strength indicator along with other indicators on the price chart.

Below is a chart of JUBLFOOD from July 2020 to May 2021 plotted with a 20-period moving average and 50-period relative strength-alpha indicator against the Nifty 50 index.

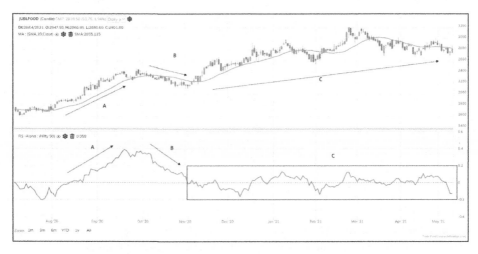

Figure 6.2: Daily Candlestick chart of JUBLFOOD with 20-period moving average and 50-period relative strength indicator to Nifty 50 index

In Period A the RS indicator was above the zero line and rising. This is the time to buy the sock either on continuation price breakouts or on pullbacks.

The zone at B was when the ratio line was trading above zero but falling. This is a period where we should be cautious for the impending major top in the price and seek more confirmation before trading price breakouts. The caution is warranted as the price is rising but is underperforming the benchmark.

Period C is when the indicator was hovering around the zero-line indicating that the performance of the stock was in line with the Nifty 50 index. This indicates that even though the price is not falling, we should look for opportunities elsewhere. A rising price not accompanied by a rising RS indicator suggests that other stocks are doing better than the numerator.

Given below is an example of the 50-period RS indicator and 20-period moving average on the price chart.

The crossover of the RS indicator above the zero line and the price above its moving average represents an ideal scenario to trade or invest. Stop-loss can be placed either below the recent swing low or below the moving average line.

Featured below is the chart of HINDUNLVR from June to November 2019 plotted with a 20-period moving average and a 50-period relative strength indicator against the Nifty 50 index.

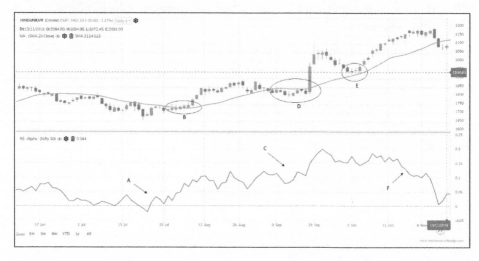

Figure 6.3: Daily candlestick chart of HINDUNILVR with a 20-period moving average and a 50-period relative strength indicator to Nifty 50 index

Point A is when the RS indicator crossed the zero line indicating the bullish performance of the numerator. The zone covered by Circle B is where the price crossed above the moving average. Zone C is where the RS indicator is rising and positioned above the zero line and the area circled as D is where the price is crossing above the moving average line. Point E captures the pullback in price to the moving average.

The price kept rising during period F but the RS Indicator was falling. This suggested that even though the price was rising, the returns were inferior to the benchmark.

Below is a chart of MARUTI from December 2020 to May 2021 plotted with a 20-period moving average and 50-period relative strength indicator against the Nifty 50 index.

Figure 6.4: Daily candlestick chart of MARUTI with 50-period moving average and 50-period relative strength indicator to Nifty 50 index

The price crossed above the zero line for a brief while in January 2021. It went below zero-line post that and the price points marked A, B and C in the above chart captures the instances where the price was rejected at the moving average line. During this period, the RS indicator was falling and placed below the zero line.

We can apply the same concept using a higher moving average length as well.

Below is a chart of AMBUJACEM capturing the price action from March 2021 to May 2021. A 50-period moving average is plotted as an overlay and the 50-period relative strength indicator is against the Nifty 50 index is plotted in the lower pane.

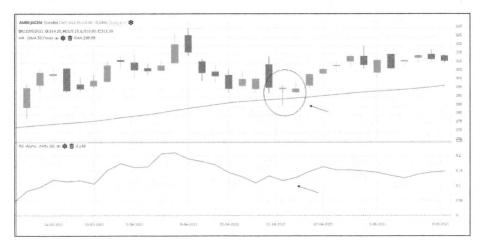

Figure 6.5: Daily candlestick chart of AMBUJACEM with 50-period moving average and 50-period relative strength indicator to Nifty 50 index

Notice the price action highlighted by the arrow mark where the RS indicator stayed above the zero line and was rising. The price however drifted below the moving average but managed to close above it, indicating strength.

All concepts that we discussed on the ratio chart applies to a period-based RS indicator as well.

It is important to remember that a falling RS indicator is a sign of caution even if it is above the zero line. A falling RS indicator line below the zero line indicates underperformance. The farther away from the RS indicator line is from the zero line, the stronger the stock is. Usually, the strong and outperforming stocks will manage to stay away from the zero line of the RS indicator. Any price pullback in such candidates is a buying opportunity.

William O'Neil and Mark Minervini use the relative strength indicator. A 52-week is a popular parameter. It is also not uncommon to see people using a 120-period or a 50-period look-back parameter to plot this indicator.

Below is a chart of ADANI PORTS from October 2019 to March 2020 plotted with a 20-period moving average and 120-period relative strength indicator against the Nifty 500 index.

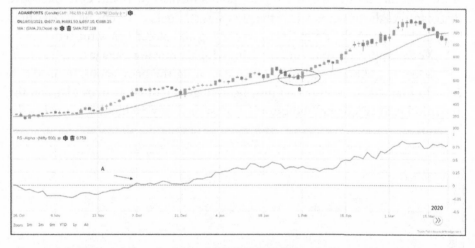

Figure 6.6: Daily candlestick chart of ADANI PORTS with 20-period moving average and 120-period relative strength indicator to Nifty 50 index

RS indicator turned bullish at point A indicating outperformance against the Nifty 500 index. Price drifted lower to the near moving average and completed a bullish crossover at point B that offered a buying opportunity on a price pullback.

We have studied instances where a look-back period of 50-period or 120-period was used to plot the relative strength indicator. Instead of defining the fixed look-back period, we can also plot the RS indicator from an important date on the chart.

The important date can be a major swing high or swing low on the chart. This approach may be called a dynamic period-based relative strength–Alpha indicator.

Given below is a chart of Nifty during early 2020.

Figure 6.7: Daily candlestick chart of Nifty 50 with 20-period moving average

There was an important top recorded on February 14, 2020, that was followed by a bearish moving average crossover and a strong downtrend. Nifty made an important low on March 24, 2020.

If we calculate the performance of stocks from February 14, we will get to know which stocks are outperforming Nifty from that date. We will get to know which stocks outperformed during the fall and the bounce after marking an important low in the index.

Below is a chart of JUBLFOOD from February 2020 to October 2020 plotted with a 20-period moving average. The relative strength indicator is plotted from February 14, 2020, against the Nifty 50 index.

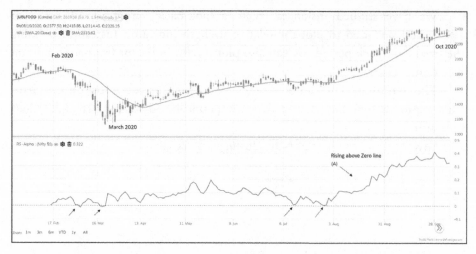

Figure 6.8: Daily candlestick chart of MARUTI with 20-period moving average and relative strength indicator to Nifty 50 index from February 14, 2020

The arrows marked in the above chart, in the RS indicator pane, indicates that the price dipped to the zero line but managed to stay above it. This suggests that sustained outperformance in terms of returns from the reference date of February 2020. The rising price indicates a bullish trend throughout this period. At point A, it started rising above the zero line and the distance between price and moving average also started widening indicating strong price momentum. At that period, the price action was bullish and the rising RS indicator line suggested outperformance of the price.

Fixed-period and dynamic-period are two formats of period-based relative strength indicator.

The advantage of the relative strength indicator is that we can easily demarcate the ratio chart between bullish and bearish zones using the zero line. The interpretation remains the same as the ratio chart.

The moving average was used in the above charts to study the price action. Any other indicator may be used to study the price action. A combination of daily RSI of the stock price trading above the 50-level and price trading above its moving average and RS indicator staying above zero is a simple system to identify bullish stock with relative outperformance.

Below is a daily candlestick chart of BAJAJFINSV with a 200-day average, 14-period RSI and 240-period RS–Alpha.

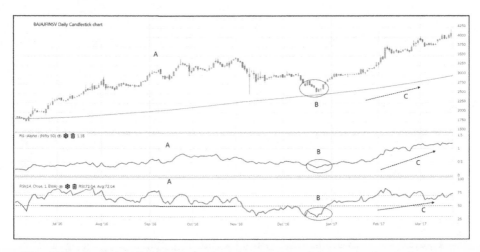

Figure 6.9: Daily candlestick chart of BAJAJFINSV with 200-period moving average, 14-period RSI and 240-period relative strength indicator to Nifty 50 index

The price was above its 200-day moving average and the RS indicator was above zero during period A. This indicates that the trend was bullish, and the stock was an outperformer. The RSI staying above 50 indicates strong momentum. Price corrected and tested its 200-day moving average at point B. The RS indicator however was still above zero. The RSI went into an oversold zone providing affordable bullish trade opportunities. This was followed by the price, RS and RSI turning bullish in zone C.

At the zones marked A and C in the above chart, all the studies were in sync and such periods are favourable for investors and traders to buy the stock. Traders should look for bullish price patterns in such cases to take fresh or additional exposures.

We can also use the RS indicator and the ratio chart together for confirmation.

Below is the daily candlestick chart of LT with a 50-day moving average, 50-period relative strength indicator and a ratio chart.

Figure 6.10: Daily candlestick chart of LT with 50-period moving average and 50-period relative strength indicator and ratio chart to Nifty 50 index

The relative strength indicator went above the zero line at A. The price went above the moving average at B and recorded a 25-day high at C. The price and ratio chart were rising and bullish at D. Price, RS indicator and ratio indicator were in sync until point E. The price moved to a new high but the ratio chart did not, at E, suggesting a bearish divergence. Price dropped below its moving average line at F.

If the denominator is the Nifty 50 index, here are some patterns discussed earlier in the current context:

If Nifty is bullish:
* If the price is bullish, and the RS indicator is above the zero line, it is a flying pattern.
* If the price is bearish and the RS indicator is below the zero line, it is a cat pattern.
* If the price is bullish and the RS indicator is below the zero line, it is a bearish star pattern.

If Nifty is bearish:
* If the price is bearish and RS indicator is below the zero line, it is a drowning pattern.
* If the price is bullish and RS indicator is above the zero line, it is a lion pattern.
* If the price is bearish and RS indicator is above the zero line, it is a bullish star pattern.

Other concepts that we discussed above such as a rising RS indicator above the zero line is more bullish whereas a falling RS indicator below the zero line is more bearish. These observations and concepts may be used to filter the stocks further.

The above template may be used to identify stocks. We can also run a screener on any group or universe using the RS indicator value and sort the stocks based on that. We can plot this indicator based on any fixed look-back period or from a chosen start date.

Below is a table of top stocks in the Nifty 500 universe. The denominator is Nifty 500 for the 50-period RS indicator.

Table 6.1: Example of list of top-performing stocks based on relative strength indicator of stocks compared to 50-period Nifty 500 index

Scrip	LCP	▼ RS Value	Trend	Status
ATGL	1334.55	1.715	Rising	Above Zero Line
TATASTLBSL	105.85	1.258	Falling	Above Zero Line
ANGELBRKG	664.15	0.992	Rising	Above Zero Line
SAIL	140.40	0.959	Falling	Above Zero Line
ALKYLAMINE	3644.30	0.796	Rising	Above Zero Line
BALRAMCHIN	326.15	0.787	Falling	Above Zero Line
SUPPETRO	704.95	0.778	Falling	Above Zero Line
BHEL	73.45	0.774	Rising	Above Zero Line
JSWSTEEL	734.25	0.749	Falling	Above Zero Line
INTELLECT	756.85	0.685	Falling	Above Zero Line
TATASTEEL	1233.90	0.661	Falling	Above Zero Line
NFL	62.70	0.619	Rising	Above Zero Line
KPRMILL	1505.05	0.619	Rising	Above Zero Line
JSWENERGY	120.75	0.614	Falling	Above Zero Line
GRAPHITE	773.65	0.599	Falling	Above Zero Line
ADANITRANS	1197.30	0.599	Rising	Above Zero Line
ADANIENT	1303.50	0.599	Rising	Above Zero Line
NMDC	196.95	0.572	Falling	Above Zero Line
MMTC	54.35	0.570	Rising	Above Zero Line
FLUOROCHEM	848.80	0.568	Rising	Above Zero Line

The table shown above captures the RS indicator value. Higher the value, the better the performance. The table also captures the status and trend of the RS indicator which can help us in quick analysis of any universe of stocks.

This relative strength indicator can also be called RS–Alpha because of its similarity to the generic concept of alpha.

Relative Strength-Alpha Volatility

The calculation of RS–Alpha compares the returns of both stocks. But let us consider a scenario detailed below.

Suppose say stock A generated 10% returns and Stock B 12% over the same period. Logically, stock B is a better performer or an outperformer. Let us introduce another layer of information here in the form of volatility. What if the volatility of stock A was 2% and that of stock B was 6%? Now, which is a better performing stock? Stock B generated higher returns but was too volatile. Why not plot relative strength indicator net returns after adjusting for volatility.

When we compare the returns of a stock versus Nifty, we also need to understand the volatility of these instruments is different. The nifty index would not move as much as stock. A stock can easily move 5% or 10% in a day, but the benchmark index would do it very occasionally.

It would therefore be advisable to consider the average volatility of each instrument while comparing the returns. I call this Relative Strength–Alpha Volatility or the RS-AV indicator.

Here are the details about the calculation of this indicator.

RS- AV Indicator = (Net return of the numerator – The net return of the denominator)

Whereas Net Return = (Return – Volatility)

When this indicator is above the zero-line, it shows that the net performance of the numerator is better than the denominator. When it is below zero-line, it shows that the numerator is underperforming the denominator.

It is not quite common to see this indicator stay in the positive territory because the average volatility of stock would typically be higher than its returns. The indicator therefore mostly remains between -1 and 1. A crossover of -0.50 may be used as an important trigger level.

If you filter the stocks using this indicator, the stocks trading above -0.50 may be considered bullish stocks. If you find stocks above zero, they are extremely bullish because they are outperforming the markets in terms of returns, as well as volatility.

As the indicator calculation considers Alpha and volatility, the outperforming or underperforming stocks captured using this indicator would be relatively less noisy.

Below is a daily candlestick chart of SRF with a 50-period Alpha–AV indicator.

Figure 6.11: Daily candlestick chart of SRF and 50-period relative strength–AV indicator to Nifty 50 index

The indicator moved above -0.5 line at point A that indicated outperformance. It went above zero line at B that indicated strong momentum and outperformance of the stock. The price did well in the next few days in terms of returns.

The RS–Alpha volatility indicator can be used in conjunction with the RS–Alpha indicator.

Given below is a daily candlestick chart of Dabur plotted with RS Alpha and AV indicators.

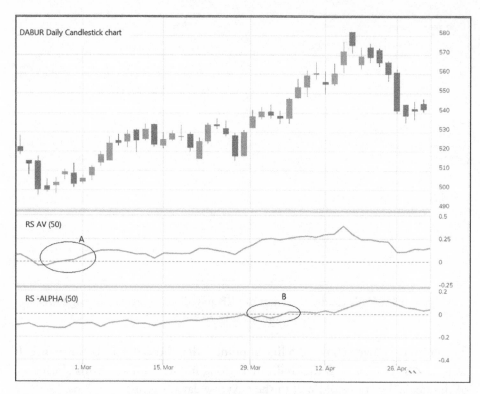

Figure 6.12: Daily candlestick chart of DABUR with 50-period relative strength and RS–AV indicator to Nifty 50 index

RS–AV indicator crossed the zero line at point A indicating strong outperformance by the stock. The RS indicator was also rising but it crossed the zero line later when there was also a breakout in price at B. When both the indicators are in the bullish zone it indicates strong outperformance.

One can experiment with different parameters for RS–AV indicator depending on the investment horizon. Using a 120- period look-back period may be a useful parameter for this indicator to get started.

Below is a daily candlestick chart of BAJAJFINSV plotted with 120-period RS–Alpha and RS–AV indicators.

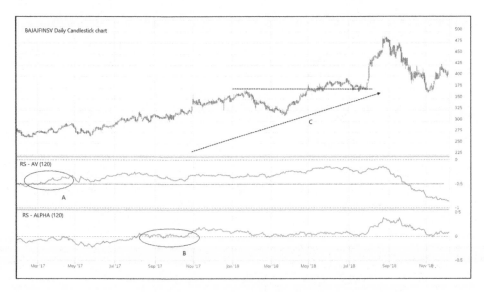

Figure 6.13: Daily candlestick chart of BAJAJFINSV with 120-period relative strength and RS – AV indicator to Nifty 50 index

The RS AV indicator crossed -0.50 at point A and that gave a hint that the stock is an outperformer. RS-ALPHA indicator moved above the zero line and sustained above it from point B. Both indicators were in sync during period C when the stock outperformed with strong momentum.

Dynamic RS–AV indicator can also be plotted from a certain period. Instead of defining the fixed-period indicator, we can also plot it from an important date on the chart.

If you rank the stocks based on the RS-AV indicator, you get the list of stocks doing better in terms of performance and volatility against the denominator.

Below is an example of the list of stocks from the Auto sector with their RS–AV value with denominator as Nifty Auto index.

Table 6.2: Example of list of stocks in Auto sector RS–AV value with denominator as Nifty Auto

Scrip	LCP	▼ RS Value	Performance	Ratio Rank	Trend	Status
BAJAJ-AUTO	4238.95	0.102	28.67%	50.83%	Rising	Above Zero Line
BALKRISIND	2175.30	0.021	32.13%	55.00%	Falling	Above Zero Line
EXIDEIND	190.00	0.014	3.37%	48.33%	Falling	Above Zero Line
MARUTI	7091.15	-0.071	-8.37%	44.17%	Falling	Below Zero Line
HEROMOTOCO	2976.75	-0.202	-5.19%	41.67%	Falling	Below Zero Line
BOSCHLTD	15108.55	-0.219	16.16%	53.33%	Rising	Below Zero Line
EICHERMOT	2665.80	-0.229	4.56%	47.50%	Falling	Below Zero Line
MRF	83083.45	-0.245	5.31%	47.50%	Falling	Below Zero Line
AMARAJABAT	739.10	-0.309	-19.31%	42.50%	Falling	Below Zero Line
TVSMOTOR	612.70	-0.336	23.00%	45.00%	Falling	Below Zero Line
M&M	806.30	-0.446	8.10%	51.67%	Rising	Below Zero Line
BHARATFORG	666.65	-0.455	23.59%	50.83%	Falling	Below Zero Line
MOTHERSUMI	237.30	-0.480	51.63%	49.17%	Falling	Below Zero Line
ASHOKLEY	121.65	-0.670	27.78%	50.00%	Falling	Below Zero Line
TATAMOTORS	318.10	-0.716	72.09%	59.17%	Falling	Below Zero Line

Stocks with a bullish number are considered outperformers in terms of price as well as noise. The trend and the status can also help in stock filtration. We shall discuss the ratio rank later in this chapter.

Like the ratio chart, RS–Alpha and RS–AV are tools that can be used to study relative strength. The advantage of the RS Indicator and RS–AV indicator is that they have reference lines to identify bullish and bearish crossovers. The advantage of the ratio chart on the other hand is that the user does not have to define any look-back period. Indicators like the 50-period moving average or RSI can be useful on the ratio chart as a substitute for zero-line crossover. If the RSI of the ratio chart is above 50, the ratio is bullish over that period.

Normalisation of ratio chart

Many analysts use a normalised ratio chart. This is nothing but a ratio chart that is calculated from a particular base date. To do this, we calculate the price of one instrument by another and start the calculation from a chosen date. The base value on the start date is 100. This makes all instruments directly comparable. If the ratio of a particular instrument is 130, it has outperformed the benchmark by 30%. If the reading is 70%, the numerator has underperformed by 30%. This helps in comparing the stocks and rank them.

Given below is the ratio chart plotted from January 1, 2020, of Bank, Pharma, Metal, Auto and FMCG sectors versus the Nifty 50 index.

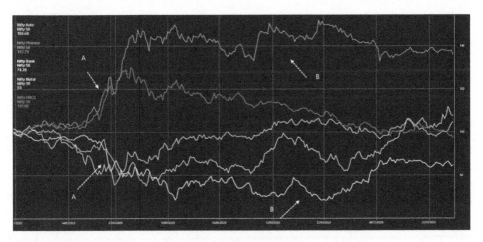

Figure 6.14: Ratio chart comparison of Bank, Pharma, Metal, Auto and FMCG sectors versus Nifty 50 index from January 1, 2020, to December 2020

It is a multi-performance ratio chart. The starting point of all charts is January 1, 2020, and the base price is 100. Looking at the image, we get to know that the Pharma (red line) and FMCG (purple line) started outperforming others at point A because those lines were rising and were positioned above others. Metals (blue line) and banks (yellow line) were falling. Pharma was the top performer at B and banks were underperformers.

This is an example of ratio charts plotted from a base price and date.

If it is for ranking, this goal can be achieved by plotting the relative strength–Alpha indicator from a particular date and measure the performance of the stocks.

Given below is a list of PSE Index stocks with the denominator as the PSE Index over the last 120-period.

Table 6.3: Example of list of PSE Index stocks with the denominator as the PSE Index over the last 120-period

Scrip	LCP	▼ RS Value	Performance	Ratio Rank	Trend	Status
SAIL	121.20	0.953	123.41%	51.67%	Falling	Above Zero Line
BHEL	71.10	0.798	107.89%	49.17%	Rising	Above Zero Line
NATIONALUM	72.35	0.439	72.06%	47.50%	Falling	Above Zero Line
NMDC	181.40	0.434	71.54%	55.83%	Falling	Above Zero Line
CONCOR	693.15	0.379	65.98%	53.33%	Rising	Above Zero Line
IRCTC	1894.60	0.094	37.48%	49.17%	Falling	Above Zero Line
GAIL	160.45	0.076	35.69%	49.17%	Rising	Above Zero Line
ONGC	117.60	0.045	32.58%	47.50%	Rising	Above Zero Line
OIL	136.10	0.024	30.49%	49.17%	Rising	Bullish Zero Crossover)
HINDPETRO	281.55	-0.003	27.83%	47.50%	Rising	Below Zero Line
BEL	146.95	-0.003	27.78%	50.00%	Rising	Below Zero Line
IOC	109.90	-0.059	22.25%	43.33%	Rising	Below Zero Line
HAL	1031.70	-0.064	21.71%	48.33%	Rising	Below Zero Line
BPCL	470.85	-0.086	19.54%	47.50%	Falling	Below Zero Line
NHPC	25.75	-0.089	19.21%	45.83%	Rising	Below Zero Line
POWERGRID	224.40	-0.121	16.00%	42.50%	Rising	Below Zero Line
RECLTD	145.45	-0.131	15.03%	45.00%	Falling	Below Zero Line
NTPC	110.20	-0.163	11.82%	37.50%	Falling	Below Zero Line
COALINDIA	147.60	-0.175	10.60%	34.17%	Falling	Below Zero Line

It shows that SAIL, BHEL, NATIONALUM etc are outperformers. RS-Alpha line for BHEL is rising. Stocks such as COAL INDIA, NTPC and RECLTD are the underperformers. There is a bullish crossover in OIL, it has gone above zero-line, the RS line is rising and the ratio rank is also close to 50%.

Ratio Rank Indicator

We can measure the performance of the security over a period to find top-performing stocks, or we can scan for RS indicator and find the top-performing stocks. If there is strength in the trend, the stock will continue to outperform a greater number of sessions during the period.

If we also measure the strength of the ratio indicator during the period, it will be an extremely helpful indicator. We can study the advances of the ratio chart during the period and calculate in how many sessions the numerator has outperformed the benchmark. If it has outperformed more than 50% of the time under consideration, it is then a strong candidate. It indicates that the stock has displayed the tendency to bounce back after the underperforming phase.

If person A and B run a 100-metre race, the winner will be the one who covers the distance in the shortest time. It is easy to rank them based on the time taken. The quality of running does not matter. But that is not the case when it comes to the ranking of stocks.

For example, here are the returns of three stocks over the same period:

A – 50%
B – 48%
C – 47%

We can rank and say A is the top-performing stock. But does that mean B and C are not good? They can easily gain more than A going forward. Hence, the top rank is not a very meaningful criterion to filter stocks. Rather, the stocks in the top slot are the important ones.

Ranking based only on what has happened in the past is not sufficient. We need to assess the overall trend to get an idea about the future potential. A stock that is stuck in the middle of the ranking table can top the list tomorrow. We can assess them by the quality of the rally and the consistency in performance. Stocks that outperformed during more sessions over a period and remained less volatile during a downtrend and generated steady returns can be considered to be high-quality performers. The stocks that outperformed were driven primarily by the move in the last couple of sessions that might top the list because of the recent spike. Those kinds of stocks must be filtered.

This quality can be assessed through a ratio rank indicator. It calculates how steady the performance has been over a period. It is calculated on the ratio chart of two instruments. But we can plot it below in the price chart itself.

A ratio rank score of more than 50% is considered an effective parameter.

Below is a daily ratio chart of ADANIENT to Nifty plotted with a 50-period RS–Alpha and ratio rank indicator.

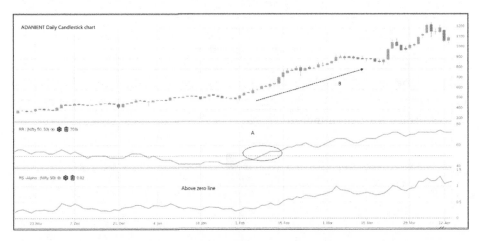

Figure 6.15: Daily ratio chart of ADANIENT to Nifty plotted with 50-period RS–Alpha and ratio rank indicator

RS indicator is above the zero line throughout the chart, suggesting that the stock was outperforming. It went through a period of correction and went above the zero line at A indicating that it is gaining momentum and outperforming sessions are increasing. This was followed by a steady price run at B, with a rising ratio rank indicator that shows strong momentum.

The ratio rank indicator reading can be useful while finding the top-performing stocks using any of the RS indicators that we have discussed.

D Cap-Shoe Indicator

We discussed techniques of plotting ratio charts separately or below the price. It is a good idea to study relative strength in candlestick charts itself as an overlay. The proprietary D cap-shoe indicator does precisely this. Let us discuss this indicator.

A box will be plotted above or below the candle to capture the behaviour of the ratio chart.

A cap is a box drawn above the candle while the shoe is a box plotted below the candle.

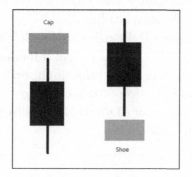

Image 6.1: Cap and shoebox

Take a look at the candle below. A strong green candle and a big box of outperformance. It shows that the price went up during the session and outperformed the denominator.

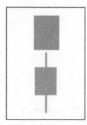

Image 6.2: Large D-Cap on a bullish candle

Price candle = Bullish

DCS candle = Bullish Strong Outperforming

See the chart given below. It shows that the price moved up during the session and it outperformed the denominator, but outperformance was not spectacular.

Image 6.3: Small D-Cap on a bullish candle

Price candle = Bullish

DCS candle = Bullish outperforming

The chart displayed below is more interesting. Price rallied during the session, but it underperformed the denominator. This is significant information, indicating that even though the numerator price candle was strong, the denominator was stronger than the numerator.

Image 6.4: Large D-Shoe on a bullish candle

Price candle = Bullish

DCS candle = Bearish Underperforming

The opposite of outperforming candles are the underperforming candles.

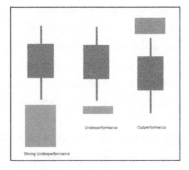

Image 6.5: D-Cap and shoe on a bearish candle

These boxes on candlestick charts help up analyze the trend of the ratio chart. Remember, a ratio chart trend comprises the trend of numerator and denominator. The height of the box captures the degree of outperformance or underperformance. A large height box shows a strong trend of the ratio chart.

A bullish price trend with more strong bullish boxes and small bearish boxes is a pattern of strong outperformance. Similarly, a chart where the size of bullish ratio boxes are reducing, and large bearish boxes are being plotted is a sign of strong underperformance.

Below is a daily candlestick chart of Tata Steel plotted with a 50-day moving average.

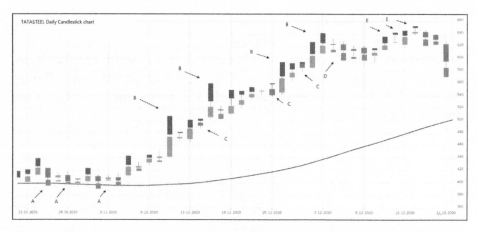

Figure 6.16: Daily candlestick chart of Tata Steel plotted with 50-day moving average and D-Cap shoe indicator

Candles during period A are bearish and underperforming but the underperformance was not significant, and the price was trading above moving average. The price remained above the moving average and started outperforming. Large caps printed above candles during B indicate strong bullish outperformance. Have a look at the candles at C during the uptrend. There were bearish candles but with a cap suggesting that the price session was bearish, but the performance was better than the denominator. It is a typical sign of a strong uptrend. There was a price correction at D, but the underperformance was not significant. During period E, the price was going up, but the size of the cap was shrinking, suggesting weakening momentum.

Below is a daily candlestick chart of GRASIM with the D Cap-Shoe indicator. Observe the important patterns that are highlighted in the chart.

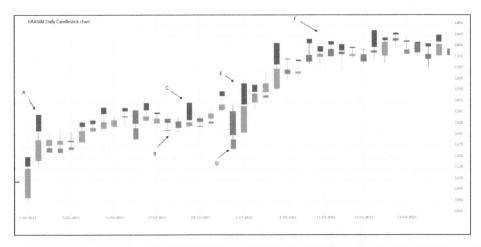

Figure 6.17: Daily candlestick chart of GRASIM with D Cap-Shoe indicator

The significant size of the ratio box at A is a sign of strong outperformance. When such type of large box is marked, the stock needs to be analyzed and monitored further. If the RS indicator is also in favour, a favourable candlestick pattern that offers affordable trade opportunities should be looked for. Take a look at the small boxes during bearish candles at B. It shows that the price candle is not bullish, but the stock is not underperforming. Look at the number of bullish boxes till that period. There were more bullish boxes than bearish, and the chart was dominated by blue indicating outperformance.

A small green candle at C but look at that large performance box. That tells us that the stock is set to outperform. A large bearish candle at D but relatively small underperformance box says that it is relatively strong. This was followed by a large bullish candle and strong outperformance box at E. The price continued to do well. There were many bearish candles in period F, but the stock outperformed the Nifty.

The D cap-shoe can be a useful indicator to study relative performance on the price chart. Observe the size of the boxes when bullish or bearish candles are printed. This can help you pick strong candidates for trading and investment.

Ratio RSI Indicator

We discussed the RSI indicator in the previous chapter. The RSI indicator can be plotted on the ratio chart as well, and it would capture the strength or the weakness of the numerator.

We typically plot the RS indicator on the price chart. But we can also plot the RS indicator of the ratio chart below the price chart of the numerator.

Displayed below is a daily candlestick chart of JSWSTEEL along with the RS indicator calculated on the ratio chart of JSWSTEEL to Nifty 50.

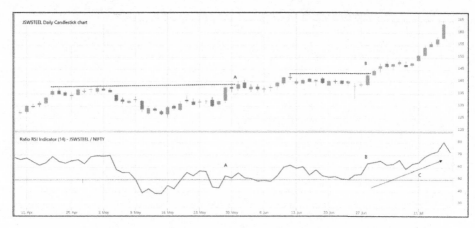

Figure 6.18: Daily candlestick chart of JSWSTEEL along with the RSI indicator calculated on the ratio chart of JSWSTEEL to Nifty 50

At Point A on the chart, the ratio RSI crossed above the 50 mark after a higher low formation and the price also completed a range breakout. The indicator hovered in the positive zone. Price breakout at B was accompanied by a rising ratio RSI indicator, suggesting the ratio chart is gaining strength. This indicates that the numerator is outperforming along with a price breakout and the ratio chart was in momentum. Ratio RSI and price were in an uptrend at C.

We discussed few indicators in this segment that we can plot below the price chart for relative strength analysis. All these indicators are useful, they can be used along with other RS studies as well.

In this chapter, we discussed:

- Different types of Relative strength indicators can be plotted below the price chart for effective relative strength analysis.
- Relative strength – alpha zero crossovers is a useful method. RS – AV, Ratio Rank, D-Cap Shoe, Ratio RSI are innovative RS tools applied on the price chart. We can also use these indicators in combination.
- Systems can be created using patterns or/and indicators on the price chart and the RS chart/indicators.

Now, you have a complete idea about the Ratio, RS patterns and RS indicator. Take a pause, spend some time on these methods, and think about the possibilities. You can create systems based on the price and the relative strength. Focus on the principles and try to be innovative. As for the price chart, there are unlimited possibilities on the RS chart.

Let's discuss different and advanced methods of using RS charts in the next chapter.

Chapter 7

NOISELESS RELATIVE STRENGTH

Until now, we discussed the ratio chart and relative strength indicators that are plotted in the line chart format and plotted using closing prices of instruments. It is not a common practice to plot ratio charts in candlestick format. A candle consists of Open, High, Low and Closing prices. It is not logical to divide these prices with another instrument. It makes a lot of sense to compare the closing price of two instruments and plot the relative strength charts.

Since we plot the ratio chart by considering a single price or the closing price of the session, we can also use one-dimensional charts such as Point & Figure, Renko, Line-break or Kagi to plot the ratio charts. They are known as dimensional charts because they only consider price to plot the chart while the time element is ignored. I call them noiseless charts because they remove noise from the data which is very vital from a trading perspective.

In the image shown below, a box is drawn in a ratio chart that is plotted in the traditional line charting format. The box is drawn connecting the current ratio line with the previous ratio line.

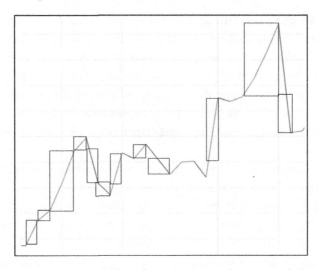

Image 7.1: Boxes are drawn on the line chart connecting the price with the previous price

I drew boxes based on the closing price of the line chart but overlapping prices were ignored. The length of the boxes depends on the distance between the lines. This in essence is a line-break chart. We can define the length of the reversal as well. This makes the approach objective. For example, if the ratio line is in a bullish box, the length of the box can be studied, and relevant rules may be framed to study relative performance.

How about if we divide the ratio line into a fixed number of small boxes?

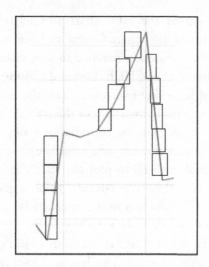

Image 7.2: Fixed-size boxes on a line chart

By doing so, we can decide the length of the move, calculate the number of boxes in the move and define objective patterns too. If the boxes are plotted diagonally, it is called a Renko chart. If the price action or the boxes are plotted vertically, they are called the Point & Figure charts. The bottom line is that the ratio chart can be plotted using these one-dimensional noiseless charting methods.

Not many people have realized the importance of noiseless charts. These charts lend a great deal of objectivity and offer more interesting insights compared to the simple line chart.

Point & Figure (P&F) can be an effective method to plot ratio charts. P&F charts help us in counting the length and the momentum in the ratio chart. Instead of simply saying that the ratio line is bullish, we can go a step further and quantify the bullishness. The number of boxes in a current move offers insights into the strength of the move and the momentum.

Let us briefly discuss P&F charts and learn how to take advantage of this charting method in relative strength analysis.

Point & Figure

Point & Figure charts are considered as one of the oldest charting methods. The plotting and nature of these charts are different from bar or candlestick charts. It does not consider time and only the price action is considered to plot the chart. Hence, they are also known as one-dimensional charts.

But I call them noiseless charts because they filter noise from the data and present clear information about the price action. I have explained this charting method in greater detail and covered it right from the basics to the advanced use of P&F charts in my book *Trading the Markets the Point & Figure Way: become a noiseless trader and achieve consistent success in Markets.*

I will briefly explain the basics of this charting method and its important features related to relative strength analysis in this chapter.

Unlike the candlestick chart, P&F charts are plotted vertically. Let me explain how.

Given below is the image of a price move shown in a line chart.

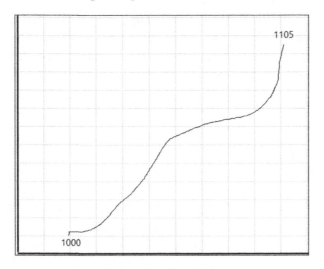

Image 7.3: Line chart

The price moved up from 1000 to 1105. We can connect the closing prices of each day and draw a line chart. Let us divide this price move into a fixed number of boxes of say 10-points each. Have a look at the chart below.

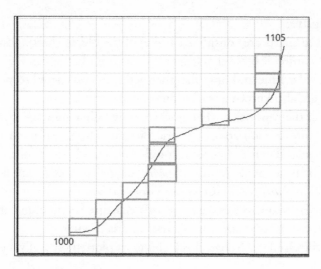

Image 7.4: Line chart divided in fixed-size 10-point box

The price is divided into fixed box sizes starting from 1000. The last box is drawn from 1090 to 1100. Box for the price move from 1100 to 1110 is not drawn because the price is still trading below 1110. Let me remove the line from the above chart and number the boxes.

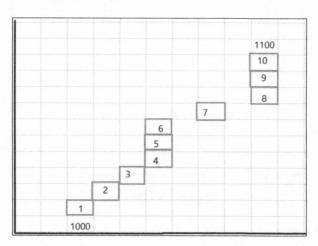

Image 7.5: 10 boxes of 10 points each

There are 10 boxes on the move. Let us merge these columns and make them a single column for better visibility.

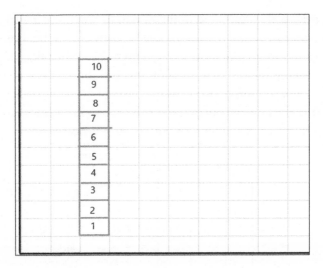

Image 7.6: Boxes brought to a single column

This vertical stacking of columns is known as vertical plotting. Let us now remove the number and plot each box as 'X'. For the price reference, we can draw the index at the left so we can come to know about the price levels at each box.

1100	X					
1090	X					
1080	X					
1070	X					
1060	X					
1050	X					
1040	X					
1030	X					
1020	X					
1010	X					
1000						

Image 7.7: 'X' replaced boxes and price index at the left

We can see in Image 7.7 that the price fulfilled the first box requirement at 1010 and went to 1100.

So, the price scale is captured in the X-axis. As we have decided to divide the price movement into boxes of 10-points each, there will be ten boxes of 'X' that will be printed to capture the move from 1000 to 1100. In a line chart, there will be a line connecting the prices from 1000 to 1100. In the P&F chart, this move will be plotted as a column of X having 10 boxes of 10-points value each.

As the price is rising, we can plot this price action in a P&F chart in a column of 'X'. When the price moves lower, we plot it in the next column.

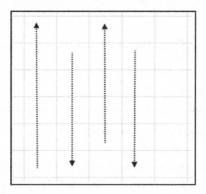

Image 7.8: Vertical plotting

As the time is ignored and only significant price action is captured in P&F charts, they are in essence swing charts. Prices are plotted in a column. There are two types of columns in P&F charts–X and O.

X	O
X	O
X	O
X	O
X	O

Image 7.9: Column of 'X' and 'O'

A column of X captures rising prices while a column of O captures falling prices.

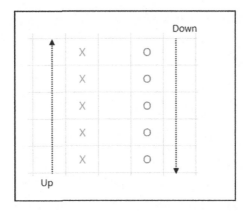

Image 7.10: Column of 'X' represents a bullish trend and column of 'O' represents a bearish trend

This fixed-size box is known as the box-value in P&F lingo. We can define the box value for any chart beforehand. For example, the above chart can also be plotted using a 5-point box-value, or 1-point box-value as well. There will be 20 boxes in the column if the chosen box value is 5. If the chosen box value is 10 points, then any move less than 10 points will not be recorded on the chart. This is an important feature of this charting method. Because of this feature, the noise or insignificant price movements are removed from the data and we get to see a clearer picture.

In the example that we discussed in image 7.7, if we choose a box value of 20-points, then there will be five boxes plotted to capture the move from 1000 to 1100. The first box capturing the move 1000 to 1020, the other one from 1020 to 1040 and so on. The price has not reached 1120 yet so that data will not get plotted.

When the price goes up, we capture the price action in the chart only if the rise or the fall is above the "qualified price". If the box value is 10 and the price is trading at 1120, the next qualifying price would be 1130. We will not mark another 'X' unless the price closes at or above the qualifying price which is 1130 in this case. We will not plot it even if the price closes at 1129.99. Similarly, we will mark a box at 1130 if the price reaches 1139.99. The box at 1140 will not be plotted as the price has not yet reached that level. However, if the price moves to 1140 or above, we will plot a box at 1140.

When the price rises, it is captured in a column of 'X'. When it turns down and falls, we plot it in a column of 'O'. There is a criterion for defining reversal in this charting method to ensure that insignificant reversals are not plotted on the chart. The three-box reversal is a popular method of plotting P&F charts. If the box value is five points, we will not plot the reversal unless the price has reversed by three times the box value or 3 x 5 = 15 points.

Take a look at the image below.

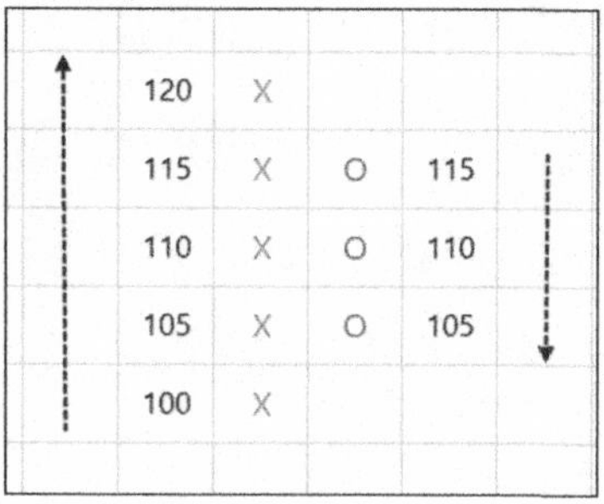

Image 7.11: 3-box reversal column turning to 'O'

The price moved up from 100 to 120 which was captured in the first column of 'X'. The chosen box value is five points and hence, there are five boxes in the column of 'X'. A fall of three boxes, that is 15-points (five points per box multiplied by three box reversals) from the high of 120 is required to trigger a column reversal from 'X' to 'O'. So, if the price falls 15-points from 120 to 105, the reversal will then be captured in the chart via a column of 'O'.

In the above example, if the price was at 120 in the column of 'X', the next 'X' will get plotted if the price moves higher by one box or five points from 120. A reversal will be captured only if the price drops 3-times the box value or 15-points to 105 or lower. There will be no plotting if the price remains between these two levels. That is how P&F charts eliminate unimportant price data and reversals from the chart.

The column reversal logic is the same for flipping over from a column of 'O' to 'X or vice versa. If the low of the column of 'O' is at 105 and the box value is five points, the price then has to rise by 15 points and close at or above 120 to trigger a column reversal to 'X'.

See the image given below.

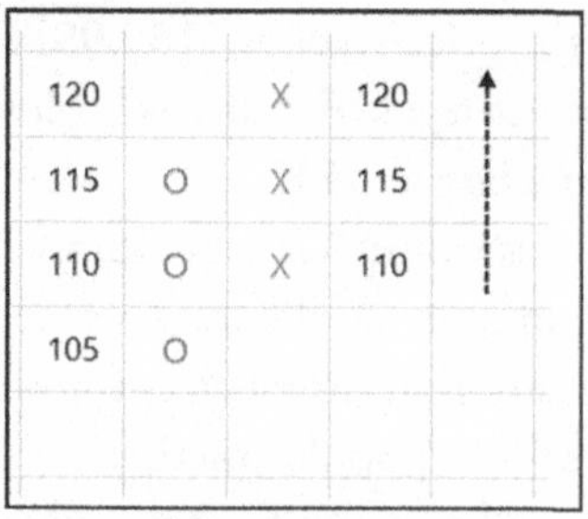

Image 7.12: 3-box reversal column turning to 'X'

If the box value is absolute five and reversal is three, it is called a 5 x 3 P&F chart. If the chosen box value is 10 and reversal is three, it then is called a 10 x 3 P&F chart.

There are other reversal values as well, but the three-box reversals are most popular and relevant. We shall stick to the three-box reversal in this book for relative strength analysis.

As you might have noticed, time is not considered in these charts while plotting. A daily candlestick chart would change every day, irrespective of the quantum of the move. A P&F chart would change only if there is significant price action. The price can remain in the same column for several days in a P&F chart. It can remain in the same column of 'X' or "O" for several days until there is a three-box reversal in the price.

Point & Figure charts are plotted using only one price for any chosen time interval. Notice that we have considered closing prices to plot the P&F charts in our examples. We will stick to the closing price to plot P&F charts throughout this book. The high/low price is also considered to plot P&F charts but that is not relevant for this discussion on relative strength analysis. Hence, we shall skip that and use the closing price to plot P&F charts.

We discussed in the earlier chapters that we only get one price in the ratio chart which is calculated based on the closing price of two instruments. If we can plot a line chart by connecting closing values of the ratio, we can use the same information to plot the data in a P&F charting format too.

The method of plotting that we have discussed above was using fixed box-values such as 5-points or 10-points. These are known as absolute box values. The problem with absolute box value is that a common or default box size cannot be used for multiple instruments owing to the differences in volatility and the price level of instruments. The other important issue is that if an instrument moves in a wide range, then using a fixed value box size may be inappropriate.

For example, if the price falls from 1000 to 500, using a fixed box size of 10-points would be misleading as the box size was about 1% of the prevailing price at 1000 and the same box value would be 2% of the price when the instrument falls to 500. So, using a fixed box size has a lot of challenges associated with it from a practical perspective. Moreover, the absolute box-value is not useful for the relative strength chart because the scale of the chart depends on the multiplier used for the ratio chart and remember that the absolute value in the ratio chart is not important. It is the trend that is more important in the ratio chart.

Instead of the fixed box value, we would use a log box value chart for relative strength analysis. Let us quickly understand the log box value method.

Log box values or box values based on percentage are very practical and useful. Instead of using the five-point box, we can use box size which is at say 1% of the price. The box value remains 1% irrespective of the price level it is trading. All other things related to the plotting of the P&F charts we discussed above remain the same. A log-based box size is a powerful tool in P&F charts. So, when we plot a 1% box value and three-box reversal, it will be called a 1% x 3 P&F chart.

Box-value and timeframe

Here are the recommended box-value to plot the relative strength chart in P&F format.

- 0.25% x 3 on Daily chart for short-term analysis
- 1% x 3 on Daily chart for medium-term analysis
- 2% x 3 on Daily chart for intermediate-term analysis
- 3% x 3 on Daily chart for long-term analysis

For lower timeframe charts, I recommend:

- 0.10% x 3 on the one-minute timeframe for very short-term trading
- 0.25% x 3 on the one-minute timeframe for momentum trading

You can always experiment with the box values. The 1% and above box sizes are more relevant for Mid-caps and Small-cap stocks on the daily timeframe chart. Smaller box sizes of 0.05% and 0.10% are relevant box values for tracking the indices on a lower timeframe of say one-minute timeframe charts.

The box value is an important tool in the P&F chart that offers the user the leeway to take trades in the lowest possible time interval using the P&F chart. When we plot a weekly or monthly timeframe chart, the chart gets locked at the end of the week or month. What we see while the week or month is in progress is irrelevant as price levels can change during the week or month. We need to wait for the chart to get locked at the end of the week or month for confirmation. This can result in higher impact costs while taking trading or investment decision based on higher time frame candlestick or bar charts.

In the P&F charts, the biggest advantage is that we can plot the chart using daily price but by increasing the box value, we can simulate the bigger time frame picture. We need not wait for the higher timeframe to get completed in P&F charts. Similarly, we can trade the lowest possible timeframe of one minute even for positional trades in P&F charts. This is the biggest advantage of box-value in the P&F chart. The importance of this is less understood hence it is a very underrated feature of this charting technique.

Point & Figure patterns:
Column Reversal
Price flipping to a column of 'O' from 'X' is known as bearish column reversal and the price turning from a column of 'O' to 'X' is known as bullish column reversal.

Image 7.13: Column reversal

When we plot a ratio chart in the Point & Figure format, a column of 'X' indicates a bullish ratio line and a column of 'O' a bearish ratio line.

Below is a chart of Bank Nifty divided by Nifty ratio chart plotted in the P&F format.

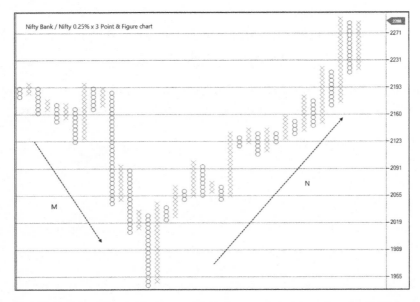

Figure 7.1: Bank Nifty divided by Nifty daily ratio chart plotted in the P&F format

More number of 'O's and bearish columns during period M in the above chart indicates underperformance of the numerator or Nifty bank in this case. More number of 'X's and bullish columns in period N represents an outperformance of the Nifty bank index to Nifty.

The biggest advantage of plotting a ratio chart in P&F format is that it becomes objective. Instead of talking about a rising or a falling ratio line, we can now talk in terms of 'X' and 'O' and also count the number of boxes in each column. The column reversal in the ratio line P&F chart is a significant piece of information. Let us consider a few important patterns in the P&F chart.

Double-top buy and Double-bottom sell

When the price moves above the high price of the previous column of 'X', it is called a double-top buy pattern. It is a bullish swing breakout.

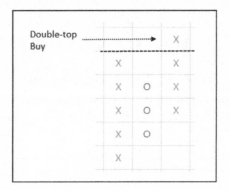

Image 7.14: Double-top buy

When the price falls below the low of the previous column of 'O', it is known as a double-bottom sell pattern. It is basically, a bearish swing breakout pattern.

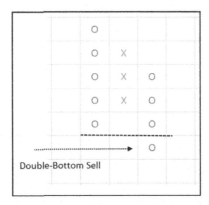

Image 7.15: Double-bottom sell

The most important aspect is that swing breakout patterns are now objectively defined in the P&F charting method. The important characteristics of the basic swing breakout patterns are:

- It is a three-column pattern, and
- If a column of 'X' breaks out above the preceding column of 'X', it is a double top buy.
- If a column of 'O' falls below the low of the preceding column of 'O', it is a double bottom sell.

In a P&F chart, the column of 'X' and 'O' always alternate. Hence, only three columns are required to complete a double top buy or double bottom sell pattern. In a double-top buy pattern, the three-column sequence would be X-O-X. The three-column sequence to complete a double-bottom sell pattern would be O-X-O.

Using such objective definitions, we can scan for these patterns using the software. Remember, unlike candlestick charts, three columns do not necessarily capture the price action of three days. This pattern has three columns, but the number of days for which the data is captured could be different. It depends on the strength of the price move.

When a double-top buy is triggered in a P&F ratio chart, it indicates that the numerator is outperforming the denominator, and a double-bottom sell in the ratio charts suggests that the numerator is underperforming the denominator.

Featured below is the same ratio chart of Nifty Bank & Nifty 50 plotted in P&F format. The green horizontal lines indicate bullish double-top buy breakout patterns while the red horizontal lines indicate bearish double-bottom sell patterns.

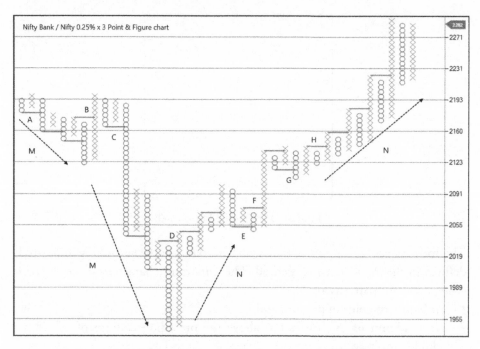

Figure 7.2: Daily 0.25% x 3 Nifty Bank to Nifty P&F RS chart

A bearish double-bottom sell pattern was triggered at point A. There were series of double-bottom sell patterns thereafter. A double top buy pattern was completed at Point B but there was no follow-through action. This double top buy was immediately followed by a double-bottom sell pattern at C. There were double-bottom sell signals at E and G but without any follow-through. A double-top buy pattern at H was followed by series of continuation double-top buy patterns, indicating sustained outperformance of Nifty Bank.

The period M in the above chart captures a series of double-bottom sell signals without any double-top buy signal. It shows a strong underperformance of the numerator. It was series of double-top buy signals without any double-bottom sell signals during period N, suggesting strong outperformance of the numerator. Objectivity and simplicity are the biggest advantages while using P&F charts.

Take a look at the image featured below. A column of 'O' after double-top buy.

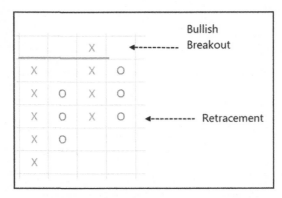

Image 7.16: Bullish breakout and retracement

The last column of 'O' is just a retracement after a bullish breakout because the low of the last column is still higher than the low of the previous column. There are two possibilities here. There could be a positive column reversal and a fresh double top buy may be triggered, or the current column of 'O' can extend lower and breach the low of the previous column of 'O'. In this scenario, a double-bottom sell signal would be completed.

If a double-bottom sell signal scenario plays out, then it becomes a bearish breakout pattern. Take a look at the image below.

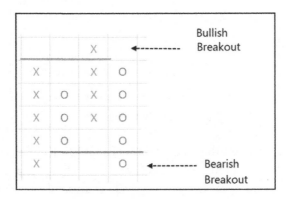

Image 7.17: Bearish breakout

Similarly, we have a column of 'X' after a double-bottom sell signal, but the buying pattern is not triggered in the current column. So, it is just a bullish retracement column.

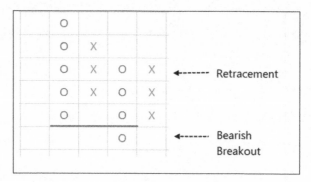

Image 7.18: Bearish breakout & retracement

We may get another double-bottom sell pattern from here in the next column, or the current column can rise further to generate a double-top buy pattern.

If a double-top buy pattern gets triggered in the current column, it becomes a bullish breakout pattern. This is captured in the image below.

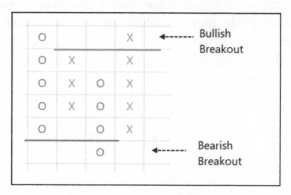

Image 7.19: Bullish breakout

It must be apparent by now that every column in a P&F chart can be defined either as a breakout column or retracement column. This clarity and the possibility of defining breakout and retracement objectively is a useful feature from a trading perspective.

A double-top buy after the double-bottom sell is a bullish reversal pattern. It is also called a fresh double-top buy pattern. A double-top buy followed by another double-top buy signal is called a continuation buy pattern. A double-bottom sell signal after a double-top buy signal is a bearish reversal pattern. It is also called a fresh double-bottom sell pattern. A double-bottom sell pattern followed by another double-bottom sell pattern is called a continuation sell pattern.

The first double-top buy or double-bottom sell pattern is a potential reversal of the prior trend. In a ratio P&F chart, such a signal would indicate a potential reversal of the prior trend of outperformance or underperformance. When a continuation double-top or a double-bottom sell pattern is triggered, it indicates the possibility that the current trend will continue.

In a nutshell, look for a double-top buy signal for bullish patterns and a double-bottom sell signal for bearish patterns in the P&F ratio chart. We can also use a combination of price and ratio noiseless charts to develop an objective trading system:

• Double-top buy pattern in price chart = Price is bullish
• Double-bottom sell pattern ratio chart = Ratio is bullish

In this scenario, go long in the numerator instrument with a stop-loss at the double-bottom sell pattern level in the price chart.

• Double-bottom sell pattern in price chart = Price is bearish
• Double-bottom sell pattern ratio chart = Ratio is bearish

In this scenario, take a short trade in the numerator instrument with a stop-loss at the double-top buy pattern in the price chart.

Before we discuss the relative strength of P&F charts, it is essential to understand a few more important patterns in the P&F chart. There are many useful P&F chart patterns and there are unique P&F based tools such as vertical count and 45° trend lines. It is beyond the scope of this book to explain these concepts in detail. Here are a few simple yet powerful patterns and studies that are useful and effective in relative strength analysis.

Anchor Column

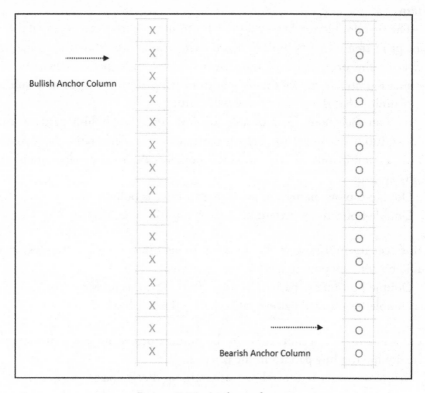

Image 7.20: Anchor column

In a P&F chart, the price would remain in a column of 'X' until it qualifies for the three-box reversal criteria. If there is a long column of 'X', it indicates that the price is moving up over multiple sessions and did not qualify for the reversal criteria, it shows that a strong trend is in place. The bullish camp is dominating. Similarly, a long column of 'O' captures the strength of bears.

We call such lengthy columns of 'X' or 'O' Anchor Columns. It indicates the presence of both, trend and momentum. Remember, unlike the bar or candlestick chart, a column in P&F does not necessarily capture the trend of a single session. The anchor column is a simple pattern yet one of the best features of a P&F chart. I would call it a gift from P&F charts to the technical analysis fraternity. No other charting method or tool can define the trend or momentum in such an objective way without considering the time element.

The other important feature of a P&F chart is that we can count the number of boxes in any column. And each box in the column captures a predefined quantum of move in price. To make things more objective we can define an anchor column as a column having more than say 10 or 15 boxes on a relative strength chart. Feel free to decide on a different parameter but be consistent with your definition of anchor column. The column should be relatively long is the key criteria here.

Ideally, we focus on anchor columns when a double-top buy pattern or a double bottom sell is also triggered. This combination of an anchor column of 'X' with a double top buy a pattern or an anchor column of 'O' with double bottom sell would qualify as a more relevant strong anchor column.

Such patterns in a relative strength chart would capture a strong trend of outperformance or underperformance.

Anchor column follow-through

It must be apparent by now that an anchor column captures strong momentum. A double-top buy that is triggered after the anchor column is called an anchor-column follow through buy pattern. It can be triggered in the immediate column of 'X', or after multiple columns.

Take a look at the below image. The bullish anchor column of 'X' is followed by a double-top buy pattern in the next immediate column of 'X'.

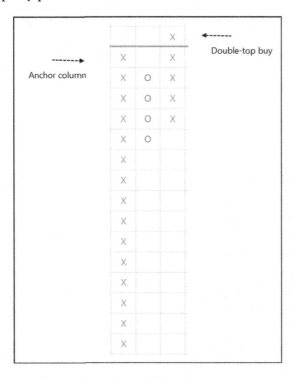

Image 7.21: Bullish anchor column follow-through in next column of 'X'

In the below image, the double buy signal is triggered after several columns were printed from the anchor column.

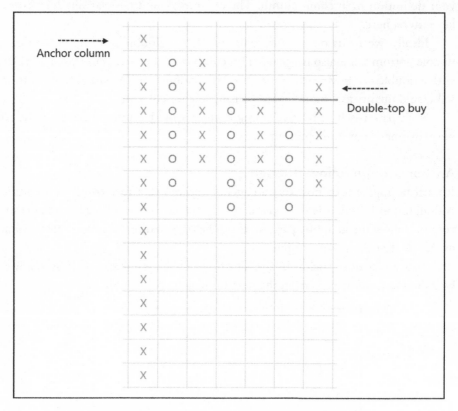

Image 7.22: Bullish anchor column follow-through

Both are valid anchor column follow-through patterns. The double-top buy pattern can occur after any number of columns, and it will still qualify as a valid follow-through pattern. What is essential is that the low of the bullish anchor column should not be breached.

The anchor column pattern is extremely important in the P&F ratio charts. The anchor column in a ratio chart captures strong outperformance or underperformance. Usually, there is a long way to go after strong anchor columns are printed in the ratio charts. After the anchor column, the sector or the numerator might cool off for a while. The completion of a follow-through signal confirms the resumption of the trend in the direction of the anchor column.

The stocks and sectors that generated bullish anchor column follow-through are interesting candidates to consider long trades.

Below is a 1% x 3 P&F relative strength chart of Ashok Leyland to Nifty 50.

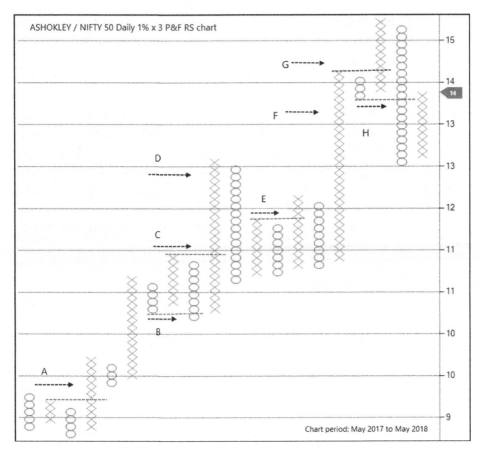

Figure 7.3: ASHOKLEY to Nifty 50 Daily 1% x 3 P&F RS chart

Pattern A is a fresh double-top buy pattern because it was triggered after a double-bottom sell pattern. Similarly, Pattern C was another fresh double-top buy pattern because it was completed after a prior double-bottom sell pattern at B. The breakout column at C turned out to be a strong anchor column of 'X' at D.

Ashok Leyland corrected and consolidated for a few columns thereafter and completed another anchor column follow-through pattern at E. The follow-through buy signal indicated the possibility of a strong outperformance by the stock against Nifty. It was indeed followed by a strong outperformance and an anchor column at F confirms this. There was another anchor column follow-through pattern completed a G. Ratio fell below the previous bottom and triggered a double bottom sell pattern at H.

In the above chart, it is fascinating to observe that the ratio chart of the entire year is captured in a few columns of X & O in the P&F chart. This is the advantage of analysing higher box-value P&F charts. The anchor column follow-through pattern was triggered in the chart in January 2018. The stock outperformed the index till April 2018. After having studied the relative performance in the higher box-value chart, the price and ratio patterns in the lower box-value charts can be considered for an entry with a better risk-reward opportunity.

When a bullish anchor column is printed after a strong downtrend and if there is consolidation after that anchor column, it could signal the completion of a major bottom. The low of the bullish anchor column mustn't be breached during the ensuring consolidation. This pattern is called an anchor strike pattern. It is important to realise and remember that an anchor column appearing after strong trends typically end up being important high or low.

In the image given below, there is a bearish anchor column immediately followed by a double-bottom sell pattern.

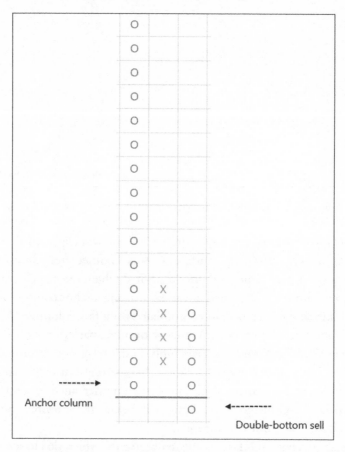

Image 7.23: Bearish anchor column follow-through in next column of 'O'

In the image below, the double bottom sell is triggered several columns after the anchor column is printed.

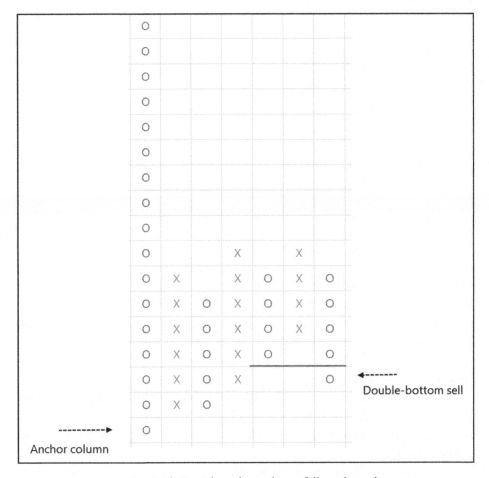

Image 7.24: Bearish anchor column follow-through

Both the charts qualify as a valid bearish anchor column follow-through pattern. Below is a daily 1% x 3 P&F relative strength chart of PEL to Nifty 50.

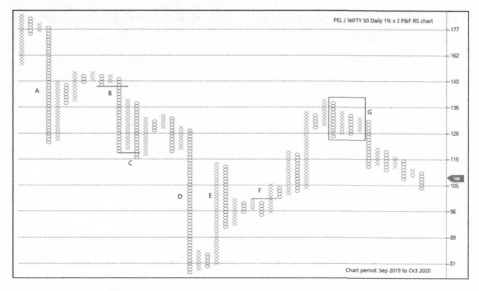

Figure 7.4: PEL to Nifty 50 Daily P&F RS chart

Pattern A is a bearish anchor column that indicates a strong pattern of underperformance. Pattern B is a bearish anchor column follow-through pattern followed by another strong anchor column. Pattern C is also a bearish anchor column follow-through. This was followed by a double top buy signal which also qualifies as a fresh double top buy. This double top buy was immediately followed by a double bottom sell.

Pattern D is a strong bearish anchor column but there was no follow-through to the downside. Pattern E was a strong bullish anchor column. Pattern F is a bullish anchor column follow-through that indicates the possibility of strong outperformance.

G is a pattern of convergence where the columns of X &O are contracting in size. This is called a triangle pattern. Let us discuss the triangle pattern in detail.

Triangle

The triangle pattern is popular in technical analysis. It is a pattern of convergence where the length of each leg is smaller than its previous price leg. In a P&F chart, a series of columns that is smaller than the previous column is called a triangle pattern.

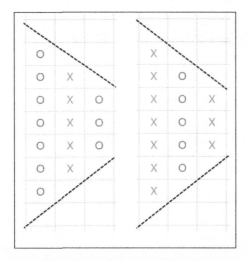

Image 7.25: Three-column triangle

The speciality of the P&F charting method is that even this pattern of convergence can be objectively defined and identified. The triangle pattern indicates congestion or a drop in volatility.

There can be any number of columns in a triangle pattern but a minimum of three columns is required to qualify for a triangle pattern. Here is an image of a four-column triangle pattern.

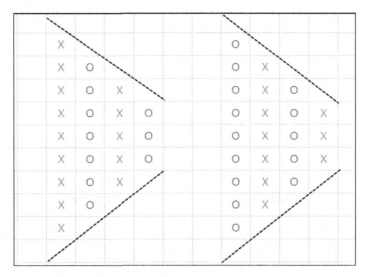

Image 7.26: Four-column triangle

Double-top buys after the triangle would be called a bullish triangle breakout. A double-bottom sell pattern triggered after the triangle pattern is called a bearish triangle breakout.

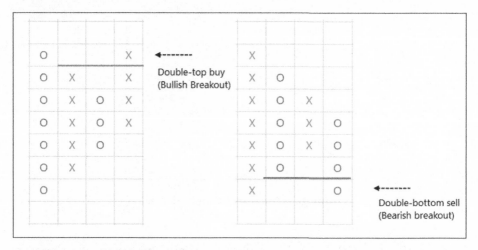

Image 7.27: Three-column triangle breakout

Below is a four-column triangle breakout pattern.

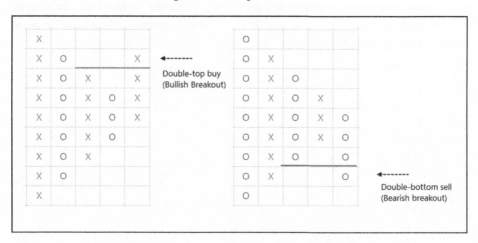

Image 7.28: Four-column triangle breakout

On the price chart, the triangle pattern is a pattern of convergence. It happens over multiple sessions, and at times cannot be identified or visible as a triangle pattern in the bar or candlestick chart. In a relative strength chart, this pattern indicates that the numerator and the denominator are trading at par.

Below is a Daily 0.25% x 3 P&F relative strength chart of the Nifty Bank Index to Nifty.

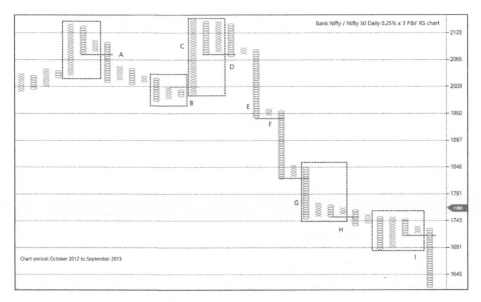

Figure 7.5: Nifty Bank to Nifty 50 Daily 0.25% x 3 P&F RS chart

Pattern A is a bearish three-column triangle breakout. Pattern B is a bullish triangle breakout followed by a strong anchor column at C. There was no follow-through to the bullish anchor column at C. But, the bullish anchor column was followed by a bearish three-column triangle breakout at D. E is a strong bearish Anchor column that indicates strong underperformance.

F is a bearish anchor column follow-through pattern that indicates the possibility of the continuation of underperformance. Pattern G is a bearish anchor column. Pattern at H is bearish anchor column follow-through as well as bearish four-column triangle breakout. Pattern at I was a bearish four-column triangle breakout pattern.

Below is the Daily 0.25% x 3 P&F relative strength chart of GAIL to Nifty 50.

Figure 7.6: GAIL to Nifty 50 Daily P&F RS chart

Pattern A, B, C and D are bearish triangle breakouts. Pattern E is a fresh double-bottom sell. Column F is the anchor column, and G is the bearish anchor column follow-through pattern which is followed by strong underperformance. Pattern H is a bullish anchor column follow-through pattern.

Turtle Breakout

Take a look at the image below.

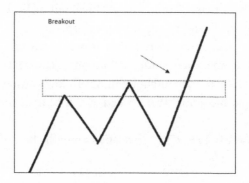

Image 7.29: Breakout

The image captures a resistance breakout pattern. Price has managed to break out above multiple highs.

Turtle trading is a popular and well-defined system that uses this concept. Let us briefly discuss the Turtle trading concept to get some background context.

It is said that during 1983, Richard Dennis–a successful and popular trader had an argument with his friend William Eckhardt about–whether great traders are born or made.

They decided to experiment. They published an advertisement in the newspaper that they would train a group of people in their proprietary system and also provide them with the capital to trade the system. They got over 1,000 applications and 13 candidates were shortlisted. They were chosen from different backgrounds. They were trained for two weeks in Chicago, the U.S. before they were given the capital to trade.

The selected students were called Turtles. Dennis said that they were growing traders like turtles in Singapore. Their trading system known as the Turtle Trading system was an objective system with rules for everything including the trading universe, entry, exit and position sizing.

They were trading stocks, bonds, commodities, currencies, and many other markets. Liquidity was their important criterion due to the huge size they were trading in.

There were two systems. Turtle Traders had the option to decide the allocation to these systems.

System 1:
- Long: When price crosses 20-day high
- Long Exit: If the price falls below the 10-day low
- Short: When the price falls below a 20-day low
- Short Exit: If the price goes above a 10-day high

Image 7.30: Bullish 20-day breakout & 10-day breakout

The entry is taken immediately after the price qualifies for the above criteria. There is no need to wait for the closing.

There was a rule here. Irrespective of direction, ignore the breakout if the last trade was a winning trade. This rule of ignoring the next breakout was applicable irrespective of whether the last signal was traded or not.

If the breakout was ignored because of this rule, then the entry should be made on System 2, detailed below.

System 2:
- Long: When price crosses 55-day high
- Long Exit: If the price falls below the 20-day low
- Short: When price falls below the 55-day low
- Short Exit: If the price goes above the 20-day high

For system 2, all breakouts should be taken irrespective of whether the previous trade was a winner or not.

Image 7.31: 55-day bullish breakout and 20-day bearish breakout

Besides these exit rules, there was a rule for stop-loss for both systems. They used ATR Indicator for stop-loss.

J. Welles Wilder introduced a concept called True Range in 1978.

Here is the formula for calculating the True Range:

True Range = Maximum of (Current High – Current Low, Current Low – Previous Close, Current High – Previous Close)

The average price of the true range over the past several candles is known as the Average True Range or ATR. It measures the volatility of the instrument.

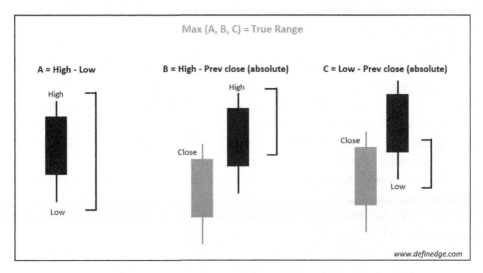

Image 7.32: True range

The stop-loss for the turtle traders was twice the 20-day ATR value. So, stop-loss would be 2-ATR below the price for long trades and 2-ATR above the price for short trades.

There were specific rules for position sizing, maximum acceptable risk, and pyramiding. There were several other rules for capping maximum position size and choice of instruments that played a key role in protecting the turtle traders in a highly volatile or unfavourable market phase. They were trading a diversified portfolio and there were rules framed to reduce the positions and risk during the drawdown phase.

There is much more to know about this system and the journey of the turtle. Those interested may read these two books–*The Complete Turtle Trader by Michael Covel* and *Way of the Turtle: The Secret Methods that Turned Ordinary People into Legendary Traders by Curtis M. Faith.*

Though the rules may appear simple today, concepts like volatility-based stop and position sizing were very advanced concepts back then. The performance of turtle traders was measured based on their discipline. It is a breakout-based trend following method and a few big winners can change the returns profile for the entire year. Missing those big winning trades because of disciplinary reasons will prove detrimental to the overall profitability of the system.

Is this system still relevant and profitable? The discussion regarding this can continue forever. People who are fixated on parameters would focus on that. System rules may differ but trend-following as a concept would perform well in a strong trending market. Methods evolve and not everyone will be comfortable with the same rules.

The story of the turtle traders is one of its kind in the history of this business. It was an important experiment that taught us several things. Richard Dennis and William Eckhardt were brilliant traders and were way ahead of their times.

Richard Dennis said, "I always say that you could publish trading rules in the newspaper, and no one would follow them. The key is consistency and discipline." And this speaks a lot about the business of trading.

Let us get back to our discussion on P&F patterns. We can adopt the turtle rules in P&F charts as well.

What is the difference, or the tweak required to adapt the turtle trading method in P&F charts?

As explained earlier, the turtle is a 20-day breakout method based on a candlestick chart. A candle will be printed in the chart irrespective of the quantum of the price movement.

In contrast, the P&F chart does not get plotted during the sideways period, which can help in reducing trades during such phases.

I recommend a 5-X turtle breakout for bullish trades. Look at the image given below to understand the concept.

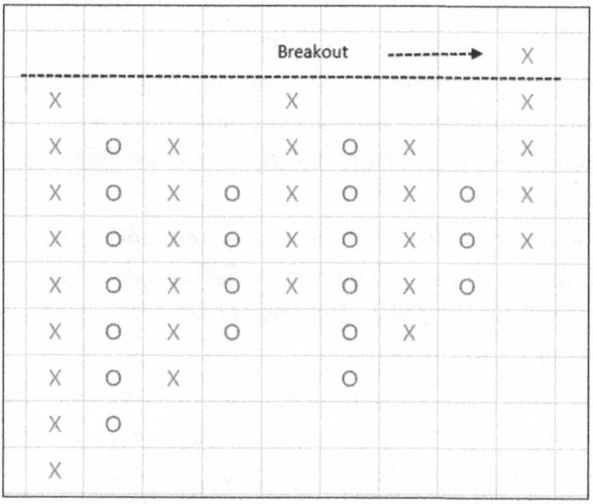

				Breakout	------▶			X
X				X				X
X	O	X		X	O	X		X
X	O	X	O	X	O	X	O	X
X	O	X	O	X	O	X	O	X
X	O	X	O	X	O	X	O	
X	O	X	O		O	X		
X	O	X			O			
X	O							
X								

Image 7.33: 5-X turtle breakout

If the current column of X moves above the highest 'X' in the last five columns (including the current column), then it is a 5-X turtle breakout.

Now ask yourself this question, when we say 5-Xs – how many days of price action does it cover? The answer is, it depends on the swing pattern and the volatility. The period may represent a price action of several days if the price is in a consolidation phase. Hence, the turtle breakout in the P&F chart is a breakout system based on price and not time.

P&F turtle breakout shows us a consolidation breakout or a range breakout. It can also be a continuation breakout which tells us that price is in a strong uptrend. In either case, the price is trading above the highest point of the last 5-Xs which is a piece of important information.

We can apply this pattern in the ratio chart as well. This pattern is extremely useful on P&F price as well as RS charts. When the ratio chart moves above the last five columns of X, it indicates that the numerator is into a fresh cycle of outperformance.

Below is a daily 1% x 3 P&F RS chart of ASTRAL to Nifty 500.

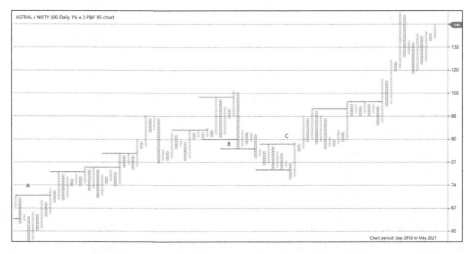

Figure 7.7: Daily ASTRAL to Nifty 500 1% x 3 P&F RS chart

In the above RS chart, there were five 'X' turtle breakouts at point A in September 2018. There were continuation moves post that and the price kept marching higher. A bearish turtle breakout was triggered at point B in January 2020. The ratio again triggered a bullish turtle breakout at C in August 2020 that was followed by continuation moves.

Look for bullish breakouts in the price chart when a bullish turtle breakout is triggered in the RS chart. The 5-X turtle breakout is the recommended parameter.

A 3-X or 10-X breakouts can also be useful box values to experiment with. This pattern is very sensible and useful on price charts too. If you are trading it on a price chart, confirmation of a bullish breakout of ratio chart can increase your chances of success.

Given below is a Daily 0.25% x 3 P&F relative strength Nifty Realty Index to Nifty 50.

Figure 7.8: Daily 0.25% x 3 Nifty Realty index to Nifty 50 P&F RS chart

A bullish turtle breakout was triggered at A in the above chart in October 2019. The realty index outperformed the Nifty 50 till January 2020. A bearish turtle breakout was triggered in March 2020 at B. The realty index underperformed significantly till May 2020. This was followed by a consolidation phase where the performance of both indices was at par.

Pattern C and E were bullish turtle breakouts that were immediately followed by bearish turtle breakouts at D and F. Bullish turtle breakout was triggered at G in November 2020. The realty index witnessed another strong leg of outperformance that lasted till February 2021. A bearish turtle breakout was triggered at H in March 2021.

These objective patterns can help us define periods of outperformance and underperformance clearly. We can pick stocks of outperforming sectors. What is even more interesting is that this approach does not need any special predictive skills to identify the patterns.

The above patterns help identify important breakouts backed by strong momentum. But P&F chart can also help in objectively identifying support-resistance and reversal patterns.

OOPs Support–Resistance Pattern

Given below is an image that shows the price at the previous important base:

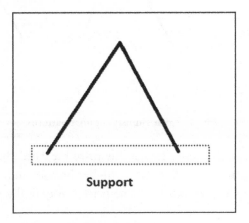

Image 7.34: Support at the previous base

This pattern can also be defined in the P&F pattern. Look at the image below.

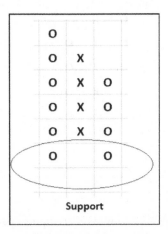

Image 7.35: Bottom of 'O' at the same level

When two columns of 'O' are at the same level, it can be defined as a pattern of support. This is a simple and objective way to identify supports.

But practically, price does not always reverse from the previous bottom or support zone. Take a look at the image below.

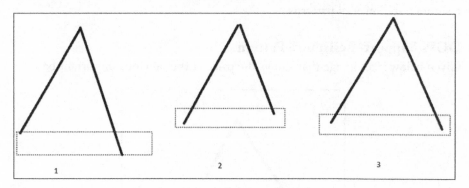

Image 7.36: Bullish support patterns

In the first pattern in the above image, the price breached the previous bottom. In the second pattern, the price makes a higher bottom and in the third image, the price is right at the previous low. The price can typically reverse after any of these patterns.

Given below is a picture that helps us define the above patterns in the P&F chart.

O				O				O		
O	X			O	X			O	X	
O	X	O		O	X	O		O	X	O
O	X	O		O	X	O		O	X	O
O	X	O		O	X	O		O	X	O
O		O		O		O		O	X	
1						O		O		
						O		3		
				2						

Image 7.37: Bullish P&F support patterns

In pattern 1, the price is right at the support at the previous low. In pattern 2, the price drops below the prior low but the maximum tolerance is two boxes. If the price drops by more than two boxes then the support possibility is invalidated.

If the price reverses within two boxes of the breakout below the prior low, it indicates the weakness of the bears. Pattern 3 indicates a scenario where the price is forming a higher bottom if there is a turnaround.

In all these patterns, there must be a price confirmation in the form of a reversal. A positive column reversal to a column of 'X' after these patterns can be considered as a confirmation that the price has reversed from support.

In the price chart, such patterns can offer precise entry locations with an affordable risk.

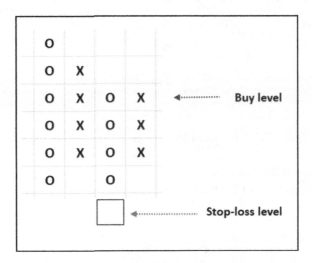

Image 7.38: Column reversal after support pattern

In the image below, a column of 'X' is printed, which confirms the support pattern.

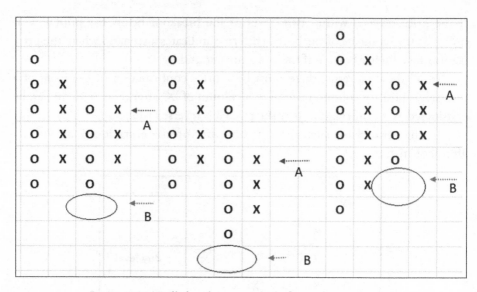

Image 7.39: Bullish column reversal after support patterns

I call them the OOPs patterns.

Below is a pattern of OOPs resistance.

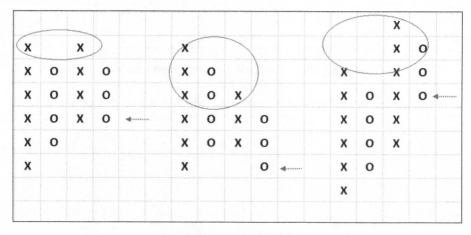

Image 7.40: Bearish column reversal after resistance patterns

The above pattern on the relative strength chart shows that the ratio has taken support and reversed.

These patterns can help to plan mean reversion strategies in ratio charts. All these patterns are simple yet objective. I have stressed enough the objectivity of patterns. The major advantage of this objective approach is that we can define them clearly, and we can scan for these outcomes.

Below is a daily 1% x 3 P&F RS chart of the Nifty FMCG index to Nifty 50.

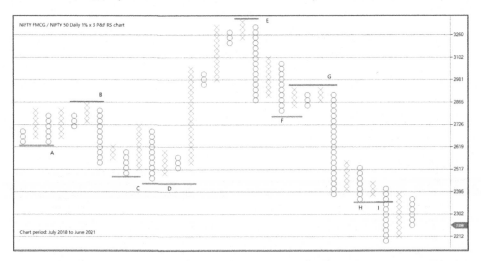

Figure 7.9: Daily 1% x 3 P&F RS chart of Nifty FMCG index to Nifty 50

Pattern A is a bullish OOPs support pattern completed in October 2018. Pattern B is a bearish OOPs pattern formed that was triggered in January 2019. FMCG underperformed until the multiple bullish OPPs pattern triggered at C and D in February 2020. The index outperformed significantly till there was a bearish OOPs pattern at E in April 2020. Bullish OOPs pattern during June 2020 was short-lived and followed by bearish OOPs pattern at G in July 2020. It was followed by a strong anchor column of underperformance. Pattern H was a bullish OOPs pattern but turned out to be a double bottom sell pattern at I in February 2021.

The purpose behind this discussion is to highlight the importance of three-to-four-column patterns in higher box-value P&F charts. They can provide a lot of information and pointers about the trend in the next few months and quarters.

Below is a daily 0.25% x 3 P&F RS chart of the Nifty Financial Services index to Nifty 50.

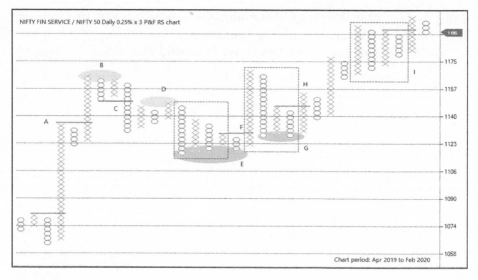

Figure 7.10: Daily 0.25% x 3 P&F RS chart of Nifty Financial Services index to Nifty 50

Pattern A is a strong bullish anchor column follow through. Pattern B is a bearish OOPs pattern followed by bearish triangle breakout at C. Pattern D is a bearish OOPs pattern followed by a triangle pattern. Pattern E is a bullish OOPs support pattern followed by a triangle breakout at F which turns out to be a strong anchor column. Pattern G is a bullish OOPs support pattern and H is a bullish triangle breakout as well as a bullish follow-through pattern of anchor column at F. Pattern I is a bullish four-column triangle breakout.

The patterns such as fresh breakouts, anchor column follow-through, turtle breakout, triangle and OOPs are important in ratio charts. These patterns help identify breakouts in the ratio chart and can help design strategies using either momentum or consolidation breakouts or mean-reversion strategy.

Recall our discussion on rising anchor lines, breakout, and convergence breakout during the discussion on ratio charts in Chapter 5. Those patterns can be clearly defined on P&F charts. The rising ratio line is nothing but a column of 'X', strong momentum in the ratio chart is an anchor column, and the convergence is a triangle pattern, swing breakouts in ratio charts are simple double-top buy and double-bottom sell patterns in the P&F chart.

Indicators and trade systems

We can plot any indicator in P&F charts as well. The formula remains the same but logic changes because they are plotted on P&F columns and not raw price data. Remember a column in the P&F chart represents a swing. Hence these indicators are plotted on swing columns.

Let us discuss three important indicators in P&F charts.

Moving average is the most basic indicator that may be used in all types of charts. It can be plotted in Point & Figure charts too. A 10-day moving average on bar or candlestick chart calculates the average price of the last 10 periods, usually the closing price. A moving average can be calculated on the P&F chart as well, but it is calculated on the last 10 columns in the P&F chart.

The calculation of the moving average remains the same in P&F charts but they are different in nature. A column represents a swing and trend and does not get printed at a fixed time interval. A column may consist of several days or months of price action and will produce just one price for calculation of moving average. So, a 10-column moving average on the P&F chart is the average price of the last 10 swings.

All other concepts associated with moving average interpretation is equally applicable and valid in the P&F charts too. Simple, exponential moving average (EMA) or weighted moving average (WMA) may be used in P&F charts.

Using moving averages, an uptrend may be defined as price trading above the moving average and a downtrend as price positioned below the moving average.

We can plot the moving average in price as well as the ratio charts.

Here is a simple trading system that one may consider.

Buy when
- Double-top buy is triggered above the moving average in the price chart indicating bullishness in price. And,
- Double-top buy above moving average in ratio chart indicating outperformance.

Exit when,
- Double-bottom sell pattern gets triggered in the price or ratio chart.

Short when,
- Double-bottom sell below moving average in the price chart indicating bearishness. And,
- Double-bottom sell below moving average on ratio chart indicating underperformance.

Exit when
- Double-top buy pattern gets triggered in the price or the ratio chart.

If you observe any other pattern that we have discussed earlier, the result can be improved further by using the moving average as a trend filter.

Below is a 0.25% x 3 Daily P&F chart of the Nifty Metal index to Nifty 50.

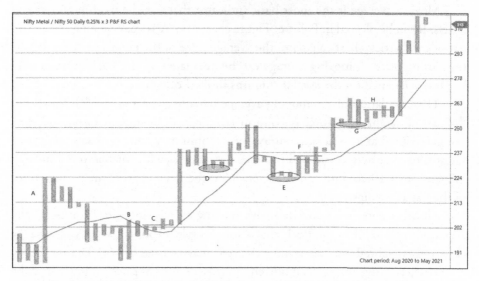

Figure 7.11: 0.25% x 3 Daily P&F chart of Nifty Metal index to Nifty 50

Pattern A is a fresh breakout and strong anchor column marked during July-Aug 2020. It indicated the possibility of strong outperformance. The metal index went through a period of consolidation but remained above the low of the bullish anchor column. At B, an anchor column follow-through pattern was completed but the ratio chart was hovering near the moving average line. At C, there was a double-top buy pattern above the moving average which was also a follow-through buy to the anchor column. The metal index got into a strong outperformance phase and there was a strong bullish anchor column above moving average. Pattern D is a bullish OOPs support pattern above the moving average.

There was a temporary phase of underperformance and the price dropped below the moving average, but a bullish OOPs pattern was completed at E. This was followed by a bullish double-top buy pattern at F. Bullish OOPs support pattern at G was triggered above the moving average. There was a continuation buy signal at H where the price was above the moving average. The metal sector marked a strong performance and proved to be a big winner during the August 2020–April 2021 period.

Moving average and price crossover is a traditional technique that is simple and successful that has stood the test of time. The major problem with this technique on time-based charts is the whipsaws during sideways price movement.

That problem is effectively dealt with, in P&F charts. As the P&F charts filter out much of the noise, it results in fewer columns of 'X' & 'O' getting printed during the sideways phase. The moving average will therefore remain flat during such a phase. As the trades are initiated based on price-based patterns instead of the crossovers, there will be far fewer trades and comparatively fewer whipsaws using moving averages in the P&F chart.

Below is 0.25% x 3 daily P&F RS chart of LT to Nifty 50.

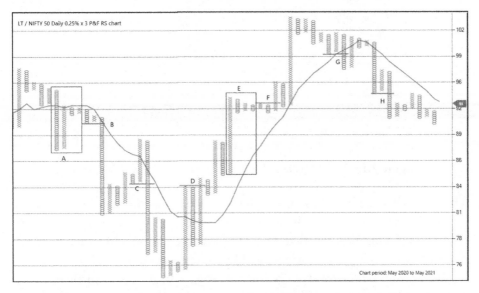

Figure 7.12: Daily 0.25% x 3 daily P&F RS chart of LT to Nifty 50

At A, a four-column triangle was triggered. This was followed by a bearish double bottom sell pattern below the moving average at B. At C, there was a bearish anchor column follow-through pattern below the moving average. Pattern D is bullish anchor column follow-through above moving average. Pattern E is a four-column triangle breakout pattern. At F, there was a bullish anchor column follow-through pattern above the average line. Pattern G is a fresh double bottom sell pattern below the moving average. Pattern H is a bearish anchor column follow-through pattern below the moving average.

Take a look at the daily chart given below of Nifty Media index to Nifty 50 in the 2% x 3 P&F chart format.

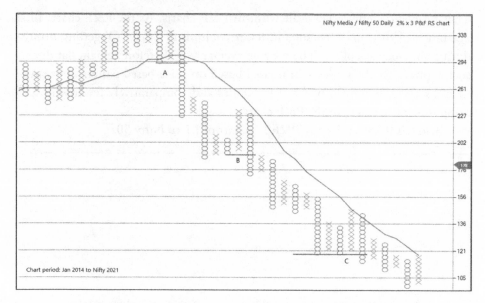

Figure 7.13: Nifty Media index to Nifty 50 daily 2% x 3 P&F chart

The above chart is plotted using a higher box-value chart that captures the bigger picture. This chart captures the data of more than seven years in a few columns of 'X' & 'O'. This indicates that the price was in a persistent downtrend. At A, a double bottom sell pattern below moving average was completed. At B, a fresh double-bottom sell below-average line was triggered. A bearish turtle breakout and fresh double-bottom sell below the average line was triggered at C.

The ratio chart was unable to cross above its moving average line after A. If we stay away from such sectors and stocks, we can avoid having losers in the portfolio.

Keeping the higher box value trend in mind we can improve our stock selection in the short-term as well. We will discuss this aspect while discussing matrix tables.

XO Zone

I introduced P&F based indicators in my book on Point & Figure charts. A fixed-size box is a unique feature of P&F charts. A price swing is divided into a fixed number of boxes that are plotted vertically. We can count the number of boxes in every column. Every box in a column of 'X' is a bullish print and every box in a column of 'O' is a bearish print.

Vertical plotting and boxes of 'X's and 'O's are unique properties of P&F charts. Using these unique features, we can count the number of bullish and bearish prints for a chosen number of columns. In the past several columns, if the bullish prints are more than the bearish prints, it is a sign of bullishness. Similarly, if bearish prints are more, it is a sign of a strong downtrend.

The cycle of expansion and contraction in markets is a popular concept in trading. Logically, the price will produce more boxes during strong trends and fewer boxes during the congestion. The number of boxes can also be plotted as an indicator on P&F charts that will display the count of boxes in the pattern or the last 'n' number of columns. The XO Zone indicator on the P&F chart captures the net count of the number of boxes.

XO Zone = Number of 'X' boxes - Number of 'O' boxes

Remember that the boxes of 'X's are bullish prints and boxes of 'O's are bearish prints. XO zone shows the net prints. A lookback period of the last 10-columns or 20-columns is the recommended parameter to plot the XO Zone indicator.

If the XO zone indicator is above zero, it indicates a bullish zone or outperformance zone of the ratio chart. XO zone indicator below zero indicates bearish zone or underperformance zone in ratio chart.

Below is the 0.25% x 3 daily P&F RS chart of the Nifty IT Index to Nifty 50.

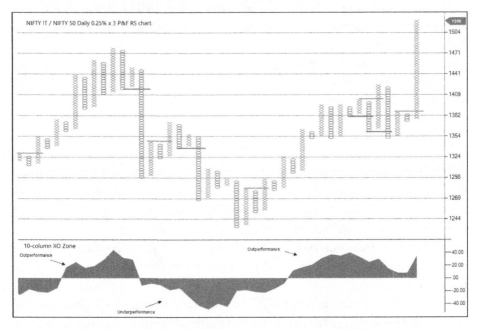

Figure 7.14: 0.25% x 3 daily P&F RS chart of Nifty IT Index to Nifty 50

A 10-column XO zone and fresh double-top and double-bottom patterns are marked on the above chart. The indicator above the zero line or green zone is a bullish outperformance zone. The indicator below the zero line or in the red zone is a bearish underperformance zone.

Bullish patterns in the outperformance zone and bearish patterns in the underperformance zone can help to know favourable phases of sectors and stocks.

Let also discuss another interesting indicator called the PMOX Indicator which is unique to P&F Charts.

PMOX Indicator

We plot indicators on the price chart to read momentum and identify extreme zones. Usually, what happens is stocks may remain in an overbought zone for a long period during strong uptrends. They can also remain in the oversold zone for a while during a strong downtrend.

Extreme zones are well respected when the market is in a sideways range-bound phase. Hence, oscillators or indicators moving between a particular range are more useful in a sideways or range-bound market. In simple words, Overbought and Oversold zone are more useful in a range-bound market.

I am introducing an interesting indicator called PMOX. It stands for Price Momentum with O and X. It is calculated using the XO zone and the number of boxes in a recent swing pattern.

It is divided into four zones:

- Bullish Momentum
- Bearish Momentum
- Overbought
- Oversold

PMOX indicator oscillates between 0 and 100 with above 75 and below 25 being the extreme zones. When the indicator moves above 75 and the price is in a strong uptrend, it means that the price is in a bullish momentum zone. In this case, a green dot is marked and the uptrend is expected to continue.

When the indicator moves past 75, but if the trend is not strong, it is considered an overbought zone. In this case, a red dot is marked and a trend reversal is expected.

When the indicator falls below 25, but the trend is bearish, it indicates strong bearish momentum. A red dot indicates that the trend is expected to remain bearish.

When the indicator falls below 25, but the trend is not bearish it becomes an oversold zone and presents an opportunity to look for a bullish strategy. In this instance, a green dot is marked and the trend is expected to reverse.

Hence, a green dot above 75 shows a strong bullish momentum. The green dot below 25 shows an oversold zone in a bullish trend. Similarly, a red dot below 25 shows strong bearish momentum while a red dot above 75 indicates an overbought zone in a downtrend.

When we apply this indicator on the relative strength chart, we can read whether the trend of outperformance or underperformance is expected to continue or reverse.

Given below is a Nifty Auto to Nifty 50 with a PMOX indicator chart.

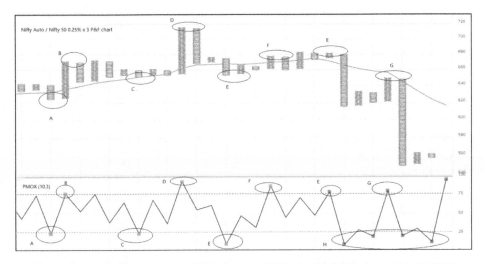

Figure 7.15: Daily 0.25% x 3 Nifty Auto to Nifty 50 P&F RS chart with PMOX indicator

At A, a green dot is printed that shows the oversold zone and the possibility of outperformance by the Auto sector. The green dot at B indicates strong momentum. The green dot at C again indicates the oversold zone and the possibility of outperformance. This was followed by a strong anchor column at D, suggesting strong outperformance by the Auto sector. At E, there was a green dot below 25, indicating an oversold zone and the green dot at F indicated strong momentum.

At E, the red dot above 75 suggested overbought conditions and the possibility of underperformance of the Auto sector. It was followed by a strong bearish anchor column. Point G showed that bounce in the Auto sector was temporary and a red dot was marked in the overbought zone. It was followed by a bearish anchor column indicating strong underperformance. The dots in circle H showed a strong bearish trend and underperformance by the Auto sector.

This indicator is a combination of momentum and oscillator indicators that helps in identifying the trend. The overbought and oversold zones identified by the indicator can help in timing the entries in the short term. Bullish column reversal pattern after the oversold zone and bearish column reversal pattern after the overbought dots are reversal patterns. The double-top buy pattern after the bullish momentum dot and the double-bottom sell pattern after the bearish momentum dot are continuation patterns.

Below is the Nifty FMCG sector chart versus Nifty 50 along with the PMOX indicator.

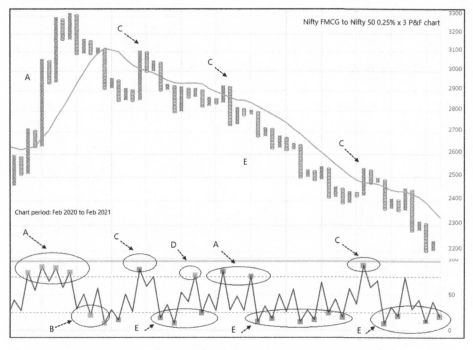

Figure 7.16: Daily 0.25% x 3 Nifty FMCG sector chart versus Nifty 50 P&F RS chart along with PMOX indicator

At A, there was a series of green dots that indicated that the FMCG was in strong momentum and outperforming the Nifty. The green dots at B in the oversold zone indicated the possibility of a continuation of bullish trend or outperformance. This was followed by a rally at C which resulted in a red dot getting printed in an overbought zone. This indicated weakness as the number of 'O's increased compared to 'X's. Circles and red dots at C showed an overbought zone and indicated the trend of outperformance is a short-term phenomenon. Circles and red dots drawn at 'E' showed strong bearish momentum and expectation of continuation in the trend of underperformance by FMCG.

All other types of indicators can be plotted on P&F charts. Remember, they are plotted on swing columns on P&F charts. Hence, their calculations remain the same but dynamics change. Any indicator that you are comfortable with and help you to define bullish and bearish zone can be used in P&F charts.

When P&F price and Ratio charts are bullish, they are bullish and outperforming stocks that could turn out to be big winners.

Let us try to relate the RS patterns studied in the earlier chapter in the P&F chart context. In the scenario listed below the denominator is the Nifty 50 index.

If Nifty is bullish and:
• If the P&F price and RS chart are bullish, it is a flying pattern.
• If the P&F price and RS chart are bearish, it is a cat pattern.
• If the P&F price is bullish but the RS chart is bearish, it is a bearish star pattern.

If Nifty is bearish and:
• If the P&F price and RS chart are bearish, it is a drowning pattern.
• If the P&F price and RS chart are bullish, it is a lion pattern.
• If the P&F price is bearish but the RS chart is bullish, it is a bullish star pattern.

If you are using trading systems based on price charts, then a confirmation from the RS chart would improve the odds of success. The confirmation may be a simple breakout in the ratio chart or it could be the ratio line staying above its moving average or any other logical tool that helps you objectively define a bullish and bearish trend in ratio charts.

A simple rule could be, remain invested in stock until the price and relative strength P&F charts are above their moving averages.

We discussed P&F charts in this chapter. We can plot the ratio chart in other noiseless charting methods such as Renko, Line-break and Kagi charts as well. The concepts and patterns discussed until now are applicable in the ratio charts plotted in these formats too. The discussion on these charting methods is avoided as they are beyond the scope of this book.

Let us discuss a few more advanced concepts that can be used in the P&F charts.

Fusion and Ultimate Matrix
In any chart, a swing move can be broadly categorised into two types–impulse and corrective.

Impulse and Corrective

When the price is trading above its previous swing high and there is an established trend, it is an impulse move. When the price is correcting, it is called a corrective move. The bullish trend is a bullish impulse and the correction during the trend is a corrective move to a bullish impulse.

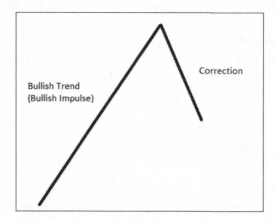

Image 7.41: Bullish impulse and corrective

Similarly, a bearish trend is a bearish impulse and the correction to the bearish trend is a corrective move to the bearish impulse.

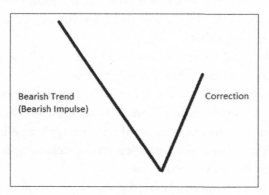

Image 7.42: Bearish impulse and corrective

But these swing patterns are too simplistic and real-life scenarios may be more complicated in terms of patterns depending on the trend and volatility. Hence, it is essential to explore these patterns further.

Though there are several different types of swing and price patterns all these patterns would broadly fit into five categories. These five categories are relevant in any instrument and any time frame. Here is a brief discussion on these patterns.

Bullish breakout

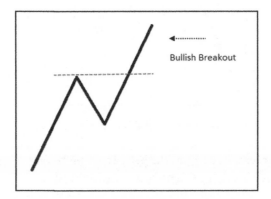

Image 7.43: Bullish breakout

Bullish breakout is the pattern where there is a price breakout above its previous swing high. Price has moved to a fresh high.

Bearish breakout

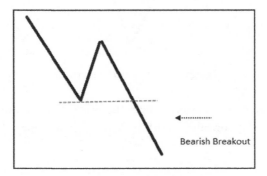

Image 7.44: Bearish breakout

Bearish breakout is triggered where the price falls below the previous swing low. Price in essence is making a new low.

Bullish retracement

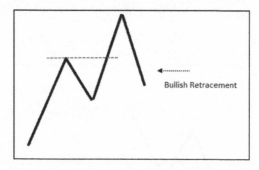

Image 7.45: Bullish retracement

In the bullish retracement pattern, the price is falling but it is a corrective move to the previous bullish breakout. There is no bearish breakout yet.

Bearish retracement

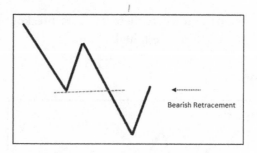

Image 7.46: Bearish retracement

A bearish retracement is a pattern where the price is rising but the rise is just a corrective move to the previous bearish breakout. There is no bullish breakout yet.

Consolidation

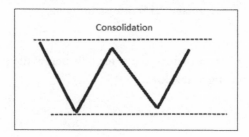

Image 7.47: Consolidation

The price would be in a consolidation pattern if it is confined to a narrow range where there is no breakout on either side.

These are the only five possibilities on any given swing chart.

As Point & Figure charts are swung charts, it allows us to define and identify the above patterns in an objective manner. In any P&F chart, have a look at the last four columns and try to identify the above patterns. It should be fairly straightforward to identify these patterns in a P&F chart. Once these patterns are identified, we can also assign scores based on the patterns. The score based on these patterns is called the performance score. The purpose behind this scoring mechanism is to identify and filter out strong and weak stocks or sectors.

Performance Score

Bullish Breakout

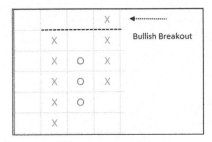

Image 7.48: Bullish breakout

A bullish breakout in the P&F chart is nothing but a simple double-top-buy pattern and the last column is of 'X'. It is a bullish pattern, and we assign a score of 2 for this pattern.

Bearish Breakout

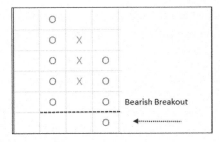

Image 7.49: Bearish breakout

The bearish breakout is a simple double-bottom sell pattern and the last column is of 'O'. It is a bearish pattern and a score of -2 is assigned.

Bullish Retracement

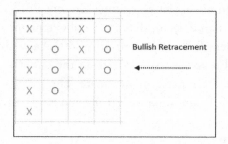

Image 7.50: Bullish retracement

In a bullish retracement pattern, the price is in a column of 'O' after a double-top buy and a double-bottom sell signal is not triggered. It is a semi-bullish pattern and carries a score of 1.

Bearish Retracement

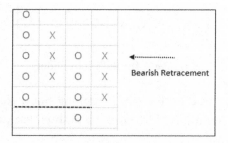

Image 7.51: Bearish retracement

In a bearish retracement pattern, the price is in a column of 'O' after a double-bottom sell but a double-top buy is not triggered. It is a semi-bearish pattern and carries a score of -1.

Consolidation

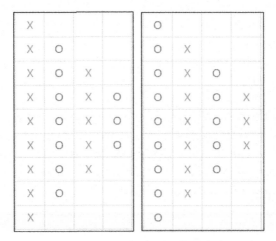

Image 7.52: Consolidation

Broadly speaking, if the price action does not fit into the above four categories, it will most likely be a consolidation pattern. In a consolidation pattern, there is no buy or sell pattern triggered in the last three columns. It can be a triangle or a horizontal pattern of consolidation. The trend is neutral and a score of 0 is assigned for this pattern.

We have now categorised all pattern possibilities in the price chart and assigned scores for each pattern.

Now, think about these patterns in a relative strength chart. Here are a few scenarios in the Relative Strength chart:

- Bullish breakout: Numerator is outperforming
- Bearish breakout: Numerator is underperforming
- Bullish retracement: Numerator is an outperformer but underperforming in short-term, pullback opportunities.
- Bearish retracement: Numerator is an underperformer but outperforming in short-term, pullback opportunity.
- Consolidation: The numerator and denominator are moving at par.

Once the patterns are identified, we can calculate the scores based on these patterns in the price chart as well as the relative strength chart. Things get more interesting now. We can assign these scores based on the patterns in multiple time frames too. The cumulative scores in multiple time frames would provide a holistic picture of the patterns in the price chart as well as the RS chart.

Below are the recommended timeframes on daily three-box reversal Point & Figure charts:

- 0.25%: Short-term
- 1%: Medium-term
- 2%: Intermediate-term
- 3%: Long-term

We can calculate the total of these scores on multiple box sizes to identify stocks that are bullish or bearish over multiple timeframes.

If the score is eight, it means that the pattern is a bullish breakout in all the four chosen timeframes. If the score is -8, that means there is a double-bottom sell signal or bearish breakout in all four timeframes.

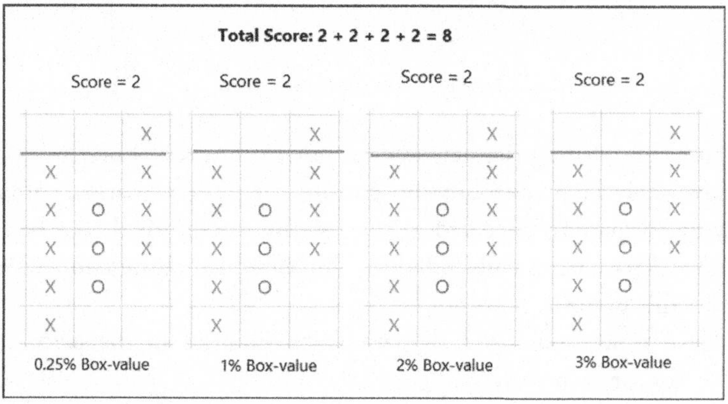

Image 7.53: P&F Matrix performance score calculation

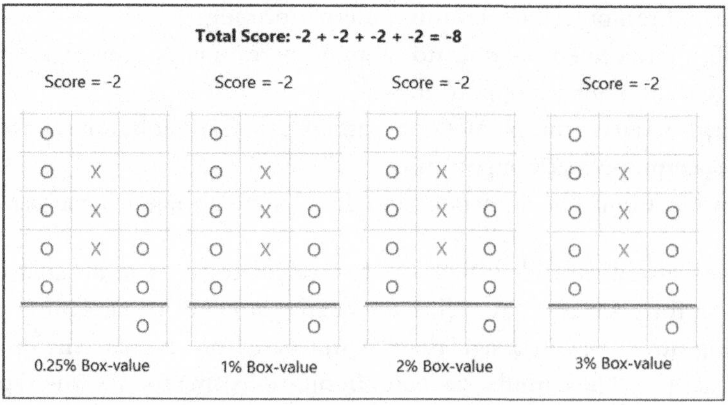

Image 7.54: P&F Matrix ranking score calculation

In essence, the stocks having a score of +8 are bullish on multiple timeframes and the ones having a total score of -8 are bearish on multiple timeframes. It is important to remember that stocks may remain in this bullish zone with a score of eight for several months. We will come back to this discussion later.

The calculation of the performance score was discussed until now where the score was based on the swing pattern. Let us discuss another scoring possibility which is called a ranking score.

Ranking Score

While the performance score helps identify bullish or bearish patterns, it does not capture the degree of bullishness or bearishness. Take a look at the image below.

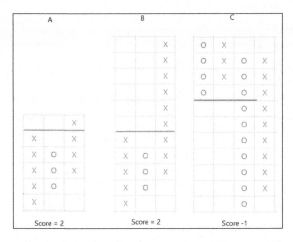

Image 7.55: Ranking score of the bullish column

Both A and B are double-top-buy patterns, and the performance score will be two in both these cases. But it should be obvious that the breakout and the price action in B are more bullish as we have a long bullish anchor column.

In Pattern C above, a double-top buy pattern is not triggered, the price is still tracing out a bearish retracement pattern, but the retracement is significant and overall, there is more number of 'X' printed in the last column indicating strong recovery. But the performance score will still be -1. The performance score does not consider the strength of the breakout or the strength in the pullback.

This specific problem associated with the performance score is addressed by the ranking score. The ranking score focuses on the length of the column or in effect, the strength of the current move. There are two advantages in a P&F chart:

- We can count the number of boxes in the last column. The distance covered in the swing move can be measured by the number of boxes printed in the last column. It will capture the strength or momentum in the swing.

- We also know the box value for each timeframe.

The ranking score is calculated by multiplying the number of boxes in the recent swing move by the box value. The ranking score in each time frame captures the momentum and trend of the current swing in that timeframe.

If there are 10 boxes of 'X' in a 1% box-value chart, the ranking score will be 10-boxes multiplied by the box size which is 1 in this case. The ranking score therefore will be 10. The ranking score will be a positive number if the last column is a column of 'X'. The ranking score will be a negative number if the last column is of 'O'.

This scoring method also gives more weightage to the higher timeframes. For example, if there are 10 boxes in all four timeframes, the ranking scores will be:

In 0.25% box-value: 0.25 x 10 = 2.5

1% box-value: 1 x 10 = 10

2% box-value: 2 x 10 = 20

3% box-value: 3 x 10 = 30

Similar to the performance score, the total ranking score across different time frames can be calculated. This will provide an overall picture of the momentum in multiple time frames. Take a look at the image below.

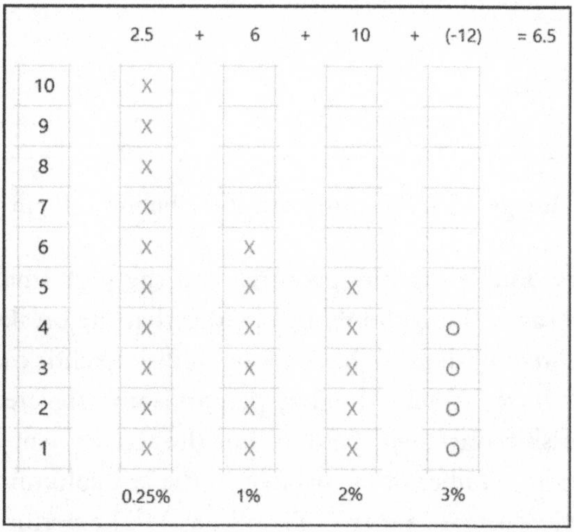

	2.5	+	6	+	10	+	(-12)		= 6.5
10	X								
9	X								
8	X								
7	X								
6	X		X						
5	X		X		X				
4	X		X		X		O		
3	X		X		X		O		
2	X		X		X		O		
1	X		X		X		O		
	0.25%		1%		2%		3%		

Image 7.56: Ranking score of bullish columns on different box values

In the above image, the last column with the number of boxes in each column is displayed. Several bullish boxes in the short-term column are more. Though the last column is bearish in the higher time frame of 3%, the number of boxes is relatively less. It means that the stock is in a downtrend on a higher timeframe but has turned bullish on lower timeframes. The total ranking score is positive because of more bullish boxes printed in other timeframes but the weightage of the bigger timeframe is the highest.

Here is a scenario where the last column is a column of X in the 3% box size. Have a look at the same chart as above but the last column is a column of X with three boxes. Let us understand how the ranking score changes in this scenario.

	2.5	+	6	+	10	+	9	= 27.5
10	X							
9	X							
8	X							
7	X							
6	X		X					
5	X		X		X			
4	X		X		X			
3	X		X		X		X	
2	X		X		X		X	
1	X		X		X		X	
	0.25%		1%		2%		3%	

Image 7.57: Ranking score of bullish columns on different box values

The total ranking score would now be a bigger positive number.

Recall the earlier discussion where the scoring was done based on the relative strength patterns in Chapter 10. Bullish patterns such as is flying, lion or bullish star would get a positive score and bearish patterns such as drowning, cat or bearish star would attract a negative score. Scoring based on the pattern is logical, but it does not consider or indicate the strength of the move. The strength can be studied by using the ranking score. The rising ratio will be a column of X and the ranking score would be positive. As the ranking score is calculated using the number of boxes or the length of the move, we would in essence capture the strength or intensity of the move. So, the ranking score is a step ahead in filtering and ranking candidates.

We can calculate the ranking score in a price as well as a relative strength chart. The performance and ranking score can be calculated in different box sizes and the output can be presented in a single table. This table would capture the trend and momentum in the price chart as well as the relative strength chart across multiple timeframes. This cumulative table is called the Fusion Matrix in the TradePoint software which is developed by Definedge Solutions.

Featured below is the P&F Performance and Ranking Matrix score of the Pharma index on four different box values.

Table 7.1: P&F Performance and the ranking score of Pharma index on four different box-values

Scrip	LCP	0.25%	1%	2%	3%	PF Performance Score	0.25%	1%	2%	3%	PF Ranking Score
DIVISLAB	4261.60	2	2	2	2	8	5.75	25.00	26.00	24.00	80.75
LUPIN	1231.50	1	2	2	2	7	-1.25	5.00	22.00	24.00	49.75
ALKEM	3164.95	2	2	2	0	6	8.75	8.00	20.00	18.00	54.75
CADILAHC	636.50	2	0	2	2	6	2.50	4.00	42.00	39.00	87.50
CIPLA	946.40	2	2	0	2	6	1.75	7.00	6.00	21.00	35.75
TORNTPHARM	2811.55	2	2	2	-1	5	3.50	11.00	16.00	15.00	45.50
SUNPHARMA	673.95	-1	1	2	2	4	1.00	-5.00	20.00	21.00	37.00
DRREDDY	5255.00	0	2	2	-1	3	-0.75	10.00	22.00	21.00	52.25
AUROPHARMA	959.05	-2	1	1	2	2	-7.25	-7.00	-8.00	24.00	1.75
BIOCON	384.90	0	-1	-2	0	-3	1.50	3.00	-10.00	-9.00	-14.50

The list is sorted in descending order of the P&F performance score. DIVISLAB has the highest performance score of eight in the above example. The total ranking score of all stocks is positive except Biocon.

We can do a similar exercise in the RS charts too. Here is the RS matrix score of the above stocks versus the Nifty 50 index.

Table 7.2: Relative strength performance and the ranking score of Pharma index stocks versus Nifty 50 index on four different box-values

Scrip	LCP	0.25%	1%	2%	3%	RS Performance Score	0.25%	1%	2%	3%	RS Ranking Score
DIVISLAB	4261.	2	1	-1	0	2	2.00	-3.00	20.00	18.00	37.00
LUPIN	1231.	1	1	2	2	6	-1.75	-5.00	18.00	18.00	29.25
ALKEM	3164.	2	0	2	-1	3	5.75	5.00	14.00	15.00	39.75
CADILAHC	636.	-1	1	1	1	2	2.00	-10.00	-10.00	-9.00	-27.00
CIPLA	946.	-2	-1	1	1	-1	-1.25	4.00	-10.00	-9.00	-16.25
TORNTPHARM	2811.	0	1	2	-1	2	1.25	-4.00	8.00	12.00	17.25
SUNPHARMA	673.	0	-2	1	-1	-2	-0.75	-10.00	-10.00	18.00	-2.75
DRREDDY	5255.	-2	-2	0	-1	-5	-1.75	-6.00	-6.00	21.00	7.25
AUROPHARMA	959.	-2	-2	-2	0	-6	-11.50	-11.00	-12.00	-9.00	-43.50
BIOCON	384.	-2	-2	-2	-2	-8	-4.50	-14.00	-12.00	-12.00	-42.50

The above table shows many stocks have a negative total ranking score.

DIVISLAB, LUPIN and ALKEM are the stocks from the above list having total positive scores in the performance as well as ranking scores.

The denominator in the above table can also be the Pharma index. We will discuss more about that in Chapter 11.

Here is a screenshot of the Fusion Matrix feature from the TradePoint software. This table captures the performance and ranking scores across multiple box sizes in both the price chart and the RS chart.

Table 7.3: P&F Fusion matrix table showing price and relative strength performance and ranking score on four different box-values of Bank Index stocks versus Nifty 50 index

Scrip	LCP	PF Performance Score				PF Performance Score	PF Ranking Score				PF Ranking Score	RS Performance Score				RS Performance Score	RS Ranking Score				RS Ranking Score
		0.25%	1%	2%	3%		0.25%	1%	2%	3%		0.25%	1%	2%	3%		0.25%	1%	2%	3%	
AUBANK	1001.95	2	-1	-1	1	1	4.50	9.00	8.00	9.00	30.50	1	0	0	2	0	1.00	3.00	-20.00	33.00	-57.00
AXISBANK	742.05	0	2	-1	-1	1	-0.75	8.00	16.00	12.00	35.25	0	0	0	1	1	-1.00	3.00	8.00	-12.00	-2.00
BANDHANBNK	314.85	1	-1	-1	0	2	-0.75	11.00	10.00	9.00	29.25	-3	2	-1	1	-3	3.75	5.00	-24.00	24.00	39.25
FEDERALBNK	87.85	0	-1	2	0	3	2.50	3.00	20.00	18.00	37.50	1	-1	2	0	1	1.75	-4.00	12.00	12.00	21.75
HDFCBANK	1500.95	1	2	0	1	4	-1.00	8.00	8.00	15.00	0.00	-3	2	0	1	-3	-3.25	-3.00	-12.00	-15.00	-33.25
ICICIBANK	642.70	1	2	0	0	3	2.75	10.00	20.00	18.00	45.25	-1	2	0	0	-1	-3.25	3.00	10.00	12.00	15.75
IDFCFIRSTB	59.80	1	2	2	0	3	-1.75	11.00	16.00	18.00	43.25	3	2	-1	2	3	-2.25	3.00	8.00	9.00	19.75
INDUSINDBK	1009.30	2	2	2	0	2	-2.00	13.00	14.00	18.00	43.00	-2	2	1	0	-2	-2.50	-3.00	14.00	12.00	20.50
KOTAKBANK	1811.20	2	2	2	2	2	1.50	6.00	14.00	-15.00	-21.50	-3	2	2	2	-3	0.75	-14.00	-12.00	-21.00	-46.25
PNB	43.10	1	2	2	2	7	-1.75	19.00	28.00	27.00	72.25	5	2	2	2	5	-2.25	-15.00	16.00	18.00	46.75
RBLBANK	214.75	1	2	-1	1	1	-2.75	19.00	22.00	21.00	59.25	1	2	-1	2	1	-3.25	13.00	12.00	12.00	33.75
SBIN	433.60	1	2	2	2	7	-1.25	22.00	28.00	24.00	72.75	5	2	2	2	5	-1.25	19.00	18.00	15.00	50.75

If you notice, we have four sections in the above fusion matrix:
- PF Performance Score = Scoring based on the pattern in the price chart.
- PF Ranking Score = Scoring based on swing momentum in the price chart.
- RS Performance score = Scoring based on the pattern in the RS chart.
- RS Ranking score = Scoring based on swing momentum in the RS chart.

Stock picking

There can be many ways to identify trading opportunities using this table.

A simple and common rule is to focus on buying opportunities in stocks where the total performance and ranking scores are positive. Look for short trades in those stocks where the total performance and ranking score are negative. Do not remain long in stocks having negative total performance or a negative ranking score. Using this simple template, you can ensure that the weak or underperforming candidates are eliminated from the portfolio.

As a rule of thumb, for trading and investment, stocks with total performance and ranking scores above zero should be on your bullish watch list. These stocks are bullish on price and relative strength charts on multiple timeframes. You can analyze them further to identify affordable breakout or retracement entry opportunities. Similarly, the stocks with a total performance and ranking score below zero should be on your bearish watch list.

Buy a stock once its total score turns eight and keep a stop-loss on the price chart at the double-bottom sell level. This way, you will be buying outperformers and high momentum. Stocks with a total performance score of seven must be on the bullish watch list. Long positions may be considered at the bullish swing breakout level in the shorter timeframe. Once the breakout happens, the total performance score will then turn eight. There can be instances where the total performance score is less than seven but may turn eight when the trend turns bullish.

Hence, focus on stocks having a total performance score above four and a total ranking score above zero. This combination typically captures bullish candidates that can offer fresh entry opportunities. Similarly, stocks with a total performance score below -4 and a total ranking score below zero are considered bearish. Focus on such candidates for shorting opportunities.

Stocks whose total performance or ranking score turning positive, or negative are the ones where reversal is in progress. I have studied the mean reversion techniques using this table. Stocks having a total score of eight would exhaust at some point so a reversal trade may sound interesting or logical. The problem with this approach is that these reversal trades work at times but the overall success ratio is low.

A better approach to trade reversals would be to focus on candidates where the total performance and ranking scores are flipping over from a negative to positive score or vice versa in the fusion Matrix. Remember, the scores in the fusion matrix are not calculated based on a single column or a pattern of one timeframe. It is calculated over multiple timeframes and on price and relative strength charts. When they turn from a negative number to a positive number, these stocks offer affordable long trade entries.

If you spend more time on the fusion matrix, you will realise there are unlimited possibilities. Even if you are trading based on any other price-based systems, shortlisting candidates using the Fusion matrix would be a logical step forward.

Bullish candidates are the ones where the total performance score and the total ranking score in the price and relative strength charts are positive.

Bearish candidates are the ones where the total performance score and the total ranking score of price and relative strength are negative.

Ratio and Price Divergence patterns

Based on the discussion thus far, it must be clear about the price patterns in the ratio charts and how to interpret the patterns and conclude about the performance of the numerator and denominator.

Often, the price and ratio chart would typically be in sync during strong trends. But the instances of divergence between the price and RS chart is when things get more interesting and must not be ignored.

When the price has broken a prior low, but the ratio chart has not, then it qualifies as a bullish star divergence pattern. It indicates that ratio score minus price score can offer interesting insights.

Take a look at the image below.

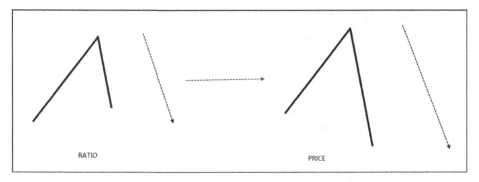

Image 7.58: Ratio and price bullish divergence

If the score in the price is deducted from the score in the ratio chart, it will be a positive number indicating bullishness. This is a bullish divergence where the numerator is falling but the denominator or the benchmark is weaker.

Take a look at the UBL chart that we discussed earlier.

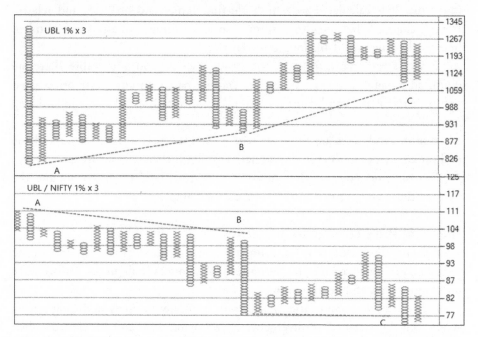

Figure 7.17: Daily 1% x 3 P&F UBL price chart and RS chart compared to Nifty 50 index

A is bottom in price recorded in March 2020. The price moved up until October 2020. At point B, the relative strength chart versus Nifty however recorded a fresh low. The bearish anchor column at B in the RS chart indicates severe underperformance by UBL in October. The price moved up further at point C during April 2021. The relative strength charts continued to drift lower during this period.

Overall, the price was rising from March 2020 to April 2021, but the relative strength chart was bearish indicating that the Nifty delivered better returns than the stock. If you had invested in this stock based on the bullish price action, your portfolio might have yielded positive returns, but it would have underperformed Nifty returns.

Below is a price and the P&F RS chart of BALKRISIND in 1% box-value.

Figure 7.18: Daily 1% x 3 BALKRISHIND P&F price chart and RS chart compared to Nifty 50 index

Price and RS both were falling and both charts recorded a low at A in July 2019. Price again tested the prior low at point B in March 2020, but the RS charts were bullish and stayed above their moving average. This indicates that the price was falling but the stock was a relative outperformer. This is a classic bullish star pattern.

Such divergences can occur in different timeframes either in relation to the sector or the market index. Let us discuss this divergence in the fusion matrix context.

Matrix Divergence

Take a look at the below image. Consider this as a relative strength chart. The performance score will be two.

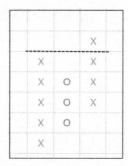

Image 7.59: Bullish breakout

It indicates that the numerator is outperforming the denominator. Consider the image below of the price chart of the numerator.

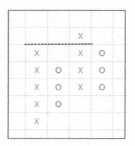

Image 7.60: Bullish retracement: Scenario A

The performance score will be one because the pattern is a bullish retracement. Let us call this scenario A.

Let us consider scenario B where the price has triggered a bearish breakout, and there is a bullish breakout on the RS chart.

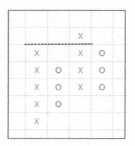

Image 7.61: Bearish breakout: Scenario B

The performance score in this case will be -2.

In both scenarios, the relative strength chart score was bullish. In scenario A, the price was retracing, but it was still outperforming the denominator. In scenario B, the price was making a fresh low, but the price was still outperforming, suggesting that the denominator was weaker.

Here comes the interesting part. How about deducting the price score from the RS scores?

In scenario A, the net score will be $2 - 1 = 1$.

In scenario B, the net score will be $2 - (-2) = 4$.

Let us call this the Net RS score. When the net RS score is positive, the relative strength chart is bullish even if the price is not. In essence, this is a bullish divergence. Candidates having a net positive score shows is that there is a bullish divergence.

P&F charts generate so much information in one go that people get confused and are unable to take advantage of the unique features of this charting method. Box value is a key feature of the P&F chart and you can get a clearer picture by increasing the box values.

Below is a chart of Adani Enterprises from March 2020 to early June 2021.

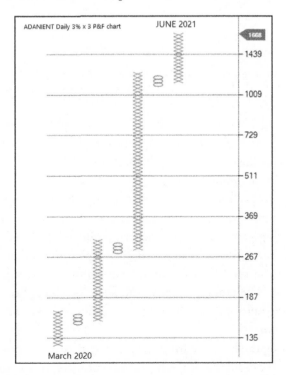

Figure 7.19: Adani Enterprises daily 3% x 3 P&F chart

The price moved up from around 127 to above 1660 during this period. The price action of more than a year is captured in these few columns of X & O.

Featured below is the same chart of Adani Enterprises with the RS chart in the 3% box size.

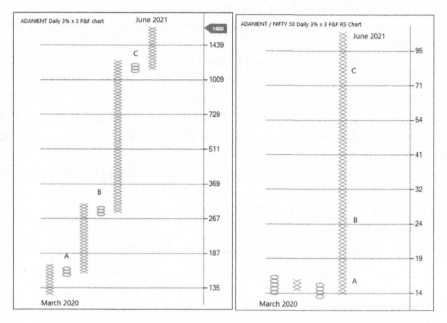

Figure 7.20: Adani enterprise daily 3% x 3 P&F price chart and RS chart compared to Nifty 50 index

Both the price and RS charts were bullish on multiple timeframes during this period. In the above chart, the price flipped to a column of O at A, B and C in the price chart. But the relative strength chart was bullish all along and remained in a column of X throughout.

This is a classic bullish divergence that we have been discussing.

In the fusion matrix, the performance score will be one on all three instances above. The ranking score in the price chart would have turned negative as the price was in a column of O. In the RS chart, the picture would be different. The performance score in the RS chart would be two and the ranking score would be a positive number. The ranking score would keep increasing because the column of 'X' was growing taller indicating that more number of boxes are getting printed in the same column.

By subtracting the RS score from the price score, we can shortlist bullish and bearish divergence candidates. If the net score is positive, it is a bullish divergence candidate and if the net score is negative, it is a bearish divergence candidate.

The example above covered the identification of divergence in a single time frame or box size. But fusion matrix offers the facility to perform this exercise on multiple time frames to identify divergence candidates.

Identifying net bullish divergence or net bearish divergence stocks is just a click away in the Fusion matrix feature in TradePoint.

Ultimate Matrix

We can consider the price and relative strength for ranking the stocks. But for relative strength, it is imperative to choose an appropriate benchmark for comparison to decide the ranking. Typically, the denominator will be a broader market index or a sector index. How about a third possibility? Why not compare the performance of an instrument with its peers. By studying the performance of an instrument with others in the group, we can identify the best performing stock in the universe. It is like an individual arm wrestling match of each instrument versus every other instrument in the universe.

For example, let us consider a sector with 10 stocks. Let us also assume that this sector is bullish and outperforming the benchmark. There is a possibility that many stocks from this sector might outperform the sector average. If we compare the performance of each of these stocks against every other stock in the group, we can gain insights into the relative performance of the stock against its peers.

Take a look at the matrix table displayed below.

Table 7.4: Group Matrix table

	A	B	C	D	E	F
A		A/B	A/C	A/D	A/E	A/F
B	B/A		B/C	B/D	B/E	B/F
C	C/A	C/B		C/D	C/E	C/F
D	D/A	D/B	D/C		D/E	D/F
E	E/A	E/B	E/C	E/D		E/F
F	F/A	F/B	F/C	F/D	F/E	

The same set of stocks are listed in the rows and columns. Stock A is divided by B, C, D, E and F and the result is captured in the first row. Similarly, each stock is divided by every other stock in subsequent rows.

Criteria for outperformance or underperformance would be a rising and falling ratio line. The rising ratio line is bullish for the numerator and the falling ratio line is bearish. We can therefore assess the behaviour of each stock against others in the group.

If A is compared to every other stock in the above image, in the first box, A is the numerator and B is the denominator. In the second box, A is the numerator and C is the denominator, and so on. So, in each row, the numerator is unchanged but the denominator changes. The behaviour of the stock is compared with other stocks. If a stock is outperforming against most of the other stocks in the group, it is considered a strong stock.

This kind of analysis is more relevant in noiseless charts such as the P&F because they are time-independent and the bullish or bearish swing can be identified easily and objectively.

If the last column is a column of X in the RS chart, then the ratio line is rising or bullish. If the last column is a column of O in the RS chart, then the ratio line is falling or bearish. A similar approach may be adopted using Renko or Line break chart charts too but we shall confine to P&F charts in this book. The log box-value P&F chart is an extremely useful tool in this context.

Let us look at the same matrix table again with additional information.

Table 7.5: Group matrix table with more information

	A	B	C	D	E	F
A		BULLISH	BULLISH	BEARISH	BULLISH	BULLISH
B	BEARISH		BEARISH	BEARISH	BULLISH	BEARISH
C	BEARISH	BEARISH		BEARISH	BULLISH	BULLISH
D	BULLISH	BULLISH	BULLISH		BULLISH	BULLISH
E	BEARISH	BEARISH	BEARISH	BEARISH		BEARISH
F	BEARISH	BULLISH	BEARISH	BEARISH	BULLISH	

This is called the Ultimate Matrix table. We calculated the performance of each stock against others. The total score for each stock may be calculated and the stocks can be ranked based on the total score. This is a very useful tool for reviewing the performance of all sectors or groups of stocks at a glance. If the performance of all sectors needs to be analyzed, then just divide the price of each sector with that of every other sector. We get to study the relative performance of every sector against every other sector. We can then check its price and relative strength charts for further analysis.

Below is an example of the Ultimate Matrix of six major indices.

Table 7.6: Ultimate matrix table of six major indices

Scrip	Total	Nifty 200	Nifty 50	Nifty 500	NIFTY MIDCAP 150	NIFTY MIDSML 400	NIFTY SMLCAP 250
Nifty 200	1	0	1	0	0	0	0
Nifty 50	0	0	0	0	0	0	0
Nifty 500	2	1	1	0	0	0	0
NIFTY MIDCAP 150	4	1	1	1	0	0	1
NIFTY MIDSML 400	4	1	1	1	1	0	0
NIFTY SMLCAP 250	4	1	1	1	0	1	0

A score of one means outperformance of the numerator and zero indicates underperformance. In this manner, we can analyze the performance of different sectors or a set of stocks from a chosen sector. The total score helps analyze the performance of the sectors or stocks at a glance. A score of one indicates that the RS chart is in a column of 'X'. The score will be 0 if the last column is of 'O'.

We can run this matrix on a group of all major indices, sectors, different stock groups or groups of stocks within a sector.

If we run it on a group of all sectors, we can identify outperforming and underperforming sectors. For instance, the bank sector's outperformance versus most of the other sectors in the group. The next step is to run the same matrix using the stocks from the bank sector.

Table 7.7: Ultimate matrix table of bank sector

Scrip	LCP	Total	AUBANK	AXISBANK	BANDHA...	FEDERAL...	HDFCBA...	ICICIBANK	IDFCFIRS...	INDUSIN...	KOTAKBA...	PNB	RBLBANK	SBIN
BANDHANBNK	314.05	10	1	1	0	1	1	1	1	0	1	1	1	1
KOTAKBANK	1811.20	10	1	1	0	1	1	1	1	1	0	1	1	1
FEDERALBNK	87.85	8	1	0	0	0	1	1	1	0	1	1	1	1
INDUSINDBK	1009.30	8	0	1	0	1	1	1	1	0	0	1	1	1
AXISBANK	742.05	7	1	0	0	0	1	1	1	0	0	1	1	1
AUBANK	1001.95	6	0	0	0	0	0	1	1	1	0	1	1	1
HDFCBANK	1500.95	5	1	0	0	0	0	1	1	0	0	1	1	0
SBIN	433.60	5	1	0	0	0	0	1	1	0	0	1	1	0
ICICIBANK	642.70	3	0	0	0	0	0	0	1	0	0	1	1	0
PNB	43.10	2	0	0	0	0	0	0	1	0	0	0	1	0
IDFCFIRSTB	59.80	1	0	0	0	0	0	0	0	0	0	0	1	0
RBLBANK	214.75	0	0	0	0	0	0	0	0	0	0	0	0	0

Each stock in the above matrix is compared with every other stock in the group and stocks are sorted based on the total score. BANDHANBNK, KOTAKBANK, FEDRALBNK are outperformers and RBBANK, IDFCFIRSTB and PNB are underperformers.

The above table shows us the list of strong and weak performers in the banking sector.

Once the strong stocks among the strong sectors are identified, price analysis in these stocks can help identify trading opportunities. In essence, this is like an arm-wrestling match between two indices or instruments. It gives a clear perspective of how one instrument is performing with others. This helps to fine-tune the selection after having identified the strongest sectors to the benchmark.

Now the question that might arise in the ultimate matrix table is what time -period or box size to use. This matrix may be studied using multiple timeframes. Here are some recommended box size settings.

- 0.25% - Short-term
- 1% - Medium-term
- 3% - Long-term

An important aspect to remember is that we are running this matrix on the P&F charts which are time-independent. If the box value is 1%, a stock remains in the same column unless the reversal criteria are met. It means we are comparing the swing moves of each stock versus others. It is not necessarily the performance of a single day or week or month. P&F charts are about price and momentum.

We can do a similar study in regular time-based charting methods such as candlesticks, but I believe time-independent matrix makes a lot more sense and are extremely useful.

We can take this concept further and run it on multiple timeframes at a time and score the outcome accordingly. If a stock is outperforming other stocks in multiple timeframes, it is a bullish stock with strong momentum.

Take a look at the multi-timeframe ultimate matrix table of bank indexes.

Table 7.8: Multi-timeframe ultimate matrix table of the banking sector

Scrip	Score-0.25%	Score-1%	Score-3%	▼ Total
SBIN	5	7	11	23
BANDHANBNK	10	11	0	21
PNB	2	9	10	21
FEDERALBNK	8	3	8	19
INDUSINDBK	8	3	7	18
KOTAKBANK	10	6	2	18
AXISBANK	7	4	5	16
RBLBANK	0	6	10	16
IDFCFIRSTB	1	8	5	14
AUBANK	6	6	1	13
ICICIBANK	3	2	7	12
HDFCBANK	5	3	2	10

In the table shown above, the constituents of the Bank Index are analyzed in the Ultimate Matrix on three different box-values of 0.25%, 1% and 3%. The stocks are ranked based on the total score across these three box sizes. This is a method through which we compare each instrument with every other instrument of the group on multiple timeframes and rank them accordingly.

In this chapter, we discussed:

- How to leverage the very important property of the oldest charting method of P&F and take our RS analysis further.
- Objective patterns and the noiseless nature of these charts prove extremely useful for relative strength analysis. Patterns to define trend, momentum & convergence are objective in these charts that can prove very useful from a practical trading perspective.
- Patterns like AFT, Triangle, Turtle breakout, OOPs and indicators such as XO Zone and PMOX are very useful for effective relative strength analysis on noiseless charts.
- Fusion matrix is an advanced objective system that helps us in scoring and ranking instruments using the price and relative strength analysis on multiple timeframes. All types of candidates like breakout, pullback, retracement, divergence on price and RS charts can be derived using it.
- Ultimate matrix ranks instruments based on the relative strength compared to each instrument in the group. This is another interesting aspect of the relative strength analysis.

The unique and innovative methods that we have discussed in this chapter can add value and significantly change the way people have been using relative strength analysis.

Chapter 8

RANKING AND TRADING

. . . .

Ranking the stocks based on some criteria is easy and useful. We can rank the stocks based on numerous parameters such as price action, momentum and price performance.

You can also develop your ranking method for stocks by understanding these concepts. Typically stocks are ranked based on the price charts, but you can rank them using relative strength as well.

There are many possibilities when it comes to ranking the stock using momentum methods. It can even be done using simple momentum indicator readings, or just averaging it on multiple periods. Ranking based on a combination of price momentum and relative strength can be useful. For example, RSI is a popular momentum indicator. You can plot RSI on ratio chart and rank stocks based on that. Higher the RSI, the better it is. You can also rank stocks based on their performance. The important factor to decide is the look-back period in this case.

For ranking, the period to consider depends on the approach and the trading time frame. For instance, a short-term trader needs to focus more on short-term momentum and use it as the ranking criterion.

Renowned author, Thomas J. Dorsey beautifully explained DWA Relative Strength Matrix in his book *Point & Figure Charting: The Essential Application for Forecasting and Tracking Market Prices*, where he divided the price of each instrument with that of another in the group.

William J. O'Neil developed a concept of ranking the stocks based on relative strength. It gets published every week in the *Investor's Business Daily*. It compares all financial instruments in the database to see which are stronger compared to others. He calculates the stock's percentage price change over the last 12 months, which means over the last four quarters. A 40% weight is assigned to the latest three-month period, and the remaining three quarters receive 20% weight each. All stocks are assigned a percentile rank from 99 to 1.

The fusion matrix that we discussed in the last chapter is also a useful method of ranking. It takes price and relative strength patterns over multiple periods and the scores are assigned accordingly. We discussed the ultimate matrix, relative strength indicator, ratio trend matrix and ratio rank indicator etc and ranking or sorting the stocks based on these criteria.

Typically, there must be a method that would rank stocks based on relative performance and momentum. I would suggest that the quality of stock performance should also be considered during this study. For example, If you are using a scanner for relative strength–Alpha indicator, you can sort stocks based on the performance but you should also check the ratio rank index along with that.

But ranking the stocks based on some criteria is the first step. The trading or investing based on that is the next step which is not that simple. You need to develop a set of rules to trade objectively.

Trading based on ranking

When we rank the stock based on some criteria, we usually expect top-ranked stocks to perform the best. But that is not always relevant or valid in real life, especially in stocks. For example, if you are ranking based on momentum, the topmost candidates are in strong momentum. But that does not mean the remaining ones do not have the potential to improve. And there is also a possibility of exhaustion in the stocks that are right at the top of the list. The method of ranking the stocks is fine, but there are a few other aspects that must also be considered.

Try not to focus only on the top-ranked and bottom-ranked stocks. Look instead for the stocks at the top slot and/or bottom slots. The stocks in the top slot would be ones having bullish potential. The stocks in the bottom slot are the ones to focus on bearish opportunities.

Broadly there are two ways of using the ranking:

1 - Buy the ones in the top slot and short those in the bottom slot: Top slot captures strong candidates and bottom slot weak candidates, and we expect the current trend to persist.

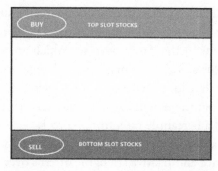

Image 8.1: Buy top slot, Sell bottom slot - Continuation

2 - Buy what is at the bottom slot: The stock and sector rotation keep happening in the market, and the ones at the bottom slot could see a mean reversion or buying interest. Stocks go through a trend and corrective cycle and hence what is at the bottom can reverse and might perform better.

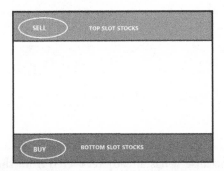

Image 8.2: Sell top slot, buy bottom slot - Reversal

Both approaches come across as viable options. But in the second approach, trading a potential reversal may sound exciting but if it is a weak stock, you might end up catching the falling knife which can be extremely dangerous.

It is essential to realise that the market will go through phases where both strategies will work. There may be instances of sudden reversal where strong stocks will fall more and the weaker ones may outperform. The reversal strategy will work well in such phases. The ones following the continuation strategy by buying the strongest and selling the weakest might be in trouble during this phase. We need to accept the pitfall or such an adverse period of one strategy and learn to live with it.

For buying the stocks in the lower slot, focusing on the eagle relative strength pattern will be effective. Meaning, if the stock is correcting in the short-term but it is bullish on the higher timeframe.

So, we have discussed two approaches to trading.

1. Buy what is in the top slot, sell what is in the bottom slot.
2. Buy bullish eagle stocks in the bottom slot and sell bearish eagle stocks in the top slot.

There is a third approach as well wherein the focus is on trading the stock with a moderate score or the ones in the middle of the heap. These are the candidates that might get into either the top slot or the bottom slot in the future.

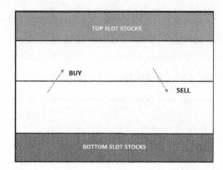

Image 8.3: Trading moderate score stocks

In the journey from zero to hundred, the stock has to cross the 50-Mark sometime. It has the potential because it has already recovered from the lows and may have the potential to reach the top.

Hence, the stocks in the middle slot can be at an important support or resistance level in price charts. So, if there is say an eagle pattern, they turn out to be more interesting ones.

For example, the ratio trend matrix and the ratio rank score of more than 50% are highly effective. Fusion matrix stocks above zero are also quite effective.

All these approaches can help you diversify your picks. Broadly, there are three approaches:

1 – Focusing on continuation trades in the top or bottom slots.

2 – Focusing on reversal trades in the bottom / top slots.

3 – Focusing on the moderate scores to catch on to a potential outperformer or underperformer.

Remember, buying top rank candidates and selling bottom rank candidates is a continuation strategy. You expect the same trend to continue. Reversal trades can work as a hedge. You can decide allocation in your portfolio based on this understanding. The portfolio can have say, an 80% allocation between continuation and moderate candidates and 20% for reversals.

Allocation or position sizing can be tweaked based on the prevailing phase of the market. The market phase can be determined using relative strength and breadth studies that we shall discuss in Chapter 10.

We discussed that ranking the stocks using different methods is possible, but it was important to discuss different aspects of trading them. In the next chapter, let's discuss a topic that must have come to your mind while reading about ratio charts–pair trading.

Chapter 9

PAIR TRADING

As the ratio chart is calculated using the price of two instruments, this methodology may be used for pair trading too. Pair trading essentially means taking contra trades in two different instruments. For instance, you may take a long trade in instrument X and simultaneously go short in instrument Y. This is a pair trade, and it must be exited simultaneously.

We can develop a strategy to trade instruments in pairs using relative strength charts and techniques. All techniques that we have discussed in trading and analyzing relative strength charts are applicable for pair trading as well; the only difference being that a pair of securities are traded instead of a single instrument.

The relative strength chart is considered bullish when the numerator is outperforming—and is bearish when the numerator starts underperforming. Thus, when we buy or sell a relative strength chart, we are betting on outperformance, or underperformance, of the numerator against the denominator.

When a relative strength chart is used for pair trading, then:

- You buy the numerator and go short in the denominator if there is a bullish pattern in the ratio chart.
- You take a short trade in the numerator and go long in the denominator if there is a bearish pattern in the relative strength.

Below is a daily ratio chart of Nifty bank to Nifty 50 along with a 40-period simple moving average line.

Figure 9.1: Daily ratio chart of Nifty bank to Nifty 50 along with the 40-period simple moving average line

If we delineate the trend using moving average in the ratio chart, we may simply state that the trend is bullish if the price is above the moving average and vice-versa.

The numerator in this example is the Nifty Bank index and the denominator is the Nifty 50 index. The ratio was bullish at point A as the ratio line was above the moving average. From a trading perspective, we may buy Bank Nifty and sell Nifty at point A because the trend is bullish. This trade would be reversed at point B where the ratio drops below the moving average. The trade now will be to sell Bank Nifty and buy Nifty. Buying Bank Nifty and selling Nifty was the logical trade at point C when the ratio line moved above moving average. At D, selling Bank Nifty and buying Nifty would have been the logical pair trade.

Bank Nifty was outperforming Nifty at M and underperforming significantly at point N when this strategy would have proved beneficial. Both the instruments may be falling at N, but Nifty is falling more than Bank Nifty that will make the strategy profitable.

The strategy is similar to taking trades on a price and moving average crossover in a line chart. While doing a pair trade, we enter and exit the trades in two instruments simultaneously.

As the price chart with indicator, there will be phases of whipsaws using the indicator on a ratio chart also, but there will be trends that will make up for these whipsaws. The biggest advantage of pair trading is a sense of hedge for overnight positions, which gives relief to traders. That psychological relief is the biggest advantage of pair trading.

The buying and selling should be based on the pattern in the relative strength chart; the individual price patterns or charts should not be tracked in such cases.

Below are important factors to consider while pair trading.

Derivatives

You need to trade in derivatives for pair trading. As you have to go long in an instrument and simultaneously go short in another instrument, you must choose a derivatives market for pair trading. Remember, you cannot take positional short trades in the cash segment. Hence you need to trade in the derivatives segment for pair trading.

Value Neutral

A pair should always be value-neutral. This means that the contract value of both instruments should be equal.

Contract value = Lot size x Price

For example, if the price of a particular instrument is Rs. 500 and its lot size is 1,000 then the contract value of that instrument is Rs. 5 lakhs.

5,00,000 = 1000 x 500

In such a case, the contract value of the other instrument should also be Rs. 5 lakhs for an effective pair trading strategy. You may need to add some quantities from the spot segment to even things out, but in pair trading, the value of both contracts are equal. This is an extremely important aspect of pair trading. If the value-neutrality is not adhered to, you may not be able to capture the full potential of the trade based on the chart analysis.

Practically, it is also a big task because contract values are not equal most of the time and adjusting the value by buying in the cash market may be difficult at times. But we need to handle this problem to be able to execute pair trading successfully.

Simultaneous trade

You need to treat the pair as a single instrument. Buying a pair is–buying the numerator and selling the denominator. Selling a pair means selling the numerator and buying the denominator. When you buy a pair, it is a single trade for you. That means you need to enter and exit simultaneously.

If you involve individual charts and their analysis after initiating a pair, it is difficult to stick to the pair trade plan. If you exit one instrument and hold another, you break the important rule of pair trading. It would no longer qualify as a valid pair trade. Hence, avoid engaging in analysis of the individual instruments after initiating a pair trade.

Trades based on Relative Strength

It is difficult to execute pair trade without ratio or relative strength charts. You cannot shortlist a pair based on the analysis of a single instrument. The relative strength chart makes the job easier. Enter and exit based on patterns or trading systems based on the relative strength chart.

Instruments

While deciding on pair trading instruments, indexes like Nifty and Bank Nifty are the most liquid and sensible options, to begin with. We can trade them as a pair based on the ratio or relative strength charts on various timeframes.

Positional, intraday or momentum strategies may be considered similar to the price charts. For stocks, instruments from the same sector must be preferred. For example, when you perform Matrix or rank the stocks using any other method for the same sector, you get to know about strong and weak stocks of the same sector. You can create a pair of strong and weak stocks from the same sector. This essentially removes sector risk from the equation.

For example, if the Pharma sector is doing well against Nifty, it is an outperforming sector and you may want to create positions in the Pharma sector. You also worry that the sector might underperform tomorrow, so you are also seeking protection. Let us assume that Dr. Reddy is outperforming in the Pharma sector. We now have a leading stock of the leading sector, and both are doing well. This is nothing but a flying pattern.

Let us take this imaginary situation forward. Suppose say Sun Pharma is an underperformer from the Pharma sector. The Pharma sector is doing good, but Sun Pharma stock is not participating. Hence this is a case of a bearish star or a cat pattern.

If the Pharma sector corrects or consolidates, it is possible that Sun Pharma may fall more compared to Dr. Reddy. We can therefore create a pair strategy of buy buying Dr. Reddy and Selling Sun Pharma. Plot the ratio chart of Dr. Reddy and Sun Pharma and look for the appropriate level to initiate the pair trade opportunity.

A set of instruments can be shortlisted and traded consistently as pair trades. If the selection is based on the market scenario, then I recommend picking the outperformer of a sector as the numerator and the underperformer of the same sector as the denominator. The outperformer is expected to continue its outperformance while the underperformer is likely to see further underperformance if the trend in the underlying sector reverses. Strength analysis of a sector *vis-à-vis* the broader market index plays a key role here.

Practically, it is not easy to find a trade in such stocks. The ratio chart is already trending when you pick an outperformer and an underperformer. You need to wait for correction or consolidation to identify trade opportunities in such types of trades, or you can trade it on a lower time frame for better risk-reward.

This was an example of a continuation trade, buy strong and sell weak stocks in the same sector. Another possibility that we discussed in the previous chapter is trading reversals. Buy strong and sell less strong in the same sector. For example, buy the flying pattern and sell a bearish star pattern. In case of a sudden reversal in the sector, when all strong stocks reverse, the bearish star candidate can underperform more and prove beneficial in pair trading.

Taking pair trades in stocks not related to each other have no logic, but if you see a pattern in the ratio chart of two different instruments, you can trade them based on the pattern on the relative strength chart.

The logic for two instruments for different sectors could be–in the above example–that the Pharma sector is outperforming Nifty and the Metal sector is underperforming. You want to buy Pharma and sell Metal sector stock. You can pick an outperformer or flying pattern candidate from the Pharma sector to go long and look for shorting opportunity in the underperformer or drowning pattern candidate from the metal sector.

You can plot the ratio chart of both and create a pair.

Here are some pointers to remember before venturing into pair trading. Select major sectors that you want to trade regularly. For example, Metal, Pharma, FMCG, Banks and IT. Select liquid instruments from the chosen sectors and shortlist the value-neutral candidates. Track their charts regularly and look for patterns that may offer logical trade entry.

Here is an example. Featured below is a daily 0.25% x 3 P&F RS chart of DR REDDY / SUN PHARMA.

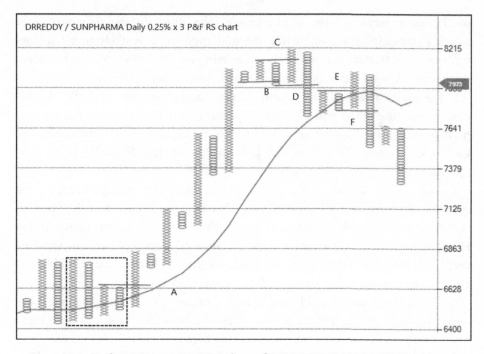

Figure 9.2: Daily 0.25% x 3 P&F RS chart of DR REDDY / SUN PHARMA with 10-column moving average

Pattern A is a four-column triangle breakout that indicated the outperformance of DR REDDY versus SUN PHARMA. It was a strong rally till the double bottom sell pattern triggered at B. Pattern C was a continuation double top buy the pattern. Pattern D is double bottom sell above moving average. Pattern E is a fresh double top buy above moving average that was followed by a fresh double bottom sell below the moving average at F.

If you spot a triangle breakout pattern as shown at A above, such patterns in relative strength charts of value-neutral candidates would offer a pair trade opportunity with an affordable risk. Along with triangle pattern, one can also trade turtle breakouts, anchor column follow-through or any other pattern that offers a trade with an affordable risk.

Pair Trading portfolio

Using the pair trading concept, one can create a portfolio of different pairs similar to a portfolio of stocks.

You can have four to five pair trades running at a time of different nature. You can run it on some instruments regularly–for example, Nifty and Bank Nifty. You can select stocks from the same sector, or different sectors too.

You can also consider diversification based on different methods. Broadly, there are two types of strategies you can adopt using relative strength charts for pair trading:

- Breakout and trend following
- Mean-reversion and Pullback trades

Breakout

When an indicator or pattern triggers a breakout on the ratio chart, the logical trade would be to buy the numerator and sell the denominator.

Here is an example using daily 0.25% x 3 P&F RS chart of DR REDDY / SUN PHARMA.

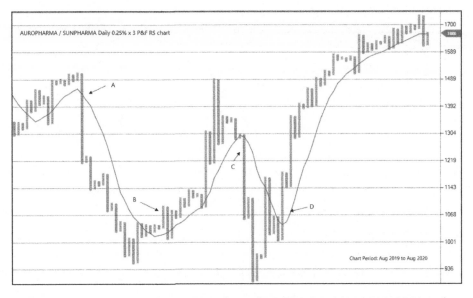

Figure 9.3: Daily 0.25% x 3 P&F RS chart of DR REDDY / SUN PHARMA with 10-column moving average

At A and C, the ratio chart was below the moving average, indicating underperformance of the numerator. Pattern B and D are positive prices moving average crossovers, indicating outperformance by the numerator.

You can consider bullish patterns for trading when the ratio chart is in the outperformance zone and trade the bearish patterns in the bearish zone. You can also ignore patterns and trade based on moving average line crossovers alone.

In the above pattern, we are trading breakouts and buying the numerator when it is showing signs of outperformance.

Mean Reversion

Another commonly used pair trading strategy is to trade the reversals or mean-reversal strategies.

When the ratio line reaches a level where you expect a reversal possibility, you may initiate the pair trade. For instance, if there is reason to believe that the ratio chart is at key support, then buy the pair or vice-versa.

This kind of approach is applicable in instruments that you think move within a range to each other. When you adopt a mean-reversal strategy, when the ratio chart is bearish and you anticipate bullish reversal–buy numerator and sell denominator to initiate a pair trade. When the ratio chart is rising and you anticipate bearish reversal–sell numerator and buy denominator to open a pair trade.

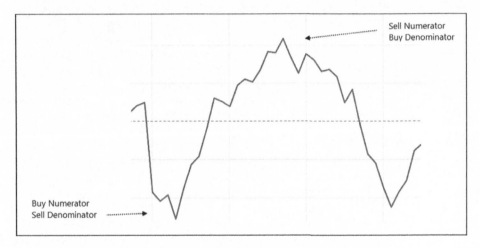

Image 9.1: Reversal pair trading on the ratio chart

Bollinger Bands

Bollinger Bands® is a wonderful invention of John Bollinger.

This indicator is based on the concept of standard deviation. Let us explore the concept of standard deviation using a simple example.

Imagine there are a group of people of varying heights. Some are short and others tall.

We can calculate the average height of this group and let us assume the average height is 165 cm. This is the average height and there can be a few people taller or shorter than the average height.

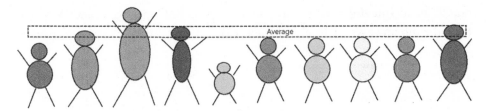

Image 9.2: Average height of a group of people

If I say that most people (roughly around 70%) will be covered in 10 cm band from the average number (Band = 10 cm above average and 10 cm below average). Meaning, most people in the group are within 175 cm and 155 cm.

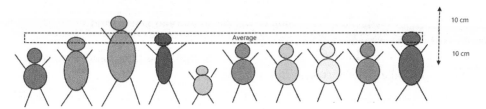

Image 9.2: 10 cm deviation from average height of a group of people

So, we now know that most people are covered in this range. This is known as standard deviation. The 10 cm in this example is a standard deviation.

If we consider 20 cm instead of 10 cm from average height, then even more people will be covered in this range. In simple words, this is a two standard deviation from the average number.

Statistically, around 68% of data gets covered within one standard deviation from the average. Around 95% is covered within the two-standard deviation and 99% in the three-standard deviation band.

The standard deviation number would depend on the variation of the individual data points from the average number in the data. We can adopt the same concept of the average and standard deviation in the price chart too.

We can calculate the average price (moving average) on the price chart.

For example, let us consider a scenario where the average price of Nifty over the last 20 bars is 11000. There would be sessions with a wide range, narrow rage etc during this 20-day period. We can calculate the standard deviation for Nifty 50 based on the data available.

Bollinger bands are calculated based on the standard deviation from the moving average which is the middle band. The standard deviation is added to the middle band (moving average) to plot the upper Bollinger band and deducted from the moving average to plot the lower Bollinger band.

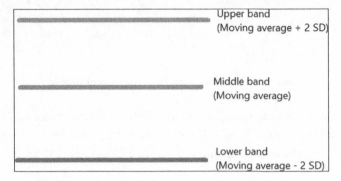

Image 9.3: Calculation of Upper, Middle and Lower band

So, there are three lines on the chart when we plot Bollinger bands. Below is a Nifty 50 candlestick chart with Bollinger bands.

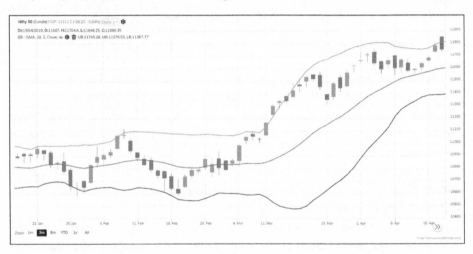

Figure 9.4: Nifty 50 Daily candlestick chart with 20,2 Bollinger bands

The moving average lookback period of 20 and a standard deviation offset of two are the default parameters recommended by John Bollinger. That means a 20-period moving average is plotted and the upper and lower bands are plotted 2-standard deviations away bands from the moving average. These bands would cover most of the data. You can experiment with other settings too.

The shape of the band is determined based on the two components–the moving average length and standard deviation.

- Moving average = trend
- Standard deviation = volatility
  To put it in simple words,
- If the trend is stronger than volatility, bands will be trending.
- If volatility is contracting than the trend, bands will be converging.
- If volatility is significantly increasing than the trend, bands will be expanding.

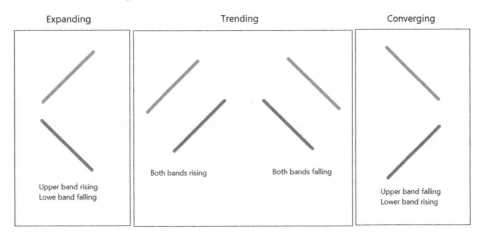

Image 9.4: Trend of bands

If volatility is higher, the gap between the upper and lower band will be higher or the bands would be expanding. If volatility is low, the gap between the two bands will be smaller or the bands would converge.

If the volatility is significantly low and two bands are in a very tight range, it is known as the squeeze pattern. According to John Bollinger, if the gap between the bands is at a six-month low, it is an ideal squeeze pattern.

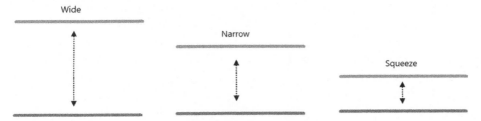

Image 9.5: Gap between bands

The narrow range is expected to be followed by a spike in high volatility or trend (Volatility cycle). Extremely low volatility (Squeeze) is a precursor to high volatility. Look for the breakout after a Squeeze.

Walking the bands

Mean reversion strategies may be adopted at band extremes but it needs confirmation from other tools or indicators. It would be a huge mistake to treat the upper band as resistance and the lower band as support. Rather, the price closing above the upper band or below lower bands is more reliable continuation signals and not reversals. John Bollinger calls this Walking the Bands.

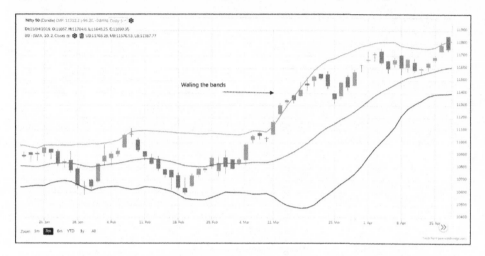

Figure 9.5: Nifty 50 daily candlestick chart with 20, 2 Bollinger bands showing the pattern of Walking the Bands

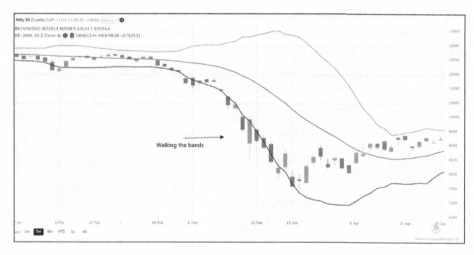

Figure 9.6: Nifty 50 daily candlestick chart with 20, 2 Bollinger bands showing the pattern of Walking the Bands

Reverse Expansion

The falling lower band and the rising upper band is known as reverse expansion. It indicates temporary exhaustion and suggests the possibility of a reversal or consolidation in the near term. Remember, bands behave this way when there is a spike in volatility. Selling options against the existing position may be a logical strategy during this phase as the option premiums might be high.

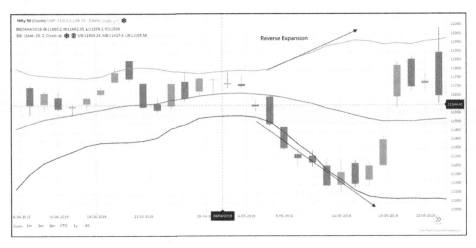

Figure 9.7: Nifty 50 daily candlestick chart with 20, 2 Bollinger bands showing the reverse expansion pattern

For Walking the Bands, a reversal from bands and reverse expansion–confirmation is required before considering a trade. It can be in the form of other indicators or volume analysis. My preference would be price pattern confirmation. It helps in planning the trades, placing the stops, and managing the trades.

Relative strength analysis, when there is a pattern of walking the bands in the price chart, is useful. For example, if the stock is trading above the upper band and outperforming the benchmark is a significant combination. It is a method of trading breakout in relative strength charts.

Extreme market breadth zone when there is a reverse expansion in Bollinger bands can help identify reversal or mean reversion opportunities. They provide significant confirmation to the Bollinger band setups. We will discuss breadth indicators in the next chapter.

For more understanding of Bollinger bands please read the book written by John Bollinger, titled–'Bollinger on Bollinger bands'. This book is strongly recommended. We can apply the Bollinger band indicator to the ratio and relative strength chart as well. The concept of standard deviation extremes can be helpful on ratio charts.

Below is a daily ratio chart of INFY / TCS along with 20-period Bollinger bands.

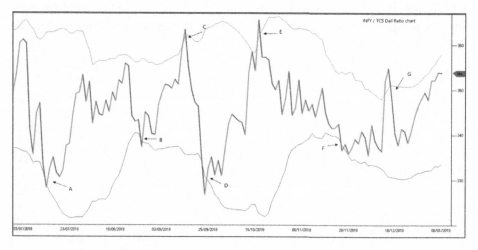

Figure 9.8: INFY to TCS Daily ratio chart with 20,2 Bollinger bands

The strategy based on the above chart would be to buy the pair when the ratio chart turns up from the lower band. A short trade in this pair may be considered when the ratio chart turns down at the upper band. The ratio chart touched the lower band and moved up at point A. It is a pattern suggesting a long trade in the pair. So, the strategy would be to take long trade in INFY and a short trade in TCS. Pattern B is also a bullish pair trade opportunity. At C, the ratio turned lower from the upper band. This is when a short pair strategy may be considered. The short trade would mean selling INFY and buying TCS. Pattern D and F are bullish patterns and E, and G are bearish patterns.

This setup is the opposite of trend following because we are looking to participate in a potential reversal.

Below is a chart of AXISBANK / ICICIBANK along with 20-period and two-standard deviation Bollinger bands.

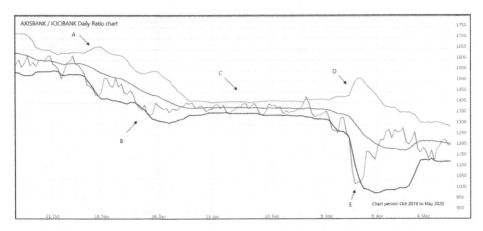

Figure 9.9: AXISBANK to ICICIBANK Daily ratio chart with 20.2 Bollinger bands

Pattern A is when there was a reverse expansion. The Bands were trending lower at B. C was a tight squeeze showing that the performance of both the instruments was at par. Pattern D is expanding bands. The ratio went above the lower band at E after the pattern of walking the bands.

All methods of reading Bollinger bands are equally applicable to ratio charts as well. Let us consider another popular indicator for mean-reversion based on the standard deviation which is the Z-Score.

Z-Score

Edward Altman, a professor at New York University, developed the Z-score formula in the 1960s. Z-Score is a statistical indicator that measures the difference between price and means and divides it by standard deviation.

Z Score = (Price – Moving average) / Standard Deviation

We can plot this as an indicator below the price chart or ratio chart. If the Z-score is 0, it shows that price is trading at its average. If Z-score is positive, it shows the price is trading above average. A negative Z-score shows price is below the moving average.

A Z-score of +2 means the price is two standard deviations above the mean. A Z-score of -2 means that the price is two standard deviations below the mean. 99% of values have a Z-score between -3 and 3, meaning they are within three standard deviations above and below the mean.

Most of the time the indicator remains between 2 and -2.

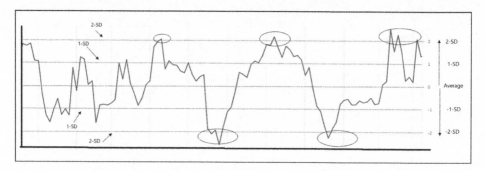

Image 9.6: Z-score between 2 and -2

The mean reversion strategy based on Z-score on the ratio chart is to buy pair when the indicator reaches below -2-SD and turns up. Close this trade when the indicator moves above the zero line. Sell the pair when the indicator reaches 2-SD and starts falling. Exit the trade when the indicator falls below the zero line.

Below is a daily ratio chart of Nifty bank to Nifty plotted with 20-period Z-Score.

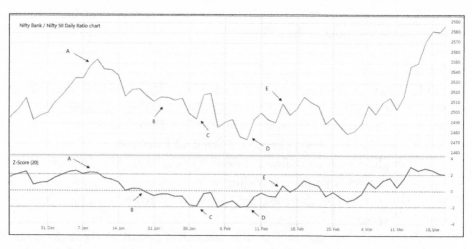

Figure 9.10: Daily ratio chart of Nifty bank to Nifty plotted with 20-period Z-Score

Point A is when the indicator falls below the 2-SD band after exceeding it. This is when you sell Nifty bank (Numerator) and buy Nifty (Denominator) in the above chart. The indicator went below the zero line at B which is when you exit the trade. The ratio fell hence it was a profitable trade. Pattern C is when the indicator touched -2 and started turning up. Ratio again touched lower band of -2-SD and went up at D. These are the occasions when you buy numerator and sell denominator. The ratio went above zero line at E, where you can cover or exit the long pair trade.

You can experiment with this strategy. You can also follow ratio patterns for confirmation. Notice the occurrence at C in the above chart where the ratio fell further initially which resulted in a loss initially in the pair trade. I recommend limiting the initial loss by following a stop-loss based on the ratio chart pattern. Even a fixed money stop will do. The idea is to limit the maximum risk in a trade at a predetermined level.

Scan for Z-score approaching 2-Sd or -2-SD. It can show instruments that may offer mean-reversion trade opportunities. Study historical data of ratio to know if and how it respected standard deviation bands.

Below is a daily ratio chart of BANK BARODA to CANBK with a 20-period Z-Score indicator.

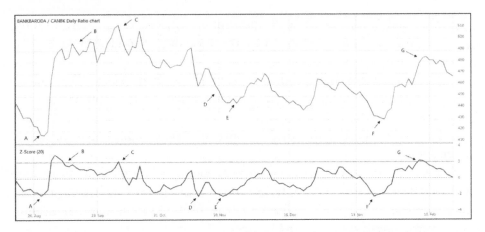

Figure 9.11: Daily ratio chart of BANK BARODA to CANBK with 20-period Z-Score indicator

Both stocks in the above chart are from the PSU Bank index. Pattern A, D, E and F are instances when the indicator reached -2-SD when you should buy numerator and sell the denominator. Pattern B, C and G are instances when the indicator reached the upper extreme when you can sell ratio, by shorting the numerator and buying the denominator.

OOPs

Below is a Daily 1% x 3 P&F RS chart of Maruti to Tata Motors.

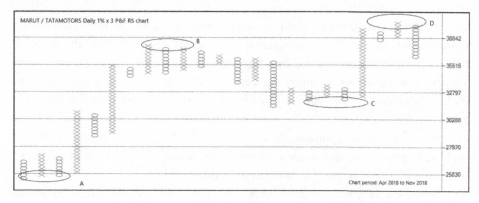

Figure 9.12: Daily 1% x 3 P&F RS chart of Maruti to Tata Motors

Pattern A and C are bullish OOPs patterns and B, and D are bearish OOPs patterns. You can look for reversal patterns in candidates to identify such types of trades.

There are many other indicators and possibilities. Mean reversion or reversal strategies that we apply on the price chart are also applicable on the ratio chart.

Identify instruments that tend to move in a range to implement the mean reversion strategy.

When the instrument is in an uptrend, trading bullish means reversion is a bullish pullback strategy. When the instrument is in a downtrend, trading bearish mean reversion is a bearish pullback strategy. Identify strong trends and short-term corrections to apply pullback strategy.

Trend following or breakout strategies in strong trending sectors and instruments can be a logical approach. While trading breakouts, prefer to trade major pattern breakouts in pair trading.

Pair trading through a ratio chart can be amazingly effective. Like price charts, you can apply trend following and mean reversion or pullback strategies on ratio charts as well for pair trading. Create a pair trading portfolio and treat them as a single instrument for entry and exit using a ratio chart. Plan strategy diversification while initiating multiple pair trades.

In this chapter, we discussed:

- Mean reversion tools and indicators can be applied on the RS chart as well.
- It is important to keep in mind different aspects of pair trading for successful implementation.

Now, you understand all aspects of trading the RS charts. Buying or selling ratio, patterns, indicators, trading systems, matrix tables, ranking etc are discussed in detail. You are well equipped to take your methods of trading the markets using these tools.

In the next chapter, we'll discuss another important part of the book – The breadth analysis.

Chapter 10

BREADTH INDICATORS

. . . .

There is humongous research and study done concerning breadth indicators. Many analysts have spent years in this field and have developed many interesting indicators. I recommend reading *The Complete Guide to Market Breadth Indicators: How to Analyze and Evaluate Market Direction and Strength by Gregory Morris* if you wish to learn more about all the breadth indicators, their history, logic and interpretation. I have been studying this subject for several years and we shall discuss the concepts that I found interesting from a trading or investing perspective.

It is often said that when you are right about the market, maximum people would tend to disagree with you. Price-shocks or surprises happen when there is a consensus. Have you felt the need for an indicator that gives an idea when there is a consensus in one direction?

We plot different indicators on the price chart that help identify the momentum or extreme zones of a particular instrument. Indicators are invariably calculated on the price data of the instrument. For example, a 200-bar daily moving average on the Nifty 50 chart tells us about the broad trend of the Nifty 50 index. If the price is above average the line, the trend is bullish and vice versa.

Like any other index, the Nifty 50 index too is calculated based on individual weightage and price action of its constituents. It does not necessarily reflect the broad market sentiment as the index heavyweights would typically influence the movement in the index.

Indicators based on the Nifty 50 index price chart tells us about the strength of the price chart which could be a result of the index heavyweight stocks moving up or down. It tells us about the trend of the index. For example, when I use some indicators on the Nifty 500 index, I get to know how the index is moving. The true health of the market can be known by checking the health of all the constituents of the index.

The indicator that considers the trend of each stock in the group would be more useful to assess the broad market health. Let us consider a simple scenario. Let us plot say, a 200-day moving average on the price chart and consider the following scenarios.

If the Nifty 50 Index is above its 200-period moving average, then the Nifty 50 index is considered bullish. What if most of the stocks from the Nifty 50 universe are trading above their 200-period average? If this is the case, then the average health of the market as a whole can be considered bullish.

While the moving average captures the broad trend in the instrument, the second measure above is the "Breadth indicator" that captures the overall health of the market. Breadth indicators are not calculated on the price of an instrument. They evaluate the market sentiments by taking into account the trend or performance of all the stocks forming part of a sector or group.

There are different types of breadth indicators out there. The advance-decline ratio is among the popular market breadth indicators. It captures how many stocks advanced or declined in a particular trading session. Any indicator may be used to calculate market breadth. We often get to hear or read in the media a certain number of stocks advanced and declined during the day. That is nothing but a discussion on the breadth of the market. If a greater number of stocks advance, it is a sign of bullishness. If a large number of stocks were to decline, it indicates bearish market breadth.

We can plot the advance-decline indicator below the price chart, but it is difficult to interpret or conclude anything significant out of it. Weekly and monthly advance-decline charts may be useful to some extent.

Let us adopt a simple approach to breadth. We just need a criterion to suggest if a stock is bullish or bearish. We can use the regular indicators to calculate breadth. For example, using the moving average, we can calculate the percentage of stocks trading above their 200-day moving average in Nifty or any other index. This percentage can be plotted in the chart. This indicator would oscillate between 0 and 100. A reading of 50% means an equal number of stocks are trading above and below the moving average, suggesting a balanced market. The indicator scans all the stocks in the group and therefore provides information about the health of the overall market and the state of the trend.

It can be calculated on different timeframes but remember it is calculated on a group of stocks and not on the index value. Hence, it provides a true picture of the market sentiment. I can show you any number of examples where price keeps rising or falling without any indication of sentiment extreme in the breadth indicator. Breadth is a very logical and useful indicator for sentiment analysis.

The breadth indicator can help us in reading broad-based trends and the exhaustion phase. Rising breadth is bullish because it indicates that there is greater participation of stocks from the group. Similarly, a falling breadth is bearish because it indicates a lack of participation.

Calculation

Let us consider a simple example of using the 200-day moving average to calculate the breadth indicator for the Nifty 50 index. For example, 50 stocks constitute the Nifty 50 index. The next step is to calculate how many stocks are bullish from the group. The criteria to decide bullishness is the price trading above its 200-day moving average in this case. If say there are 25 stocks in the group trading above their 200-day moving average, the breadth indicator reading would be 50% (25 divided by 50).

This way, we can calculate this percentage daily and plot it on the chart. This indicator would give us an idea about the bullishness and participation of the index constituents.

Below is a chart showing the percentage of stocks trading above their 200-day moving average in the Nifty 50 index.

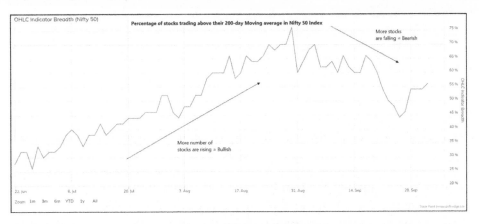

Figure 10.1: Percentage of stocks trading above their 200-day moving average in the Nifty 50 index

When this chart is rising, that means more numbers of stocks are fulfilling the bullish criteria. This is a bullish sign as there is the increased participation of the stocks from the chosen universe. Similarly, when the breadth indicator is falling, it means more numbers of stocks are turning bearish.

When the market index is rising and the breadth indicator is also rising, it is a bullish scenario. It indicates that the price is bullish, and the participation of the constituents is also increasing. It is a sign of a strong bullish trend. When the price and the breadth are falling, it is indicative of a strong bearish trend.

Which parameter to use for calculating breadth indicator depends on the horizon we are looking for. For instance, a 20-period average may be used to study the short-term breadth perspective. A 50-period moving average would capture a medium-term time frame and a 200-period average may be considered to study long-term breadth.

Below is a daily candlestick chart of Nifty along with a 50-day moving average breadth indicator.

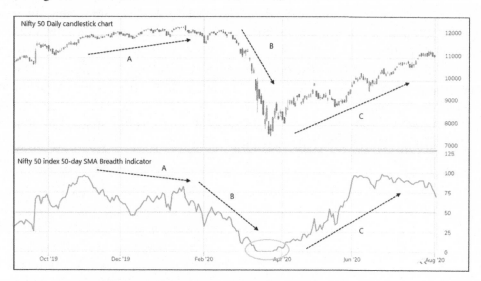

Figure 10.2: Daily candlestick chart of Nifty along with 50-day moving average breadth indicator

The price went up, but the breadth chart was falling during the stretch-marked A in the above chart. It shows that the participation is reducing and provided a heads-up of the underlying weakness. Point B is where both the price and breadth were falling which suggests a strong downtrend. Point C is when price and breadth both were increasing indicating a strong uptrend.

The indicator line shown below the chart is not a calculation based on the price. It is a breadth indicator calculated on the entire group of stocks. The 50-day moving average breadth indicator in the above chart captures the percentage of stocks trading above their 50-day moving average. It captures the participation and strength of the trend from a medium-term perspective.

Notice the circle after point B where the indicator reading was 0%. This indicates all the stocks from the index were trading below their 50-day moving average.

Extreme zones

When the stock market sentiment is bullish and stocks are outperforming, the environment is favourable and stocks that you buy would do well. This bullish phase may be followed by a phase where the market may correct temporarily. It can be either a price correction or a time correction. During this corrective phase, it is possible that you may end up exiting stocks driven by fear or may end up buying stocks at the highs before the correction. Either way, this hampers the overall portfolio return. The mistakes in this corrective phase may affect overall returns.

When everything is bullish, and things are sounding great, there must be something to caution you to slow down a bit. The proverbial boat may get over the board. It would make sense in this scenario to slow down a bit and enter later.

It is often said that when you are right about the market, the maximum number of people would tend to disagree with you. Given that price-shocks, or surprises, generally occur when there is consensus and complacency, I often felt the need for an indicator that gives an idea of the consensus in any one direction. When the visual media, magazines or analysts sound confident about the price moving in a particular direction, it is often a reason to be cautious.

Even while studying fundamental reports, one may notice too many analysts sounding extremely bullish and confident about a target level which again, is a sign of complacency. It makes sense to get an idea of what most market participants are doing but it is practically impossible to read through the reports of all analysts and know the view of all traders. Given this backdrop, would it not be handy to have a method to assess such sentiment extremes? Opinions of bench sitters are not of much importance in this context as they do not influence price in any way.

The trend of most stocks would be bullish when the overall market trend is strong and up. But this phase would inevitably be followed by exhaustion when there would be little fuel left in the tank to keep the momentum sustaining in the same direction. Taking long positions in such a "tiring" scenario is not advisable even though the trend may still be up, and the chart might still appear bullish. Breadth extreme zones indicate that there is a possibility of euphoria or panic. In simple terms, this captures sentiment extremes.

Many possible rules can be designed using breadth indicators. Overbought and oversold zone depends on the breadth indicator we are using. When the breadth reading is above 70% - 80%, it means that most of the stocks from the group are bullish. This happens when the trend is up, and strong, but it could also mean indicator exhaustion or too much bullishness. Most individual stock charts will be in a bullish mode during such an extreme phase. Remember, overbought or oversold breadth extreme zones indicate exhaustion—but not necessarily a trend reversal. Hence, fresh longs are best avoided during such a scenario when the indicator is in the overbought zone. Similarly, fresh shorts are best avoided when the indicator is at the oversold zone. The overbought–oversold zone reading also depends on the type of indicator used for the breadth study. Traders should remain cautious and reduce their position sizes during breadth extremes.

The trend of most of the stocks will be bullish when the overall market trend is strong and up. But exhaustion sets in when there is little fuel left in the tank to keep the momentum going. Taking long positions in such a scenario is not advisable even though the trend is up, and the chart patterns are bullish. Breadth extreme zones typically indicate the possibility of euphoria or panic sentiment extremes.

Featured below is a chart of the 200-day moving average breadth indicator on the Nifty 500 group.

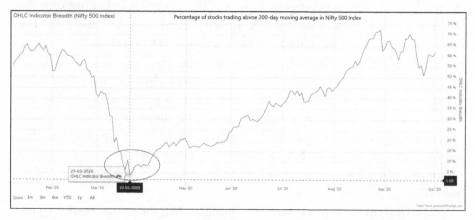

Figure 10.3: 200-day moving average breadth indicator on the Nifty 500 group

The indicator dropped sharply towards the end of the market meltdown in March 2020. The breadth indicator reading at lows suggested that only 4% of stocks from the Nifty 500 universe were trading above their 200-day moving average. This is extremely bearish because most of the stocks are in a downtrend and trading below their 200-day moving average. But this also suggests an extreme oversold or panic condition.

We can plot the breadth indicator below the price chart to get a better idea. Below is a 200-day moving average breadth indicator of the Nifty 500 index average plotted below the Nifty 50 index chart.

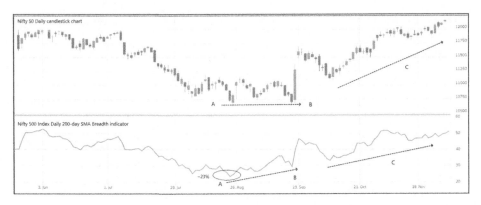

Figure 10.4: A 200-day moving average breadth indicator of Nifty 500 index average plotted below Nifty 50 index daily candlestick chart

The 200-day moving average breadth indicator in the above chart shows the percentage of stocks trading above the 200-day moving average. Price made a new low at A and the breadth indicator indicated that more stocks were turning bearish by falling below their long-term 200-day moving average. The indicator reading was around 23%, meaning 77% of stocks were trading below the moving average. Price made a double bottom support pattern at B and tested the previous low; the breadth indicator however was rising. This means participation improved and more numbers of stocks were in an uptrend and trading above their 200-day moving average. It was followed by a bullish price trend at C and the participation improved consistently.

The breadth overbought and oversold zones are hugely different from overbought-oversold zones based on price-based indicators. Breadth indicators are calculated on a group of stocks. Adopting the mean reversion setups or investing in relatively strong stocks when breadth indicators are at extreme zones can prove highly profitable. This might give you some idea about the possibility of including breadth indicators in your trading systems.

Divergences
Whenever you spot a divergence between the breadth indicator and the Nifty index, it would be a sign to turn cautious. The positive divergence between the price and the breadth indicator happens when the price makes a new low, but breadth does not. Similarly, a negative divergence occurs when the price makes a new high, but the indicator does not.

If Nifty is rising but the breadth is falling, that means there is not enough participation from most of the stocks and only a few heavyweight stocks are pushing the index higher. While this phase may happen often but such types of phases are difficult to sustain. If this situation does sustain, then, typically, a major price reversal follows.

Below is a daily candlestick chart of Nifty plotted along with a 20-period moving average breadth indicator.

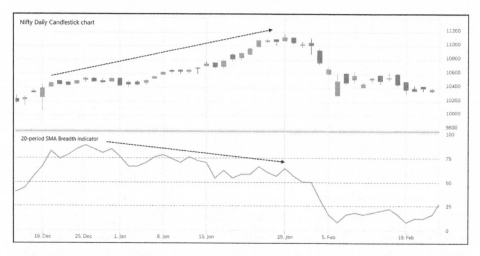

Figure 10.5: Daily candlestick chart of Nifty plotted along with 20-period moving average breadth indicator

Moving average breadth indicator of the Nifty's group of 50 stock that calculates the percentage of stocks trading above their 20-day moving average. The breadth was falling indicating that the rally was fuelled by only a handful of stocks. The other logical inference is that stocks were falling below their averages while Nifty was going up. It means heavyweight stocks were taking the index higher. Thereafter, Nifty witnessed a significant fall in February 2018.

By now it must be clear that it is important to understand the importance of the breadth indicator. The index can rise or fall due to the contribution of only a few of its constituents, but the overall market health will be positive only when most of the stocks from the group or the index are participating. The divergence between breadth and index price is an important warning sign.

If such divergences occur near the breadth extreme zones, i.e., positive divergence at or near an oversold zone, or a negative divergence at or near an overbought zone—they could end up being a sign of a major trend reversal.

The breadth leaving an oversold zone is when long trades have a better risk-reward and breadth leaving an overbought zone is when the risk-reward for short trades is more favourable. But the breadth indicator alone is not sufficient; price patterns of the respective chart need to confirm whether a trade can be initiated.

Breadth indicator can act as a confirmatory tool to the support and resistance pattern in the price chart.

Breadth indicator helps up in three ways:

1. Confirming the strength of the trend.
2. Divergences that confirms demand or supply.
3. Reading the phase of exhaustion.

Breadth Indicators

We just discussed a breadth indicator based on a 200-day moving average. The moving average look-back period can be changed based on the trading time horizon. There are also many other tools to plot breadth charts. As mentioned earlier, any indicator may be used as the breadth indicator.

Advance-decline is a very popular breadth indicator. This study calculates the number of stocks that advanced and declined in a particular trading session. Let us take the example of the National Stock Exchange in India where close to 2000-stocks are traded daily. Suppose say 1000 stocks advanced on a given day (the closing price was higher than the previous close), the advance% would be 50% because 50% of stocks advanced during the day. Now, there are many ways to present this information.

Below is the daily advance-decline breadth indicator along with the Nifty 50 index candlestick chart. Note that the indicator is calculated on the Nifty 500 index.

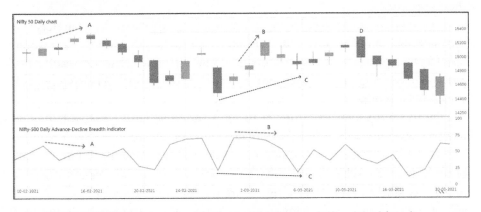

Figure 10.6: Nifty daily candlestick chart with advance-decline breadth indicator on Nifty 500 index

Plotting the indicator on a larger universe helps in understanding what happened to the broad market. Logically, more numbers of stocks should be advancing if the market session was bullish, and more numbers of stocks would be declining when the market session was bearish. In scenario A in the above chart, price when moved up over multiple sessions but more stocks were declining that indicated that the sentiment was not positive. More stocks declining would mean that portfolios are not gaining even though the benchmark index was rising.

Have a look at the zone captured by the arrow marked at B, where the price rose sharply but the participation was relatively stable. The declining stocks were more than the advancing ones. The sessions were not bullish at C, but the number of declining stocks were much more showing that there was a sharp correction across the stocks, and the fall was more than what was captured by the benchmark Nifty 50 index. We can see the price running into resistance at point D which was the same level where the breadth turned down earlier at B.

It is important to understand that any index is created as a barometer to study the broad market trend but that does not always capture what is happening across the market. While plotting the breadth, I prefer the Nifty 500 universe because it is the largest group available at the NSE, and it captures the broader picture of the overall market sentiment.

There are a variety of breadth indicators based on the advance-decline ratio. For instance, advance minus decline divided by advance plus decline, net of advances, advancing percentage, advancing minus declining issues, up volume, down volume, calculating single or double averages of these ratios etc. There are many possibilities, many analysts have made modifications as per their understanding and experience. There are pros and cons associated with each of these approaches.

What I have observed is that it gets difficult for people to track and understand the interpretation of breadth indicators and stick to the process. I think it would be effective if people use the indicators, they understand to calculate breadth. The purpose of plotting breadth indicator is to analyze the trend and behaviour of all stocks in the group.

Different types of indicators are based on price, volume, trend, volatility, or momentum. Any of these indicators may be used to calculate breadth.

For example, we can use the popular relative strength index or RSI to calculate breadth. If we consider an RSI value above 60 as bullish, then we can calculate how many stocks in the Nifty universe are trading above the RSI 60-level? This gives us an idea about how many stocks in Nifty are in a strong momentum.

The calculation or logic of all breadth indicators that we discuss in the book remains the same. Its objective here is to identify how many stocks in the group are fulfilling the chosen criteria? If the RSI-14 breadth indicator and if 20 stocks in the Nifty 50 index are trading above the chosen threshold, then the RSI breadth indicator reading would be 40%.

The breadth indicator oscillates between 0 and 100. A reading of 50 means that an equal number of stocks are trading in the bullish and bearish zone, thus suggesting a balanced market. The indicator scans all the stocks in the group and captures the health of the overall market and the state of the trend. When the indicator shows a reading of 80%, it means that 80% of stocks are in a bullish trend. On the other hand, if the indicator drops to 20%, it suggests that 80% of stocks are in a bearish trend. Like Moving average and RSI, any indicator can act as a breadth indicator.

Benefits of indicators as breadth
There are different types of indicators, averages, momentum, strength-weakness, channel indicators, volatility indicators etc. The fact that we can plot them as a breadth indicator changes their dynamics.

The market rotates through trend and volatility cycles on different timeframes. Consider this scenario:

Trend > Volatility = Trend is strong, trade breakouts – ride the move.

Volatility > Trend = Caution, trade pullbacks – adopt aggressive profit booking strategy.

We discussed trend-based breadth indicators. We can also plot volatility-based breadth indicators. There are many volatility-based indicators and ATR% is one of the popular ones. ATR% indicator that calculates the Average True Range of a particular stock. High ATR indicates that stock is more volatile and vice versa.

Below is a chart showing a breadth indicator that calculates the number of stocks with an ATR reading of 5% or more in the Nifty 500 index.

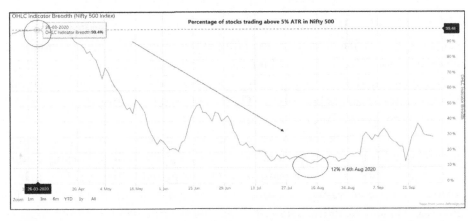

Figure 10.7: Breadth indicator that calculates the number of stocks trading above their 5% ATR in the Nifty 500 index

The chart above shows that the indicator recorded a high in March 2020 suggesting that stocks were moving in a wide range. The indicator was consistently falling till August 2020. Interestingly, Nifty appreciated by more than 30% during this period. It shows that the trend was strong, and volatility was contracting. Trend following systems, breakouts and riding the move should be a preferred strategy during such times.

Below is a Nifty daily candlestick chart along with a 14-period ATR 5% breadth indicator on the Nifty 500 Universe.

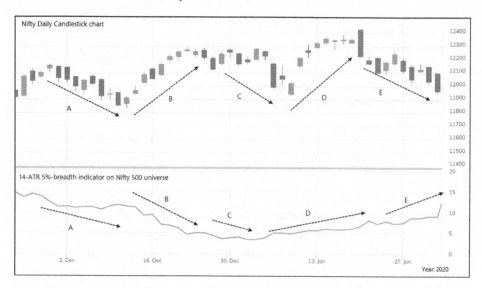

Figure 10.8: Nifty daily candlestick chart along with 14-period ATR 5% breadth indicator on Nifty 500 Universe

ATR 5% breadth indicator in the above chart calculates the percentage of stocks where the ATR is 5% or more in the Nifty 500 universe. Usually, this indicator moves in the 0-25% range. The indicator typically rises when the market falls. During period A, the price fell, and the indicator was also falling showing that the downtrend was steep but less volatile. The lack of volatility during the fall suggests a strong momentum of the downtrend.

During period B, the price was rising, and the indicator was falling, suggesting that the trend is getting stronger along with a drop in volatility. During C, the price fell, volatility started picking up later. During period D, the price was up but volatility was also increasing indicating that the trend is up but volatile. During E, the price fell, and volatility increased suggesting that the trend is getting weaker, and volatility is rising in the markets.

Knowing this can help traders tweak their strategies. During the period of low volatility, the trader can ride the trend and trend following strategies will be more rewarding. When the volatility is high, it would be advisable to switch to a lower timeframe. There will be trends in the lower time frame that will be rewarding. At times, there is higher volatility in the lower timeframe and that is when trading in the bigger time frame or box-value in P&F charts would prove more rewarding.

When an ATR based indicator moves beyond the normal range, it indicates the possibility of a strong trend, but such a situation is not usual. Usually, rising volatility is a sign of a bearish trend.

Featured below is the Nifty 50 daily candlestick chart along with the 14-period ATR 5% breadth indicator on the Nifty 500 Universe.

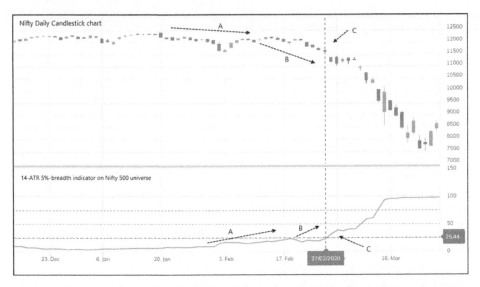

Figure 10.9: Nifty 50 daily candlestick chart along with a 14-period ATR 5% breadth indicator on Nifty 500 Universe

Indicator started increasing at point A after price made a high in January 2020. Price fell and volatility breadth indicator was rising at B. It moved beyond 25% towards the end of February 2020 at C. This was followed by a sharp fall in the index. The indicator reading was 100% in March 2020.

There are many ways to use and interpret the breadth indicators in trading. You can plot it on different charts and sectors for analysing the prevailing market phase.

Below is a daily candlestick chart of Nifty 50 along with 14-period RSI breadth for mid-level.

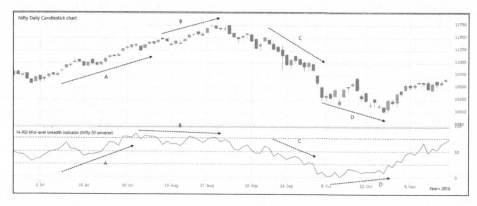

Figure 10.10: Daily candlestick chart of Nifty 50 along with 14-period RSI breadth for mid-level

The RSI breadth indicator in the above chart plots the number of stocks in the group whose RSI reading is above 50. Stock will be above RSI 50 if its trend is bullish. In a bull market, more stocks are expected to have their RSI above the 50-mark. During period A, the price is moving up and the number of stocks above mid-level RSI was also increasing. This is a classic bull market. At B, the price was rising but the indicator reached extreme levels and stopped making new highs indicating a bearish divergence. At C, the price and the stocks above 50-RSI were falling, suggesting a bear market. At D, the price made a new low but the number of stocks above 50 level started increasing. This is a typical bullish divergence scenario.

What does it mean when RSI is above 70? It indicates that the stock is in strong momentum because there were more numbers of bullish prices compared to the bearish ones. If a majority of the stocks are trading above RSI 70-level, it indicates that most of the stocks from the group are in a strong momentum. That way, the RSI breadth indicator becomes the RSI momentum breadth indicator.

Think about the possibilities now. Do not fall into the trap of what will be the best tool to assess breadth. Imagine what you can do with this information.

Here are a few major types of breadth indicators:
* Advance-Decline based indicators.
* Price based breadth indicator: High and Low indicator
* Channel-based indicators: Donchian, Bollinger band, Keltner etc.

- Average line-based indicators: Moving average, Super trend, PAR SAR, AMA etc.
- Momentum based oscillators: RSI, MACD, ADX etc.
- Volatility based indicators: Standard deviation, ATR%, Z-score etc.
- Noiseless chart swing-based indicators: Bullish percent, X-percent, DT-percent, bullish-brick percent, line-break bullish line% etc.
- 52-week high and low

The 52-week high and low is a sensible breadth indicator that captures the market sentiment. More stocks hitting a 52-week high is a bullish environment. More stocks hitting a fresh 52-week low indicates a bearish environment.

Here is the Nifty 50 candlestick chart along with the 50-period moving average. The breadth indicator displayed in the lower pane is the 52-week high low breadth indicator of the Nifty 500 index.

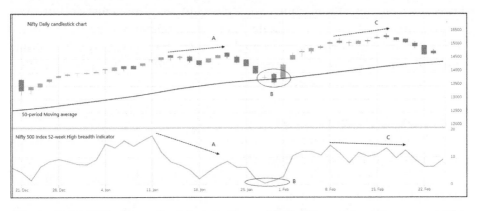

Figure 10.11: Nifty 50 candlestick chart along with the 50-period moving average. The breadth indicator displayed in the lower pane is the 52-week high low breadth indicator of the Nifty 500 index

At A, the price was rising and was trading above the moving average, but the number of stocks recording 52-week highs was reducing. It was followed by a short-term correction where the price pulled back to the moving average at B while the breadth indicator dropped to the oversold zone. The price holding above the average and oversold breadth indicator provides the ideal environment to consider pullback trading opportunities. The price moved up to hit a peak at C, but the breadth indicator was not keeping pace.

At times, these indicators reverse before the price. When several stocks hitting 52-week high prices start dropping, it is a bearish sign. Similarly, if stocks hitting a 52-week low starts reducing in a downtrend, it is a sign that the downtrend is weakening.

When you see more number stocks registering new 52-week highs from a sector, it means re-rating of the overall sector is happening and stocks are getting into a new zone. Identifying the price breakout in this sector would be a logical trading strategy. This is like a classic top-down approach. Always remember, when most of the stocks in sectors are positive (breadth chart is extremely bullish), the sector is strong from the medium-term perspective and there is a strong possibility of follow-through action.

When a 52-week high or stocks at a new high surpasses stocks at new lows, it is a bullish sign. This is a traditional observation that has stood the test of time. It shows a significantly bullish environment and sentiments.

When the breadth starts improving, meaning a greater number of stocks are showing strength, be aggressive in buying. The major issue in a bull market is many stocks are moving at a time. We cannot buy the entire universe, but when multiple stocks are rising, it indicates that the sentiment and participation are strong. So, it would make sense to hold on to the long positions and probably even add to the winners. The portfolio in such conditions will outperform if we have strong stocks in the portfolio.

High–Low Momentum Index

Breadth indicators based on price high or low and moving average are more useful breadth indicators as per my experience.

Here are a few aspects to consider while studying the breadth readings of major indices, groups, or sectors.

- Stocks trading above or below the average line.
- Stocks trading above important high or low, such as 52- week high low.
- Stocks in strong momentum.

A 52-week high low is a weekly timeframe breadth indicator. We can convert it to a 250-day high-low indicator. We can also plot a 20-day high-low indicator for short-term health and a 100-day high-low indicator to study medium-term health.

If we plot a 250-day high-low indicator on the candlestick chart, it will plot lines at 250-day high or low levels. We will also draw lines for stocks trading within 10% from their 250-day high and low. The stock trading within 10% from high is considered as the ones in bullish momentum. Stock trading within 10% from the low are the ones in bearish momentum. Stocks trading above the average line of the high and low bands are in a bullish zone. The stocks trading below the average line is in a bearish zone.

Below is a chart of Siemens with a 250-period high-dow Momentum Index with a 10 percent band.

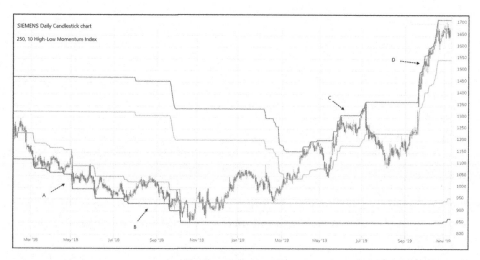

Figure 10.12: Siemens daily candlestick chart with 250-period high-low momentum index with 10 percent band

The lower band is falling at A that shows price slipping to new 250-day lows. If the price is in between the red and yellow bands, it indicates that the price is in a bearish extreme zone. At C, the price was between the green and blue upper band indicating that it was trading near high and in a bullish extreme zone. The upper band is rising at D indicating that the price is marking a new 250-day high.

The chart below captures the percentage of stocks in a bullish zone using the 120-period high-low momentum index breadth indicator.

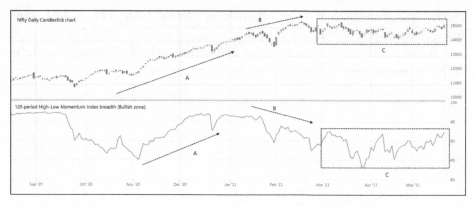

Figure 10.13: Nifty daily candlestick chart with the percentage of stocks in a bullish zone using the 120-period high-low momentum index breadth indicator

Price and breadth indicators, both were in a strong uptrend at A. Price went up, but the breadth indicator was declining at B indicating that more stocks were sliding to the bearish zone. It was followed by a range-bound market during the C period.

Featured below is a chart that displaying the Nifty daily candlestick chart along with the HLMI breadth indicator.

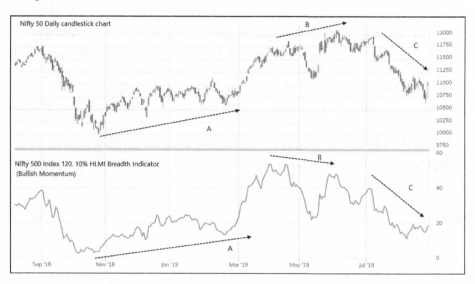

Figure 10.14: Nifty daily candlestick chart along with HLMI breadth indicator

The above breadth indicator chart is a 120-period and 10% bullish momentum index chart of HLMI. It shows the percentage of stocks trading within 10% of their 120-period high.

The number of stocks in bullish momentum was rising during period A and this was followed by a strong uptrend in Nifty 50. Price was rising at B, but the breadth indicator was falling, which indicated reducing the momentum of stocks. This was followed by period C, where price and breadth declined.

At times, the momentum acts as a lead indicator and provides early warning about the market sentiment and probable exhaustion of the trend.

It would be interesting to see the bearish momentum breadth indicator chart of HLMI during the same period. Below is the chart of Nifty daily candlestick chart along with the HLMI bearish momentum breadth indicator for the same period.

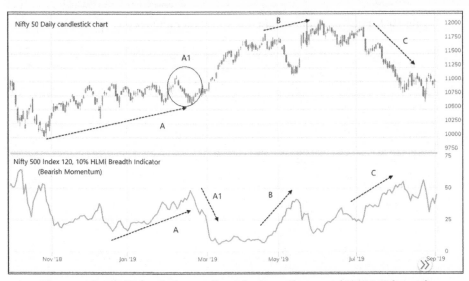

Figure 10.15: Nifty daily candlestick chart along with HLMI bearish momentum breadth indicator.

Period A is when the price was increasing but there was a lack of momentum. Bullish momentum stocks and bearish momentum, both were increasing during the period suggesting more of a range bound and stock-specific market. At A1, the price fell but stocks in bearish momentum also fell. It was followed by rising prices and a falling bearish breadth indicator. At B, the price was rising, but the bearish momentum breadth indicator was also rising while the bullish momentum indicator was falling. This is a classic negative divergence and suggests underlying weakness in the market. At C, the price was falling while the bearish momentum indicator was also rising, and the bullish momentum indicator was falling. This was a clear indication of bearish sentiment.

So, this HLMI Momentum based breadth indicator will capture six aspects of the chosen group:

- Percentage of stocks trading at highs.
- Percentage of stocks trading at lows.
- Percentage of stocks trading in bullish momentum.
- Percentage of stocks trading in bearish momentum.
- Percentage of stocks trading in the bullish zone.
- Percentage of stocks trading in the bearish zone.

Below is an example of high-low momentum index breadth numbers on different sectors.

Table 10.1: High-low momentum index breadth numbers on different sectors

Group	At High	At Low	High momentum	Low Momentum	Bullish zone	Bearish zone
Energy Index	30.00%	0.00%	100.00%	0.00%	100.00%	0.00%
CPSE Index	25.00%	0.00%	91.70%	0.00%	100.00%	0.00%
Commodities Index	20.00%	0.00%	90.00%	0.00%	100.00%	0.00%
Pharma Index	0.00%	0.00%	90.00%	10.00%	90.00%	10.00%
FMCG Index	20.00%	0.00%	86.70%	6.70%	93.30%	6.70%
IT Index	10.00%	0.00%	80.00%	0.00%	100.00%	0.00%
Metal Index	6.70%	0.00%	80.00%	0.00%	100.00%	0.00%
PSE Index	25.00%	0.00%	80.00%	0.00%	100.00%	0.00%
Realty Index	20.00%	0.00%	80.00%	0.00%	90.00%	0.00%
Infrastructure Index	23.30%	0.00%	73.30%	0.00%	100.00%	0.00%
Consumption Index	10.00%	0.00%	70.00%	3.30%	96.70%	3.30%
MNC Index	10.00%	0.00%	63.30%	6.70%	86.70%	13.30%
PSU Bank Index	7.70%	0.00%	61.50%	0.00%	92.30%	7.70%
Auto Index	6.70%	0.00%	60.00%	0.00%	93.30%	6.70%
Bank Index	0.00%	0.00%	58.30%	0.00%	91.70%	8.30%
Media Index	0.00%	0.00%	50.00%	0.00%	100.00%	0.00%
Pvt Bank Index	0.00%	0.00%	50.00%	0.00%	80.00%	20.00%

The table shown above is sorted based on the high momentum stock breadth reading. All stocks in the Energy index are trading in the bullish zone and within 10% from their-250day high. 30% stocks are at a 250-day high. The sector is in strong momentum. Followed by the CPSE index. With this table, we get all the important information about how stocks in the group are behaving.

Below is an example of the high-low momentum breadth index for all major averages.

Table 10.2: High-low momentum breadth index on all major averages

Group	At High	At Low	High momentum	Low Momentum	Bullish zone	Bearish zone
Nifty 50	16.00%	0.00%	82.00%	2.00%	98.00%	2.00%
Nifty 100	16.00%	0.00%	81.00%	2.00%	96.00%	4.00%
Nifty Next 50 Index	16.00%	0.00%	80.00%	2.00%	94.00%	6.00%
Nifty 200	15.00%	0.00%	71.00%	1.50%	95.00%	5.00%
Midcap 150 Index	12.70%	0.00%	63.30%	1.30%	93.30%	6.00%
Nifty 500 Index	9.20%	0.00%	63.30%	1.20%	91.20%	6.60%
Midcap 100 Index	14.00%	0.00%	61.00%	1.00%	94.00%	6.00%
Mid-Small Cap 400	7.50%	0.00%	59.00%	1.00%	90.00%	10.00%
Midcap 50	14.00%	0.00%	58.00%	0.00%	96.00%	4.00%
Small Cap 250	4.40%	0.00%	56.40%	0.80%	88.00%	12.00%
Small Cap 50	6.00%	0.00%	48.00%	2.00%	82.00%	18.00%
Small Cap 100	6.00%	0.00%	47.00%	2.00%	85.00%	15.00%

The table is sorted based on a percentage of stocks in high momentum. If you pay attention, it should be easy to assess how each index is behaving. Nifty 50 stocks are closer to their 250-day high than other groups. Large caps are outperforming. However, the whole market is bullish because no stock in any group is trading at a 250-day low.

The high-low momentum index is an extremely useful breadth indicator that captures how stocks are behaving in each group and index. It plots the average, high-low and momentum and shows us the percentage of stocks qualifying for these important parameters in each group of stocks. It is a price-based indicator that captures all important information and is useful on the price chart as well as a breadth indicator tool.

The look-back period to plot the indicator may be chosen based on the time horizon. Apart from the popular 250-day or 52-week lookback period, I found 120 days, 60-day and 20-day to be useful from a medium-term and short-term perspective.

Open Interest-based Breadth:

Open interest breadth is another useful indicator for short-term derivative trading.

As the name suggests, open interest shows how many parties have interest open in the instrument. The interest here means their trade is still open.

Derivatives are contracts. A contract is opened when there is a buyer and a seller. The bid price on the trading terminal is from the buyer and the offer price is from a seller. A contract takes place when both these prices match. Below is how open interest is calculated:

- When a new contract takes place, open interest increases.
- When the existing contract is closed by any party, the contract is just shifted to another party. Hence, open interest remains the same.
- When both parties close the contract, the open interest would decline.

Below is a table that broadly captures how open interest is interpreted.

Table 10.3: Price and open interest analysis

Price	Open Interest	Remark
Increase	Increase	Long build-up
Decrease	Increase	Short Build-up
Increase	Decrease	Short Covering
Decrease	Decrease	Long Unwinding

When price and open interest are increasing, it shows new bullish contracts are being opened as the price rises. It is a long build-up.

When the price is declining but open interest is increasing, it means new bearish contracts are being opened. it is a short build-up.

When the price is increasing but open interest is not increasing, it means that current bearish contracts are being closed. It is short covering.

If price is reducing and open interest is also reducing, it means that current bullish contracts are being closed, it is a long unwinding.

This is the basic interpretation of price and OI data. We can perform other forms of analysis on instruments filtered based on the above criteria.

In a bullish session, it is expected that more stocks will be participating. That means the percentage of long build-up should be more. Similarly, the percentage of stocks having short build-up should be more on bearish days.

Open interest may be used as an interesting breadth indicator for short-term trading and derivative analysis.

If we see the percentage of long build-up and short-covering together, it will act as a proxy for the percentage of advances. It will be similar to the advance-decline ratio because the price is rising in both cases irrespective of open interest. Short build-up and long unwinding numbers are the percentages of declining stocks.

Long build up% is a bullish indicator, it shows us numbers of stocks advancing with an increasing contract in the universe. Short build up% is a bearish indicator, it shows numbers of stocks declining with increasing contracts.

One can get to know about the market sentiment during the session by tracking this indicator. I recommend plotting it on the entire derivative universe to get a broader perspective.

Look for bullish opportunities when the long build-up percentage is more than the short build-up percentage. Look for bearish opportunities when the short build-up percentage are more than the long build-up percentage.

Pay attention to instances where the market action is not in sync with these indicators. If for instance, the market is bullish but long build up% are not supportive, the uptrend then is not strong. If the Nifty is bearish and if the short build% stocks are not rising, it indicates that the downtrend is not strong. It is a signal to remain cautious with short trades.

This indicator is more useful from an intraday and short-term derivative trading perspective. Let us discuss a few breadth indicators based on noiseless charts.

Noiseless chart indicators

I prefer to track breadth indicators based on noiseless charts because it considers both price and volatility. Thomas Dorsey in his book mentioned that Earnest Staby was trying to create an indicator that is bearish when the market is at the top and bullish when the market is at the bottom. He said that charts of most of the stocks would be bullish when the market is strong and most of the stocks would be bearish when the market is at the bottom. A. W. Cohen created an indicator with a similar philosophy in 1955 which is called the–Bullish Percent Breadth indicator. It is Point & Figure (P&F) chart-based breadth indicator.

Bullish-Percent

We discussed earlier the basic double-top buy pattern in P&F charts. The bullish-percent breadth indicator calculates how many stocks in the group have the double-top buy signal as the last generated pattern. Unless a fresh double bottom sell is triggered, the buy signal would remain valid.

The calculation and interpretation remain the same. For example, if the indicator reading is 50%, it means that a double-top buy signal has been triggered in 50% of stocks in the group. In other words, 50% of stocks from the group are in a bullish trend.

Below is a daily candlestick chart of Nifty with a 1% bullish percent indicator.

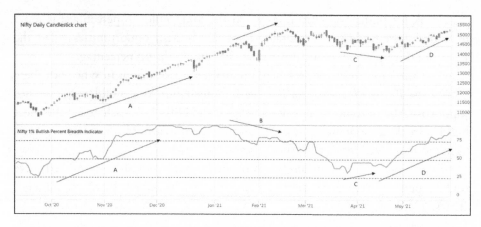

Figure 10.16: Daily candlestick chart of Nifty with 1% bullish percent indicator

At A in the above chart, the price was bullish and the breadth indicator was also rising, indicating that more stocks were turning bullish. The price moved up during B, but the breadth indicator was falling, suggesting that many stocks that were bullish earlier, are now in a corrective mode, and hence the participation is falling. The index was essentially making new highs on the back of a few index heavyweight stocks. At C, though the price made a new low, the indicator was rising. This is a positive divergence and suggests that the correction in the market is probably over as the participation is increasing. At D, indicator, and breadth indicator both were rising, indicating a strong price trend with increasing participation.

Bullish percent is a useful and relatively stable indicator. It does not fluctuate too aggressively from one extreme to another. Some aggressive indicators may provide more opportunities from a short-term trading perspective. Let us consider a few such aggressive indicators.

X-Percent

One of the unique features of P&F charts is that the last column in the chart can either be a column of 'X' or a column of 'O'. Simply stated, if the price is in a column of 'X', it is considered bullish and vice versa. Jeremy Du Plessis explained the X-percent breadth indicator in his book *The Definitive Guide to Point and Figure: A Comprehensive Guide to the Theory and Practical Use of the Point and Figure Charting Method.* The percentage of stocks in the group that are trading in the column of 'X' is known as the X-percent indicator.

X-percent breadth indicator is calculated by counting the number of stocks where the latest column is bullish and dividing it by the total number of stocks in that group or sector. This result is expressed as a percentage.

Below is the Nifty 50 chart with bullish X-percent indicator of 50-stocks that constitutes the Nifty 50 index. The calculation is done on the 1% box-value P&F chart.

Below is a daily candlestick chart of Nifty plotted with a 1% x 3 X-percent breadth indicator.

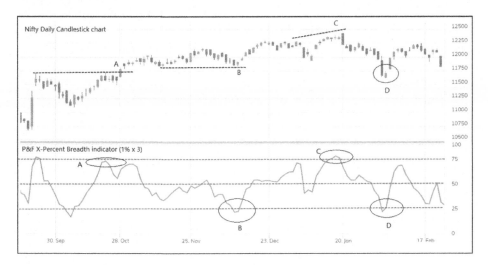

Figure 10.17: Daily candlestick chart of Nifty plotted with 1% x 3 X-percent breadth indicator

Price triggered an important breakout from a cup-and-handle pattern at A. The breadth was above the mid-level but not at the extreme zone. If a breakout is triggered in the price chart when the breadth indicator is at an extreme zone, it shows that there is a lack of fuel and the breakout may not result in any significant move. Price often gets into a correction after such breakouts.

Getting back to the above chart, the price was testing the previous bottom at point B. Price was also pulling back to retest the prior breakout level at A. Previous resistance turning support is popularly known as the principle of polarity. A bullish polarity pattern was completed in the price chart while the breadth indicator was at the lower extremity or oversold zone. Have a look at the overall price trend at B, it was bullish. Hence, oversold breadth was an opportunity to participate in the uptrend with an affordable risk.

Price made a new high at C and the breadth indicator moved into the overbought zone or the yellow zone, suggesting caution. It was followed by a price correction to D. Breadth indicator entered oversold zone at D indicating the possibility of a bounce as the correction was exhausted.

The breadth indicator in the above chart is calculated based on the 1% box-value P&F chart of the index constituents. This indicator calculates the percentage of stocks trading in the column of 'X' on a 1% box value. The indicator oscillates between 0 and 100. A rising breadth is a bullish sign because it indicates that there is participation from more stocks from the group. Falling breadth is bearish and indicates a lack of participation.

Featured below is a daily candlestick chart of the Nifty 50 index along with an X-percent breadth indicator on the Nifty 500 universe. The X-percent indicator is calculated on the 1% box size and three-box reversal P&F chart.

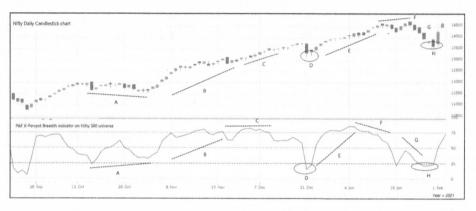

Figure 10.18: Daily candlestick chart of Nifty 50 index along with 1% x 3 X-percent breadth indicator on Nifty 500 universe

Period A is when the price made a new low, but X-percent breadth was rising. This indicated that more stocks are turning to a bullish column. Simply stated, this was a classic case of bullish divergence. Price and indicator were bullish and rising at B. The price was rising but the breadth indicator was hovering around the overbought zone at C.

There was a period of consolidation where a series of Doji like small candlestick patterns were printed which was followed by a strong red candle at D. The breadth indicator in the meanwhile dropped to the oversold zone indicating that stocks have corrected significantly. Breadth and price were both rising at E. Price made a new high at F but the falling breadth indicator suggested that more stocks were turning into a column of O. This is a classic negative or bearish divergence. Price and indicator were falling at G. Breadth indicator formed another bullish divergence pattern at the oversold area at H.

DT-Percent

I have explained another breadth indicator called DT% breadth indicator in my book on the Point & Figure chart. DT% breadth indicator captures the number of stocks trading in the double-top buy column, meaning several stocks trading in the breakout column, and are therefore in a strong momentum.

Below is the Nifty 50 candlestick chart along with the 1% x 3 DT% breadth indicator on the Nifty 500 index.

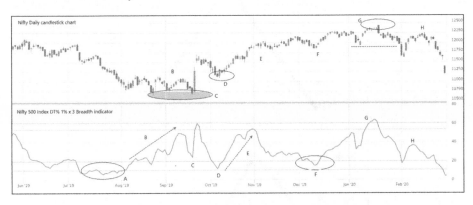

Figure 10.19: Nifty 50 candlestick chart along with 1% x 3 DT% breadth indicator on Nifty 500 index

The price was falling during period A, the breadth indicator was in an extreme zone which shows strong bearish momentum. Very few stocks were above their swing highs during that time. The price made a new bottom and formed a range during B, while DT% went up significantly during that period. This shows that many stocks broke their previous swing high and turned bullish. This was a bullish indication. The index made a double bottom at C when the breadth indicator was also corrected. After the breakout, the breadth indicator corrected till the lower extreme point D and the price also corrected but maintained its previous bottom. It was trading near its previous peak that formed a bullish polarity pattern. Price and DT% went up during period E, showing a strong uptrend. The breadth corrected during F, but the price maintained its previous bottom that indicated a bullish correction. The breadth indicator went to the upper extremity during period G. Breadth and price made lower high at H.

Note the point C and F again. Breadth indicator corrected but price maintained its previous bottom. After the sudden spike in the breadth indicator, when it corrects but the price maintains the previous bottom, it is a bullish corrective pattern suggesting the possibility of a strong continuation move in price.

DT% breadth indicator is not expected to remain below 15% for a longer period during bull markets.

Beamer pattern

See the image given below.

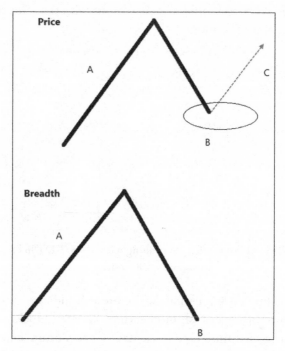

Image 10.1: Beamer pattern

The breadth indicator suddenly moves up during period A. It means a greater number of stocks are crossing their previous highs. Price may or may not be going up at point A. The breadth indicator corrects at point B. Price corrects but stays above its previous bottom. The breadth indicator may or may not breach its previous bottom at B. It may not come in an oversold zone, but if it comes below 20% it would be a more favourable scenario. The up move in the price indicated at C is expected if the price stays above the previous bottom of B. Price going above high of move A would be more bullish, positions can be added there.

Look for buying opportunities at B, if the bottom remains protected. Risk-reward would be favourable and a big continuation move in price is expected. I call it a Beamer pattern. Big move and momentum expected with better risk-reward opportunity.

Look at the chart below. It's a Nifty 50 candlestick chart along with a 1% x 3 DT% breadth indicator on the Nifty 500 index.

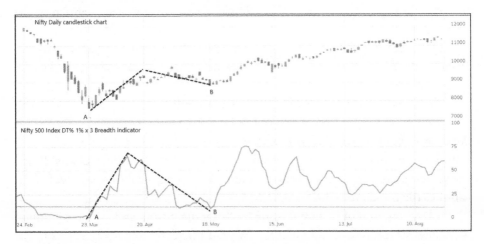

Figure 10.20: Nifty 50 daily candlestick chart along with 1% x 3 DT% breadth indicator on Nifty 500 index

Solid spike in breadth indicator at point A. Breadth moved back to point B but price maintained its previous bottom. It's a Beamer pattern at B.

I closely track the DT% breadth indicator. It often turns out to be a leading indicator. The extreme zones for this indicator would be at 55 – 60 on the higher side and 15 - 20 on the lower side.

Below the chart is the Nifty 50 candlestick chart along with a 1% x 3 DT% breadth indicator on the Nifty 500 index.

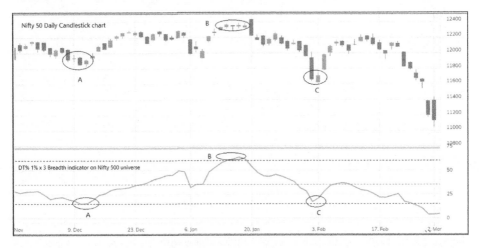

Figure 10.21: Nifty 50 daily candlestick chart along with 1% x 3 DT% breadth indicator on Nifty 500 index

Point A is when DT% went to oversold zone showing that a greater number of stocks are in a column of O. The indicator turned overbought at B followed by correction in price and breadth indicator. The indicator again came near the oversold zone at C.

DT% breadth indicator is a combination of X-percent and bullish percent. It shows the number of stocks in a breakout column and falls when stocks turn to the column of O.

The opposite of DT% is the DB% breadth indicator.

Anchor column breadth indicators

I am introducing a couple more breadth indicators based on P&F charts. Recall the earlier discussion on the Anchor column. The Anchor column in a P&F chart captures the trend and momentum.

A large column of X shows strong bullish momentum, and a large column of 'O' shows strong bearish momentum. We can calculate how many stocks in the group are in strong bullish momentum and strong bearish momentum. They can be very useful for short-term or medium-term trading and investing. It can also be very useful to understand the market phase and sentiments.

Recommended parameters are several boxes above 15 on 0.25% box value.

The rising anchor column percentage of stocks shows that stocks are not only bullish. but they are also in a strong momentum. It shows that rally has got strong potential.

When the index is in an uptrend, the rising anchor column percent indicator is a strong sign.

Below is a daily candlestick chart of FMCG along with a 0.25% X-anchor column% breadth indicator on the FMCG index.

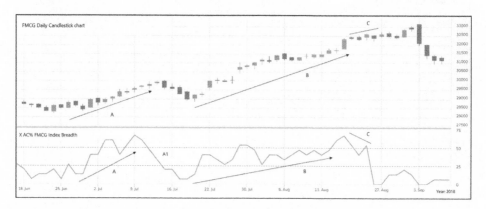

Figure 10.22: Daily candlestick chart of FMCG along with 0.25% X-Anchor column% breadth indicator

Index and breadth indicator was rising during period A. This was bullish because it shows a greater number of stocks are showing strong momentum, the rally is strong and shows strength in the price. Stocks turned to the column of 'O' and breadth indicator corrected during A1, but it bounced from the oversold zone again. Price and breadth indicator, both were rising during B. During period C, the price went up, but the indicator was falling. This divergence indicated that the stocks have started correcting. They are not in a strong momentum anymore. That is a sign of impending weakness.

Opposite of the X-anchor column percent is the O-anchor column percent. The rising O-anchor column percent indicator shows that stocks in bearish momentum are increasing, it is a strong bearish sign.

Below is a daily candlestick chart of the mid-cap 50 indexes along with a 0.25% O-anchor column% breadth indicator on the mid-cap index.

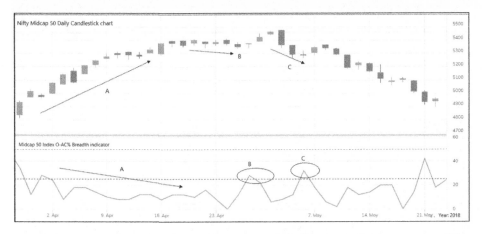

Figure 10.23: Daily candlestick chart of mid-cap 50 index along with 0.25% O-anchor column% breadth indicator

The price index was rising during period A and the O-anchor column percent indicator was falling. That is a sign of a bullish market. The price was almost flat after A, but the O-anchor column percent indicator started rising to show that more stocks are falling, and they are in bearish momentum. The price made a new top after B, but it did not sustain. When this indicator is rising the sentiments are not bullish, it shows that the top is weak. Stocks in bearish momentum increased in fall during C. It shows that sentiments have turned bearish and there is a possibility of price correction.

Usually, during a strong uptrend, bullish X–anchor column percent reading will be higher than the bearish O-anchor column percent reading, vice versa for a downtrend.

This breadth indicator captures the number of stocks in a bullish and bearish momentum in the group. If they are not in sync with the trend, when those numbers are changing–we need to analyze the price chart and turn cautious.

Breadth Zone

We discussed how we can plot different breadth indicators. We calculate the percentage of stocks qualifying for a bullish criterion. We can do something similar with bearish criteria, high volatility, high momentum etc.

With this calculation, any breadth indicator that we plot will be oscillating between 0 and 100. We have different zones on the breadth indicator in that case. See the chart given below.

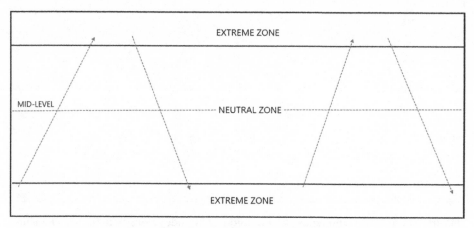

Image 10.2: Breadth indicator zones

The 50% mark is the mid-level indicator. When the indicator is above 50, it means a greater number of stocks in the group are bullish, when it is below 50, it shows more numbers of stocks in the group are bearish.

When it reaches the extreme zone, let us say 75 or above, it shows many numbers of stocks are becoming bullish. Similarly, when it falls below 25%, it shows many numbers of stocks are falling and bearish. These 75 and 25 are extreme zones. Between 75 and 25, it is a neutral zone.

So, we can simply define four categories of breadth zone:
1. Above mid-level = Bullish
2. In bullish extreme zone = Very bullish but exhaustion possible

3.   Below mid-level = Bearish
4.   In bearish extreme zone = Very bearish but exhaustion possible

This helps us in understanding the breadth zone but integrating this to trading is not quite simple. Markets like life, cannot be divided into a fixed category or circle. They are dynamic. When the breadth is at the extreme zone, the environment is bullish but exhaustion is possible. So, it is a bit tricky. We cannot trade with "ifs" and "buts" in markets.

When the market is in a range or sideways phase, this breadth indicator extreme zones works like a charm. We can call them an overbought and oversold zone during such times.

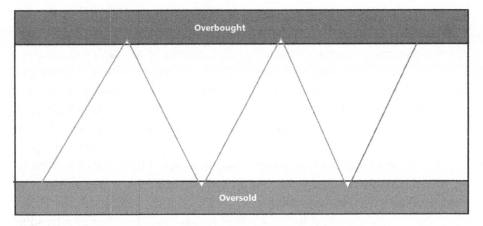

Image 10.3: Breadth overbought and oversold zone

Strategy in such period can be looking for shorting opportunity in overbought zone and looking for buying opportunity in the oversold zone. If you recognize that a market or a particular sector is in a range-bound environment, the breadth indicator can be a highly effective tool. The market can move in a strong trend after this phase that can trigger the stop-loss. To improve the chances of success you can use relative strength analysis here. While shorting, look for a relatively weak candidate. Similarly, while buying, look for a relatively strong candidate.

These extreme zones don't work this effectively when the price is in a trending mode. The breadth tends to remain in the extreme area when markets are in a strong trend.

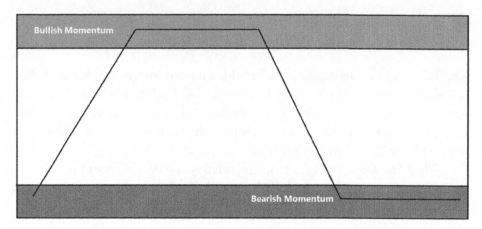

Image 10.4: Breadth bullish and bearish momentum zone

During the strong uptrend, markets tend to remain in a bullish extreme for a longer period. During a strong downtrend, markets tend to remain at the bearish extreme. These overbought and oversold areas behave like a strong momentum zone in such cases. When the market is in a strong uptrend, it is only logical that a greater number of stocks are bullish. This does not necessarily mean that the market will reverse. On the contrary, if there is a divergence between the price action and the breadth indicator, that would be a sign of temporary exhaustion.

But I have often seen that increasing exposure even in the strong momentum zone does not prove very rewarding.

When an indicator approaches a bullish extreme zone in a strong up-trending market, it means that trend is up, and a greater number of stocks are bullish. The environment is bullish for stock prices to go up. We cannot use it as a contra indicator here, but at times, risk-reward may not be favourable for initiating bullish trades in this zone. You must be more selective in such cases.

So, in all markets, breadth extreme zones may be considered a yellow zone.

There are instances when the momentum is strong and breadth is at the extreme zone. This is a sign that the market should be given some breathing space. When the breadth indicator is at an overbought extreme, the risk-reward parameter is not typically in favour of the bulls. Hence, position sizing should be reduced for fresh longs.

In the same way, oversold breadth suggests that the risk-reward ratio for fresh shorts is not favourable. So, breadth tells us what not to do. Hence, I call it a yellow zone.

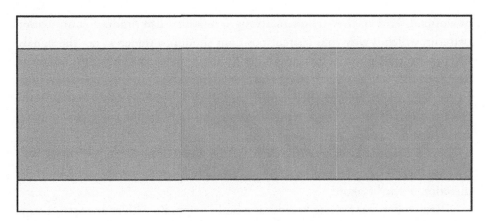

Image 10.5: Breadth yellow zone

We have three traffic signal lights: green, red and yellow. Breadth in the extreme zone is analogous to the yellow traffic signal in trading. One should take the foot off the accelerator and reduce the speed. Though markets at an extreme zone may not necessarily reverse immediately, they can get into a sideways or volatile phase. It is therefore wise to step aside until the breadth extreme condition is resolved away from the extremes.

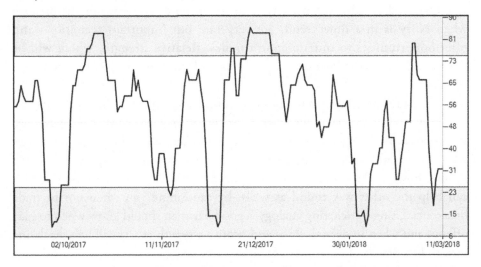

Figure 10.24: Nifty 50 1% x 3 X-percent breadth indicator

Remember, overbought or oversold breadth is not a proxy for market tops and bottoms. The breadth can remain in overbought zones for a long time while the price is in a strong uptrend—and equally so at oversold zones during a strong downtrend. Rather, they represent strong trends that can produce continuation patterns, which is why your current positions should be ridden as per the signals. There is no reason to exit existing trades or investments when breadth reaches an extreme zone. It is just that fresh trades should be curbed until the breadth returns to the neutral zone, namely between 75 and 25. Price pattern confirmation is the most important aspect for a trade decision and one should never pre-empt or trade-in anticipation.

Price breakouts when breadth is in the neutral zone tend to work well because there are no signs of exhaustion and there is enough room to move in the direction of the breakout.

Remember that a rising breadth is a bullish sign. Breadth at an extreme zone indicates exhaustion which may be followed by a time correction, something which typically happens during strong trends. A continuation breakout is often seen when breadth sustains in the extreme zone. Normally, there is the possibility of a weak high or a weak low getting formed in that zone before producing a reversal. During range-bound markets, bearish formations when the breadth indicator is above 75 and bullish patterns when the indicator is below 25, are strong alerts. Always wait for price patterns to confirm, before initiating trades based on breadth reaching extreme zones.

Oversold breadth when Nifty is in an uptrend, and overbought breadth when Nifty is in a downtrend, are very rare but important scenarios—and offer opportunities to initiate contra trades. Relative strength, which will be discussed in the next chapter, can help us pick the right stocks to trade such scenarios.

We don't know how far the breadth indicator can go after crossing above 75 or falling below 25; nor do we know how long it may remain at those extremes. It can do so for a long-time during trending markets. Breakout in price patterns when the breadth indicator is in the neutral zone is more interesting. Breakouts should, however, be avoided when the breadth is in the extreme zone. Breadth can help the other way round as well—by cautioning you when not to trade breakouts. Using a cricketing analogy, a good batsman should know when to play offence and when to defend. Price and relative strength charts will help us define how to hit: Breadth helps us decide when to be aggressive and when it's time for defence, and which balls should be left alone.

I used these 75–25 levels to explain the concept. Remember, some indicators can have different dynamics so these extreme levels need to be modified accordingly. For example, long-term or medium-term moving average breadth indicator can easily move and remain above 80% or below 20%. Their extreme levels need to be different. Check the past data and behaviour of the indicator to decide the extreme levels.

All sector breadth

You must have by now understood the concept of breadth. You can plot breadth on NSE All Sectors group to study the trend and the health of the market. Create a group of all sectors and plot its breadth chart. Think about this for a moment, what will that chart capture?

For example, there are 20 sectors in the group. If the breadth chart shows you a reading of 50%. That means, 50% of sectors are bullish.

Now think, what does it mean when this breadth chart shows 70%. It means most of the sectors are bullish. That means the market trend is strong, sector and stock participation is very strong.

This indicator often goes above 90% or falls below 10%. All sectors tend to move together during strong trends. When most of the sectors are bullish, it shows us a strong uptrend.

When all sectors move in tandem, it is a sign that the market rally is strong. When all sectors are falling, markets are weak.

Sector rotation will make the breadth go back to the neutral zone, it may or may not impact the index price. It can be followed by price correction or time correction.

When all sectors are extremely bullish, markets might consolidate. When all sectors are bullish, some are leaders, and some are in the retracement column. Look for bearish star patterns during such times to anticipate weak sectors. Same way, when all sectors are bearish and breadth is oversold, look for bullish star sectors to spot the early signs of sectors that are witnessing reversal.

Below is a daily candlestick chart of Nifty along with a 0.25% x 3 DT% breadth indicator on all sectors of NSE.

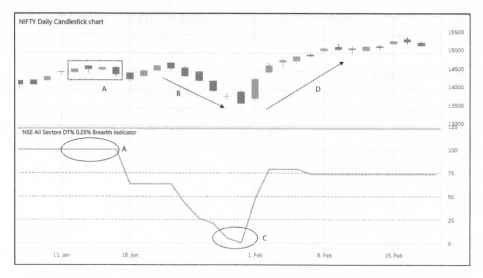

Figure 10.25: Daily candlestick chart of Nifty along with 0.25% x 3 DT% breadth indicator on all sectors of NSE

Breadth indicator reached the reading of 100 at point A. Price and breadth indicator corrected at B. In those few bearish candlesticks that appeared during the fall, all sectors turned to bearish swing and breadth indicator reading reached zero levels at C. It was followed by a reversal and uptrend in price at D.

Below is a daily candlestick chart of Nifty along with a 0.25% DT% breadth indicator on all sectors of NSE.

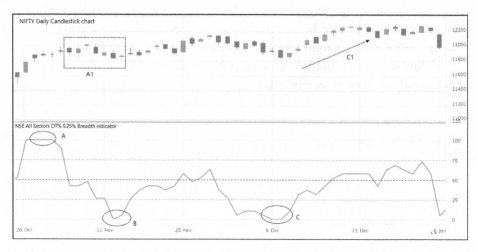

Figure 10.26: Daily candlestick chart of Nifty along with 0.25% DT% breadth indicator on all sectors of NSE

Breadth indicator reading was at the extreme zone of 100 at point A. This was followed by consolidation (time correction) at A1. During this correction, the breadth indicator reached the lower extreme zone at B. The breadth indicator again reached the lower extreme at C that was followed by a rally in price at C1.

We primarily discussed four types of P&F breadth indicators:

- X – percent which considers the number of stocks trading in a bullish swing.
- DT – percent which considers the number of stocks trading above their previous swing high.
- X – Anchor column percent which considers the number of stocks trading in a bullish momentum column.
- O – Anchor column percent which considers the number of stocks trading in a bearish momentum column.

These four indicators may be calculated on any sector or group of stocks to get the breadth details. The P&F chart-based breadth indicators can provide a complete view of the health of the index, group, or sector. Here is the information that can be discerned by using all breadth indicators mentioned above.

- Number of stocks in bullish swing
- Number of stocks in bearish swing
- Number of stocks above their swing high
- Number of stocks below their swing low
- Number of stocks in bullish momentum
- Number of stocks in bearish momentum

To recap, the above information can be captured in a P&F chart which is detailed below.

- Number of stocks in bullish swing: Number of stocks in a column of 'X'
- Number of stocks in bearish swing: Number of stocks in column 'O'
- Number of stocks above their swing high: Number stocks in Double-top buy
- Number of stocks below their swing low: Number of stocks in Double-bottom sell
- Number of stocks in bullish momentum: Number stocks in bullish Anchor column
- Number of stocks in bearish momentum: Number of stocks in bearish Anchor column

Most people fail to understand the importance of time-independent breadth tools. P&F charts are essentially swung charts. You do not even need to know the P&F charting method in detail to understand and interpret the breadth information generated using P&F charts. You can track these charts and trade price-based systems on other charting methods too. We discussed chart examples of the P&F based breadth indicators below the candlestick chart.

But do not ignore it just because you do not understand the subject. Breadth indicators based on noiseless charts such as P&F or Renko are very logical and useful tools to understand the strength of the trend. The bullish brick percent breadth indicator which is based on Renko charts was discussed in my book on Renko charting. As you may be aware, the price may remain in an uptrend for several weeks and months. If so, what is the logic in studying the price action on some chosen time interval such as daily, weekly, or monthly? An uptrend is an uptrend, and it may reverse in a day or after several weeks or months. Rather than looking at those time-based charts, why not just let the price indicate a trend reversal? If this sounds logical, then noiseless charts would be the logical tool to focus on price action.

P&F breadth calculates the strength based on the price action and provides extremely useful information about the state of the trend.

In any P&F chart, the stock or the instrument would either be in column of X or O. If we get a count of the stocks in a bullish swing (those in a column of X), we also know the stocks in a bearish swing or a column of O.

Here is a summary of the P&F based breadth indicator available in TradePoint software.

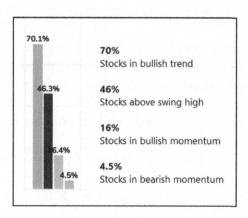

Image 10.6: Breadth bar chart

Out of the four indicators, the X% breadth indicator would typically be the biggest score. Remember, DT% stocks will be also included in the X% calculation. And bullish anchor column stocks would also be a part of X%. Hence, the X% indicator would be a bigger number.

We can run the scanner on a group of stocks to read all these numbers for a group or sector at a glance. Below is an example of All P&F breadth indicators on each sector.

Table 10.4: All P&F breadth indicators of all sectors

Group	X % Breadth	DT Breadth %	X Anchor Breadth %	O Anchor Breadth %
Realty Index	100.00	80.00	10.00	0.00
Bank Index	91.67	75.00	25.00	0.00
IT Index	90.00	50.00	0.00	0.00
Commodities Index	86.67	36.67	10.00	0.00
Infrastructure Index	86.67	63.33	23.33	0.00
PSU Bank Index	84.62	69.23	46.15	0.00
MNC Index	83.33	53.33	13.33	0.00
Consumption Index	80.00	66.67	23.33	0.00
Energy Index	80.00	50.00	20.00	0.00
FMCG Index	80.00	60.00	13.33	0.00
Financial Services Index	80.00	75.00	20.00	0.00
Metal Index	80.00	6.67	6.67	2.00
PSE Index	80.00	50.00	25.00	0.00
Pharma Index	80.00	60.00	10.00	0.00
Pvt Bank Index	80.00	70.00	10.00	0.00
Service Sector Index	76.67	53.33	10.00	0.00
Auto Index	73.33	60.00	20.00	0.00
Media Index	70.00	50.00	20.00	0.00
CPSE Index	58.33	25.00	8.33	2.00

The table is sorted based on X-percent breadth. The table shows that all stocks from the realty index are in a column of X, 80% of stocks are in the breakout column and 10% are in bullish momentum. We can study each sector in this manner.

Below is an example of all breadth readings on all major NSE indices.

Table 10.5: All P&F breadth indicators of all major NSE indices

Group	X % Breadth	DT Breadth %	X Anchor Breadth %	O Anchor Breadth %
Mid-Small Cap 400	69.50	41.50	13.75	1.00
Midcap 100 Index	76.00	52.00	15.00	0.00
Midcap 150 Index	74.00	48.00	14.67	0.00
Midcap 50	80.00	56.00	18.00	0.00
Nifty 100	82.00	59.00	18.00	0.00
Nifty 200	79.00	55.50	16.50	0.00
Nifty 50	82.00	62.00	18.00	0.00
Nifty 500 Index	71.91	44.82	14.54	0.80
Nifty Next 50 Index	82.00	56.00	18.00	0.00
Small Cap 100	69.00	38.00	14.00	1.00
Small Cap 250	66.80	37.60	13.20	1.60
Small Cap 50	70.00	34.00	20.00	2.00

Breadth indicators in the trading system

We discussed some important breadth indicators. Breadth indicators capture the percentage of stocks in a group that are:

- Bullish
- Bearish
- Bullish Momentum
- Bearish Momentum
- Neutral zone, Bullish zone, Bearish zone
- Extreme zone: Overbought, Oversold or Neutral

You can plot the same indicator for multiple periods to study the breadth in different time frames. For example, we can calculate the breadth indicators such as X% or DT% in a bigger box size of 3% to study the scenario in a bigger time frame.

We have discussed a few important breadth indicators thus far. There are however many other breadth indicators that you may plot using any of your favourite indicators. Understand the principles and frame rules to use the concept. Most important is, remain consistent with your indicator.

Following one indicator consistently will make your system objective and help you make better decisions. Using 20-day, 120-day and 250-day High low momentum index breadth indicators may be a prudent choice. I keep track of the X% & DT% breadth indicators along with the all-breadth chart of P&F to track all sectors. P&F is just a tool and the time-independent nature of breadth calculation in P&F charts helps in understanding the strength of the price swing and the strength of the trend.

All price charts would convey the same picture during strong trends. Most of the charts from the universe will be bullish during strong uptrends. Most of the charts will be bearish during a strong downtrend. Only the breadth indicator can help you not to get complacent during times where the trend enters the euphoric phase where complacency or fear sets in. In this context, market breadth indicators will act as a perfect complement to your system. Including the breadth indicators as a part of your trading system will improve the performance of your price-based systems significantly.

It must be obvious by now that the breadth analysis applies to a group of stocks. Hence, it is relevant in:

- Sectors
- Indices
- Customized group of stocks
- Portfolios
- Group of all sectors and indices

Breadth indicators are irrelevant on individual stocks.

We have seen that the constituents of a major market index like Nifty in Indian markets must be monitored to assess the breadth and overall sentiment of the market. Breadth indicators of sectors, other indices, or groups of stocks may also be studied. In the Indian context, the breadth indicator of Nifty 50, and mid-cap and small-cap indices should be monitored regularly to get a broad idea about the underlying market sentiment.

Being cautious when there is euphoria associated with mid-caps and small caps can save one from getting stuck at the wrong levels. Typically, any group having at least 30 or more constituents may be used to study the breadth. If there are fewer constituents, then increase the extreme threshold levels to 10% and 90%.

Here is a recap of important aspects that we have discussed relating to the breadth indicator:

1. Rising breadth is bullish, falling breadth is bearish.
2. Breadth indicator above mid-value indicates bullish zone and below mid-value indicates the bearish zone.
3. Breadth indicators on many occasions act as a lead indicator and they typically turn before the price does.
4. Price making a fresh high or low that is not supported by the breadth indicator is a typical sign of divergence to look for.

5. Extreme breadth zone is useful information. It is like a yellow light flashing in a traffic signal. It is a sign to turn cautious and reduce your position size during such a phase.

Breadth indicator either at the overbought zone in an uptrend or at the oversold zone in a downtrend indicates the possibility of a temporary halt in the trend. Either a time correction or a price correction can materialize when the breadth cools off.

Breadth indicator reaching extreme zones while the price is in a sideways or range-bound market is an opportunity to trade reversals.

Breadth indicator at overbought zone in a downtrend, or the oversold zone in an uptrend is an opportunity to trade pullback patterns with an affordable risk.

Now, consider this scenario where say the breadth of the Nifty 50 universe is 60%. This indicates 60% of stocks from the Nifty 50 universe are bullish. And, say if the same breadth indicator is at 75% for the Nifty 500 universe. Remember, Nifty 50 stocks are also part of the Nifty 500 basket. A look at the breadth indicators for these two indices suggests that more stocks from the Nifty 500 universe are bullish compared to Nifty 50. It means Nifty 500 stocks are outperforming Nifty 50. Can we expect this scenario to play out if the Nifty 500 to Nifty 50 relative strength chart is bullish?

Let us consider another scenario. Let us assume that the number of stocks breaking above their 20-day moving average in Nifty private banks is more than Nifty Pharma. Is it reasonable to assume that Nifty private bank sector health is bullish than the Pharma sector because many more stocks are bullish?

If so, we are performing a relative strength analysis based on Breadth. In this context, it would be appropriate to introduce the BRS principle.

BRS Principle

How does one identify if a sector is gaining momentum and doing good? A classic signal in this context would be a turnaround in the breadth of the sector. If the breadth turns bullish and sustains in the bullish zone, it would be a strong signal that the majority of the stocks are participating in the uptrend.

For example, Indian Finance Minister Nirmala Sitharaman talked about increased government spending on the infrastructure of the country during the budget session in February 2021. The cement sector breadth already displayed signs of improvement in December 2020. The sector was already bullish and many stocks from the sector registered fresh 52-week highs. That is one of the most important observations and clues. Once you identify this, all that you need to do is study the relative strength of the stocks in that sector to identify stocks showing strength.

The basic rule is: Perform relative strength analysis in sectors showing strong breadth.

The breadth and relative strength charts together can be extremely useful to perform sector, group, or index analysis.

When a sector is going through a temporary period of correction, most of the stocks would fall and the breadth chart will deteriorate sharply. When the breadth approaches the oversold zone, it is an opportunity to buy the stocks of those sectors.

How will you know if the sector is strong? The answer is simple, just use the relative strength study. If the sector index is outperforming the Nifty index in the medium-term, it is a relatively strong sector.

The rule is: Buy when the breadth is at the oversold zone while the sector relative strength setup is bullish. Sell when breadth is in the overbought zone of sectors whose relative strength setup is bearish.

When breadth is in the overbought zone of relatively strong sectors or at the oversold zone of relatively weak sectors, then adopt a go-slow approach. There is no point in taking a contra bet in such instances.

We have discussed various aspects of breadth and relative strength analysis. There are many tools and indicators to perform these studies. You can pick any of them and design a strategy with a combination of both.

Breadth helps in analysing the sectors while the RS study helps in further analysis of Sectors and helps in shortlisting stocks. By combining both, we can categorise the sector or an index trend as bullish or bearish phases. I call it the BRS principle.

Below are the principles of the strategy.

Table 10.6: BRS principles

Breadth	Relative Strength	BRS Trend
Overbought	Bullish	Strong Bullish Momentum / Exhaustion
Above Mid level	Bullish	Strong Bullish
Below Mid level	Bullish	Bullish & Pullback / Caution
Oversold	Bullish	Bullish & Oversold
Oversold	Bearish	Strong Bearish Momentum / Exhaustion
Below Mid level	Bearish	Strong Bearish
Above Mid level	Bearish	Bearish & Pullback / Caution
Overbought	Bearish	Bearish & Overbought

When market breadth is overbought and the relative strength chart is bullish, the momentum is strong. There can be exhaustion, but the trend is bullish. It is a yellow zone suggesting caution. When the breadth chart is above the mid-level, it means most of the stocks from the group are bullish, and when the relative strength chart of the sector is also bullish, it simply means the trend is strong and bullish for the sector. Your allocation should be maximum for bullish strategies in the stocks from such sectors. Trade bullish breakout in these stocks. When the breadth chart is below the mid-level, but the RS chart is bullish, there is a possibility of a short-term correction. It would be logical to look for a bullish pullback opportunity in this scenario. Also, watch the RS chart for clues regarding the resumption of the prior outperformance cycle. When the breadth chart is oversold but the RS chart is bullish, it is a rare but wonderful opportunity to trade bullish reversal patterns in the stocks from such sectors.

When market breadth is oversold and the relative strength chart is bearish, the momentum is bearish and strong. There can be exhaustion due to the breadth reaching the oversold zone, but the trend is bearish. It is similar to the yellow light in traffic signals suggesting caution or slowing down. When the breadth chart is below the mid-level, it means most of the stocks of the group are bearish, and when the relative strength chart of the sector is also bearish, it simply means the trend is strong and bearish for the sector. You should adopt bearish strategies in the stocks from such sectors.

When the breadth chart is below the mid-level and the RS chart is bearish, there is a possibility of a short-term uptrend in stocks, look for bearish pullback opportunities in stocks for shorting. Also, check if the RS chart is displaying any signs of reversal. If so, be cautious while taking bearish trades in such a scenario. When the breadth chart is overbought but the RS chart is bearish, it is a rare but wonderful opportunity to trade bearish reversal patterns in the stock from such sector.

Market breadth is a contra indicator as well as an indicator of strength. Relative strength indicators would be a perfect complement for analysing stocks from such sectors.

When the breadth chart of a sector is at an extreme zone, it indicates that the sector is in a strong momentum. If you track the breadth scanner regularly and if a sector keeps popping up in the top list, it might be an interesting sector to focus on. By studying the RS charts, you can devise a trading strategy that may offer opportunities with relatively low risk.

The sector with a limited number of stocks tends to remain in the overbought or oversold zone for a long time. As discussed earlier, their extreme levels are different. It also depends on the type of breadth indicators used. I prefer the Fusion matrix and use the X% or DT% breadth indicator in such instances. The

Fusion Matrix would offer multi-timeframe price and RS metric. This along with the breadth study would provide a holistic picture.

The breadth chart behaves differently in different market trends. They respect the overbought and oversold zone in a sideways trend, but they tend to remain in the overbought zone or oversold zone during the strong trending phase.

An overbought breadth simply means that a greater number of stocks are bullish. It does not have bearish connotations. It simply means there can be exhaustion soon. We need to understand the market trend to deal with breadth extreme zones. As explained earlier, short-term exhaustion is temporary, sectors coming in that list are interesting and should be analyzed further to capitalise on price or time correction.

When the Index makes a new low, without a similar fall in breadth or if the index is trading in a range but breadth is improving, it indicates a scenario where more returns can be generated by focusing on the stocks rather than the index.

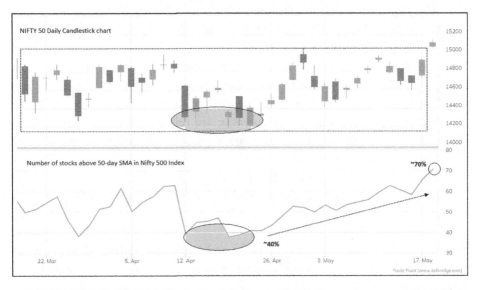

Figure 10.27: Daily Nifty 50 candlestick chart with 50-day moving average breadth indicator on Nifty 500 index

It would be extremely logical and profitable to use a lower parameter breadth indicator from a trading perspective and a relatively longer parameter breadth indicator for medium investment. Buying when the short-term breadth is at an oversold zone while the trend is bullish can generate better risk-reward trades.

Using the RS chart, one can identify if the sector or group is bullish. Check the breadth chart for confirmation. The long-term and medium-term breadth charts should be favourable. When the breadth improves, that means portfolios are doing good and the market sentiment is positive. When the market is rising without much participation from stocks, it is a sign that only heavyweight stocks are moving and hence portfolios with such index heavyweights would be performing well. The portfolio of people at large might not deliver significant returns though.

I am not discussing Renko or Line-break based indicators as you must have understood the broad concept and logic behind the breadth indicator. The breadth indicators are extremely useful, but they are less explored because of the lack of awareness. Breadth is one of the most important tools and should form part of any trading kit. The best part is that it complements other methods of analysis.

In this chapter, we discussed:

- Breadth indicators can complement price and RS based systems.
- Traditional breadth indicators are useful. Any indicator that you are using for the price analysis can become a breadth indicator.
- The trend, volatility, channel etc indicators that we use on the price chart can also work as a breadth indicator. There are benefits to doing that.
- High-low momentum index and Noiseless chart breadth indicators are very helpful to analyze the health and strength of the markets.
- Breadth extreme zones & divergences are useful concepts. Breadth zones should be treated based on the market phases, this understanding is a key aspect of breadth analysis.
- The BRS principle explores the idea of using RS and Breadth zones together to decide the trend of the market and tweak the stock-picking strategy accordingly.

We have discussed relative strength and breadth analysis in detail. Let us discuss implementing these concepts on assets and sectors to choose instruments in the next chapter.

Chapter 11

ASSET, SECTOR AND STOCK SELECTION

. . . .

Asset class analysis

Let us consider a scenario to understand the role of overall market mood or sentiment. Suppose say you are not in a good mood or feeling low and depressed. If someone were to ask you to participate in a sport or a game, what will be your response? The typical response will be that you are not in a mood to play right now. But if you are in a good mood and charged up, you would then accept that request from your friend and likely play well and perform better.

The mood or sentiment plays an important role and decides how we behave or react to a particular situation. That is why people react or behave differently to the same event under different circumstances. The same logic applies to the markets too and the prevailing sentiments are important in markets as well. Even a strong positive bullish news for a stock or sector may fail to push the prices higher in a bearish trend. Whereas even moderately positive bullish news would propel the prices higher in a strong uptrend.

Recognizing market sentiments is an important part of trading and investment. Relative strength and breadth analysis are effective tools to gauge market sentiment. There are numerous approaches and patterns to study price action. But what is even more important is to study the market sentiment.

When the sentiment is bullish, the expensive stocks would typically get more expensive. So much so that even the junk stocks would attract interest in a bullish environment. On the contrary, even the high-quality companies will also not get a fair valuation when the sentiment is not favourable.

The study of the market phase is all about recognizing the underlying trend and sentiment. Different market phases suit different trading systems and techniques. For example, momentum trading strategies will work better when the trend is strong, and sentiments are favourable. Rangebound strategies will perform better when the attention is in other sectors of the markets. Every instrument on every timeframe goes through these phases of strong trends, consolidation, correction, expanding moves and convergence.

In a strong bull market in the mid-cap stocks, any breakout technique that you use would work reasonably well. Many newcomers would have a better record than even experts during such phases. That is why we often say a bull market produces new heroes. Unfortunately, when you begin with that kind of favourable phase, the pain during the difficult time could be severe if you are not aware of managing risk. When sentiment reverses, and the market phases change, everything that was working well earlier would no longer be profitable.

Let me give you a recent example about market sentiment and its impact. During the second wave of Covid-19 in India, in April 2021 there was a shortage of oxygen cylinders in hospitals across the country. A stock called Bombay Oxygen moved from around Rs. 10,000 to around Rs. 25,000 in one month. It turned out to be an NBFC company that used to produce oxygen in its earlier avatar. But they discontinued their gas-related operations in 2019 and converted themselves to a finance company. The company was rechristened as Bombay Oxygen Investment Limited. That is the strength of market sentiment.

If the market is in a bullish trend, even negative news will have a temporary impact while not so significant bullish news will have an overwhelming impact on price. Similarly, in a bearish trend, the bullish news will have a muted impact on price but any bearish news will trigger a sharp fall.

This is an important lesson to understand the market sentiments and the state of the trend. Markets not reacting to bullish news is a bearish indication and not reacting to bearish news is a bullish indication. Let us consider another example during the second wave of the Covid pandemic. People were expecting markets to fall as they did in 2020. But the benchmark indices did not retreat much during the second wave, and they were confined to a broad range. The mid and small-cap stocks were doing better during this phase. If the market is not reacting negatively to bearish news, it indicates that the trend is bullish.

Every strategy has a favourable and non-favourable phase. Sticking to the strategy even during the non-favourable times is the key to success. But if we can identify the sentiments of the overall market and for individual sectors and stocks, we can then make changes or tweak our strategy accordingly to improve our performance.

There are many different trading and investment strategies, but the important aspect is the selection of the market or the instrument. Is it a good time to invest in Equity? Or, should I invest in Gold? Should I park my funds in the debt market or term deposits? These are more relevant and important questions to consider before deciding on the trading or investment strategy. The typical approach would be to diversify across risky and less risky asset classes based on age and risk profile. There is nothing wrong with this approach. The basic assumption in this approach is that we cannot predict the market moves so it would be better to diversify by investing in multiple asset classes.

Broadly, there are four major asset classes:
- Equity
- Bonds

- Precious metals and other commodities
- Currency

There can be other categories or subcategories of asset classes but broadly these are the ones to consider. You of course have a new asset class called Cryptocurrency but let us not get into that discussion. Retail investors, domestic funds, Hedge funds, financial institutions, prop-desks, high net worth individuals are active in most of these markets and rotate funds across these asset classes.

It would be extremely helpful to identify the trend and invest in the markets or asset classes where there is a strong momentum. Most of the time what happens is that we identify the momentum late. For example, Gold was stagnant between 2016 and May 2019 but generated returns of about 60% return in the next year or so. Nifty generated returns of more than 50% between 2016 and 2019 but it lost by almost 50% during Covid 19 pandemic driven fall in 2020.

Theoretically, we would have done better by investing in equities between 2016–2019 and shifting to Gold in 2019 and back then to equities later in 2020. Timing these asset switches to perfection is easier said than done. On many occasions, we realise much later that a particular asset class has performed well. Then we fear entering late, and the risk-reward may not be favourable. When we overcome this fear and invest, that is precisely when the trend starts reversing. This sounds so typical for many of you, right?

Relative strength charts help us in dealing with this and help identify the shifts relatively early.

As always, we can plot the ratio chart of one asset class versus another and analyze the behaviour. The strategy and patterns in relative strength charts that we studied until now are applicable in this context too.

We can analyze across say global equity markets to identify which country's stock market is performing better. If the equity market is performing better, then the next logical question would be which sector or group should focus on? Which stock to invest in?

I strongly believe that like in life, everything in markets too goes through cycles. There are good and difficult phases in life and markets. Economies and countries also go through the phases of prosperity and pain. Different markets go through these phases. They are applicable on all timeframes. It is difficult to make these studies objective and it is a bit complicated too.

In terms of trading, if a country's stock market index is going through a favourable phase, and if I plot its relative strength chart with another market that is going through a difficult phase, the former ratio will be bullish, and I can see it is outperforming. We can perform this analysis on a broader level to the stock level, to find the markets, sectors and stocks going through a favourable phase compared to others.

Below is a daily 0.25% x 3 P&F RS chart of Nifty to Dow Jones Industrial Average (DJIA).

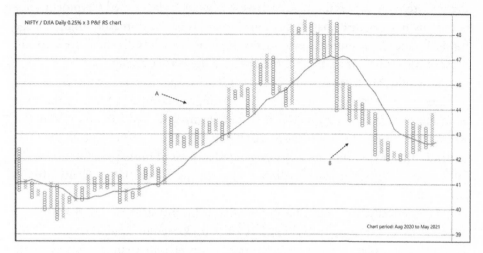

Figure 11.1: Daily 0.25% x 3 P&F RS chart of Nifty to Dow Jones Industrial Average

Nifty is the numerator in the chart shown above. The ratio line was trading above its 10-column moving average at point A indicating that Nifty was bullish in comparison to DJIA. Nifty was underperforming at B when the ratio chart slipped below its moving average.

Nifty is a barometer for Equity Markets in India. GS Composite index can be considered as a barometer for fixed-income Government securities. USDINR may be used to study the trend in the currency market.

There are favourable phases of each asset class in the economy. Law of demand and supply, various cycles and factors affecting these asset classes will influence the price of these assets. It is important to realise that these asset classes are related to each other. They have direct and inverse relationships in different situations. John J. Murphy had explained this concept in his book *Intermarket Analysis: Profiting from Global Market Relationships.* Martin J. Pring also talked about the cycle of bonds, stocks and commodities in his book *Technical Analysis Explained: The Successful Investor's Guide to Spotting Investment Trends and Turning Points.*

The money once printed will not disappear into thin air. It will remain in the system and circulate across different asset classes. By studying the relative strength, we get a heads-up on where the funds are flowing into.

Given below is a daily line chart of Nifty along with a 50-period moving average.

Figure 11.2: Nifty daily line chart along with the 50-period moving average

Price fell below its moving average at A in February 2020 and crossed over above this moving average in May 2020. We get to know about price breakout by analysing the chart.

How the price behaves concerning its moving average helps in understanding the strength of the breakout.

Displayed below is a daily ratio chart of Gold to Nifty 50 along with the 50-period moving average.

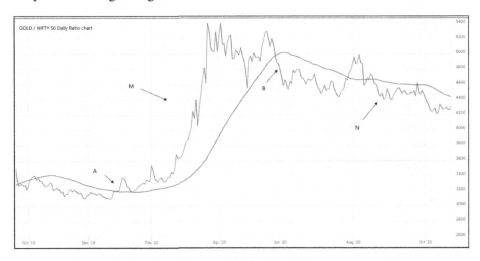

Figure 11.3: Daily Ratio chart of Gold to Nifty 50 along with the 50-period moving average

The gold to Nifty Ratio chart moved above its moving average at A in January 2020. It fell below the moving average at B in June 2020. Gold outperformed Nifty during period M and Nifty outperformed Gold during period N.

It was not only Gold that was outperforming against Nifty at point A. Check the daily ratio chart of Nifty GS Composite to Nifty along with the 50-period moving average.

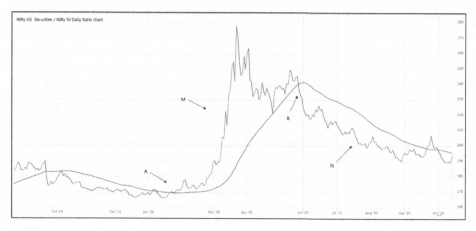

Figure 11.4: Daily ratio chart of Nifty GS Composite to Nifty along with the 50-period moving average

The ratio line moved above its moving average at A indicating outperformance. The bonds were outperforming Nifty during period M. The ratio fell below the average line at B. Nifty was outperforming bonds and also against gold during period N.

Bonds and Gold outperforming during period M suggested that the money was moving to safer assets. It happened because of uncertainty due to the Covid-19 pandemic and the non-clarity of the outcome of the pandemic. There was a global sell-off in equities.

Featured below is the daily ratio chart of USDINR to Nifty along with the 50-period moving average.

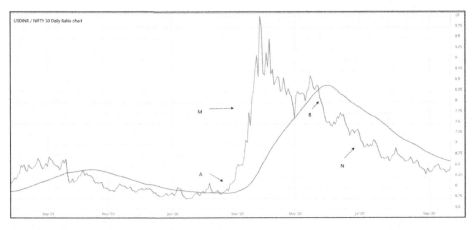

Figure 11.5: Daily Ratio chart of USDINR to Nifty along with 50-period Moving average

USDINR was also indicating outperformance at A. The ratio chart slipped below the moving average line at B. USDINR was another asset class that was outperforming against Nifty during period M. Nifty was outperforming USDINR during period N.

Currency was also outperforming during the M period indicating a global sell-off and equity was underperforming against all other asset classes.

When the equity market started underperforming all major asset classes at A, bearish signs such as price dropping below its moving average or any bearish breakout patterns in the price chart would be valuable information. It tells us that the reversal in price is extremely significant. In May-June 2020, the Covid-19 situation was worsening with the number of cases rising, and businesses being affected due to the country-wide lockdown. But Equity started outperforming against all other asset classes at B and the price also sustained above the moving average. This indicated that the money was flowing back into equity markets.

Nobody knows the reason behind the dramatic stock market recovery but the price and RS chart trends would have proved extremely useful to decide which asset class to focus on.

You can use other tools and indicators for this analysis as well. Below is my favourite screen that I track daily.

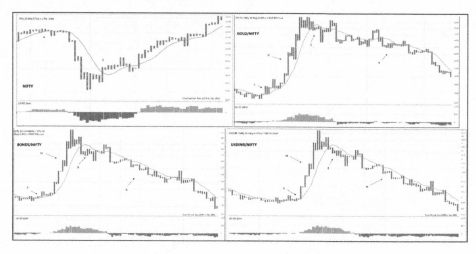

Figure 11.6: Nifty performance chart with other asset classes

Let me explain these charts individually.

Below is a daily 0.10% x 3 P&F chart of Nifty along with a 10-column moving average and a 20-column XO Zone indicator.

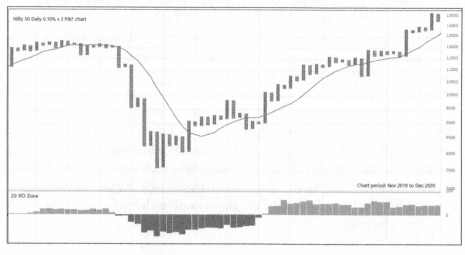

Figure 11.7: Daily 0.10% x 3 P&F chart of Nifty along with 10-column moving average and a 20-column XO zone

This is the Nifty chart used for price analysis. The moving average is used as a trend filter and the 20-column XO zone is used for confirmation. We can engage in reading price patterns in these charts for further insights.

The second chart in the window is the daily 0.10% x 3 P&F RS chart of Nifty GS Composite and Nifty along with a 10-column moving average and 20-column XO zone indicator.

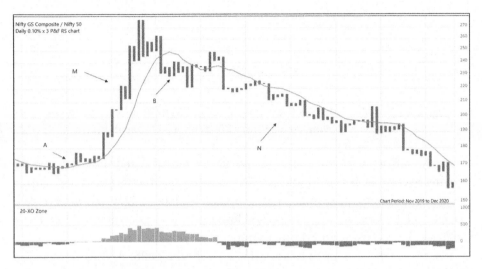

Figure 11.8: Daily 0.10% x 3 P&F chart of Nifty GS Composite to Nifty along with a 10-column moving average and a 20-column XO zone indicator

This chart is to study the relationship between bonds and equity. Bonds started outperforming versus Nifty during A. The ratio dropped below the moving average at point B, and later the XO zone too turned bearish. At M, there was series of double top buy patterns above the average line with a green XO zone that indicated strong outperformance by Bonds. Period N saw a series of bearish double bottom sell patterns below moving average while the XO zone was bearish all along, suggesting strong underperformance of bonds.

Below is a daily 0.10% x 3 P&F chart of Nifty USDINR to Nifty along with a 10-column moving average and 20-column XO zone indicator.

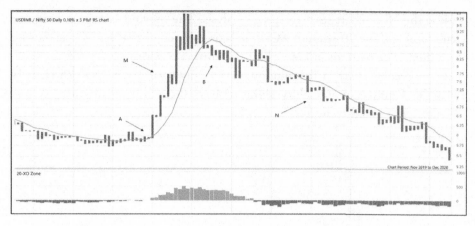

Figure 11.9: daily 0.10% x 3 P&F chart of Nifty USDINR to Nifty along with a 10-column moving average and a 20-column XO zone indicator

The price crossed over and above the moving average at A and slipped below the moving average at B. This indicates that USDINR outperformed Nifty during period A and underperformed during period N. Notice how the price pulled back to the moving average and turned lower during the downtrend at B. These pullbacks are a classic opportunity to initiate low-risk short trades.

Tracking the moving averages helps identify the pullback situations. If you are only interested in crossovers, you may plot the adaptive moving average instead of the simple moving average.

Below is a daily 0.10% x 3 P&F chart of USDINR to Nifty along with a 10-column AMA and 20-column XO zone indicator.

Figure 11.10: Daily 0.10% x 3 P&F chart of USDINR to Nifty along with a 10-column AMA and a 20-column XO zone

Notice how the crossovers are clear and there are fewer instances of prices touching the AMA average line. Periods of outperformance and underperformance are also clearly delineated.

Below is a daily 0.10% x 3 P&F chart of Gold to Nifty along with a 10-column moving average and a 20-column XO zone indicator.

Figure 11.11: Daily 0.10% x 3 P&F chart of Gold to Nifty along with 10-column moving average and 20-column XO zone indicator

Gold also moved above the average line at A and slipped below it at B. This represents the same observation of strong outperformance during M and strong underperformance during N.

The box value is an extremely useful tool in the P&F chart. I always look at higher and lower box-value charts to get a broader perspective. The chosen box size is 0.10% box value because I wish to look at a 20-column XO zone or 10-column average line. We can also increase the box value to study the price patterns.

Investors can ride the trend using the moving average in bigger box sizes. Traders can time the entry and exit based on patterns.

Below is a daily 1% x 3 P&F chart of Nifty GS Composite to Nifty along with a 10-column moving average and 10-column XO zone indicator.

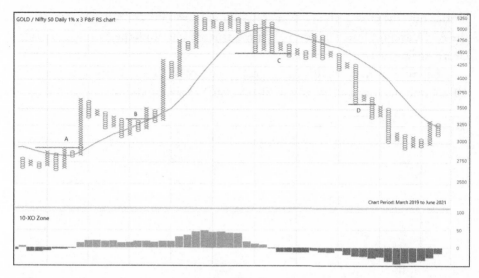

Figure 11.12: Daily 1% x 3 P&F chart of Nifty GS Composite to Nifty along with 10-column moving average and a 10-column XO zone indicator

Point A is a bullish turtle breakout above moving average and at bullish XO zone. Period B is a triangle breakout and fresh double top buy above the average line with a bullish XO zone. Point C is a bearish turtle breakout below the moving average with a bearish XO zone. Point D is bearish anchor column follow-through below the moving average and bearish XO zone.

Once we identify that an asset class is outperforming against Equity, the price chart of that asset class must be studied to identify trading or investing opportunities.

For example, Gold was outperforming Nifty during period M in the above chart. It makes sense to trade bullish patterns in the Gold chart when it is outperforming the Nifty and other asset classes.

Below is a daily 0.25% x 3 P&F chart of GOLD futures, traded at MCX in India along with a 10-column AMMA indicator.

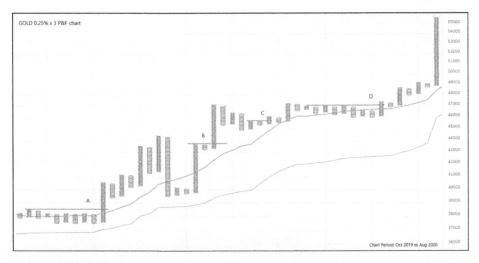

Figure 11.13: Daily 0.25% x 3 P&F chart of GOLD along with 10-column AMMA indicator

Point A is a bullish turtle breakout above AMMA. Point B is a bullish anchor column follow-through with a very affordable stop-loss above AMMA. Point C is also a bullish anchor column follow-through with a very affordable stop-loss above AMMA. Point D is a bullish turtle breakout above the AMMA indicator.

The breakout in Gold or USDINR is more important when its ratio chart is also outperforming against Nifty. That would mean a strong rally in that asset class because the money is shifting from Equity to these asset classes.

Similarly, the breakout in Equity is more effective when it is outperforming against other asset classes. That also means that the downtrend in Equity may be temporary if it continues to outperform other asset classes. Any reversal would be considered significant if it also results in an underperformance against other asset classes.

The takeaway here is that even if you are trading primarily in equities, you should be aware of what is happening in other major asset classes. The performance of Nifty vis a vis other asset classes is a key factor to decide about the strategy and exposure to the equity asset class.

If Nifty is outperforming, we should have more allocation in equities. With the breakout in stocks, the sectors and groups outperforming in Nifty are more attractive from an investment perspective. The performance of bullish trades will be better than bearish trades in such a scenario.

If other asset classes such as Gold or bonds are outperforming, then increase allocation to them. This indicates that the money is moving from equity to safer assets. Bearish and range-bound trading strategies would yield better results in Equity Markets during such times.

You can remember it as an RS switch for your trading and investment portfolio.

Image 11.1: RS switch

Many people keep searching for the best strategy or tools, but the fact is that there is none. Every tool or strategy would have its favourable and non-favourable phases. This is inevitable in all timeframes. People who follow a certain strategy tend to present it like it is the best, but that is not the case.

If you understand charts and follow risk-management rules, you do not have to worry about the bear market similar to 2008. You will be in a position to exit your trade position and initiate short trades too. The bigger problem is during periods of consolidation similar to what happened during 2010–2012. Those were painful years for those adopting trend following strategies.

But some sectors in the equity market were performing well even during this period of consolidation. That key is to identify such sectors using relative strength analysis and look for trades in those sectors.

If you prefer to adopt a price momentum or trend-following strategy, then identify markets that are currently in a strong trend. Move to outperforming or trending sectors and stocks where your momentum strategy would work. Otherwise, recognize the phase of the segment you are trading. If it is underperforming or moving in a range, shift the strategy suitable to the range market. If you are someone who prefers a range-bound strategy, find sectors and markets that are not trending. Breadth zone can be a very useful tool to trade sectors in a sideways trend. Identify stocks and sectors in a suitable environment to the nature of your trading strategy using RS and breadth analysis.

The RS switch would be ON for equities if it is favourable or outperforming. In such a scenario, increase the allocation to equities and focus on trend trading strategies. The RS Switch would be OFF for equity if it is underperforming. This concept of the RS switch applies to all instruments.

When the equity asset class is outperforming, then analyze sectors and indices that are performing better within the equity segment. Broadly, we need to analyze three segments:
- Large cap
- Mid cap
- Small cap

Nifty 50 index consists primarily of large-cap stocks. The Nifty mid-cap 150 and Nifty small-cap 250 are representatives of the mid-cap and small-cap universe respectively. There are some other indices as well. Nifty mid-small 400 indexes can also be a very useful index to keep a track of. Nifty 500 is the largest universe of stocks which includes large-cap, mid-cap, and small-cap stocks. The Nifty 500 index includes the Nifty 50 stocks. The Nifty 50 stock enjoy the highest weightage in the Nifty 500 index. But the price and breadth study in the Nifty 500 index would help get insights into the broader market performance.

If we analyze these indices, it will help identify which segment of the equity market to focus on. If the large-cap is outperforming, then adopting a breakout trading strategy in this universe would be advisable. The year 2017 was one of the best years for mid-caps. Take a look at the chart below of Nifty 500 to Nifty 50 0.15% x 3 Daily P&F RS chart.

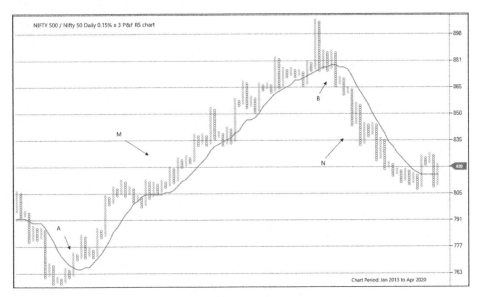

Figure 11.14: Nifty 500 to Nifty 50 0.15% x 3 daily P&F RS chart

The above chart shows that the Nifty 500 to Nifty ratio chart was trading above the average line from point A in December 2013 to Point B during April 2018. This means Nifty 500 stocks outperformed Nifty 50 during the period. Remember the Nifty 500 stocks also includes the Nifty 50 stocks. That means the performance of Nifty 450 stocks was better. It also shows that there was action in mid caps and small caps stocks. Any breakout strategy in these stocks would have yielded attractive returns. The Nifty 50 index appreciated by about 68% during that period while the Nifty 500 index generated returns of about 92%.

The Nifty 500 index underperformed Nifty 50 from April 2018 till January 2020. The Nifty 50 index was up by 20% during that period and the large caps did comparatively well. Mid-cap stocks underperformed large caps during that period. Nifty 500 index posted a moderate 10% during this period.

Any breakout buys strategy in mid-caps will have a better success rate when they are outperforming the index. Understanding this concept will help you decide when to increase allocation to mid-cap stocks.

Have a look at the below chart of Nifty mid and small cap 400 indexes to Nifty 50 index 0.15% x 3 daily P&F RS chart.

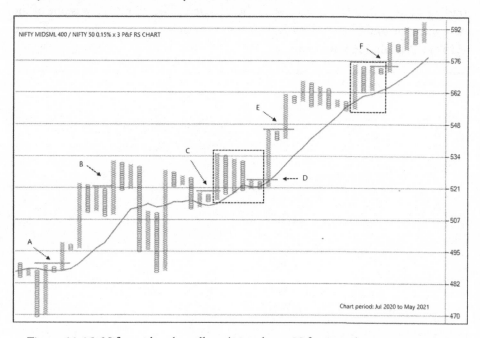

Figure 11.15: Nifty mid and small cp 400 index to Nifty 50 index 0.15% x 3 daily P&F RS chart

The mid and small cap index outperformed Nifty from August 2020 till May 2021 in the chart above. The ratio was consistently trading above its moving average. There were interesting price patterns during the period. A fresh double top buys and a turtle breakout was completed at A in August 2020. Pattern B and C were anchor column follow-through patterns. The anchor column at C was followed by a six-column triangle breakout at D. This was followed by an anchor column follow-through pattern at E. Pattern at F was also a four-column triangle pattern along with an anchor column follow-through breakout.

Other indices such as the small cap 250 and mid cap 150 were also outperforming Nifty 50 during the period.

I studied about 300 stocks that delivered returns more than 125% returns between September 2013 and January 2018. Around 73% stocks of the stocks outperformed markets between 2012–2013. They were lions and bullish star stocks. The threshold of 125% was considered because the Nifty 500 index was up by about 125% during that period.

Around 115 stocks delivered returns more than 500% returns and 46 stocks yielded more than 1000% returns during this period. About 68% of stocks outperformed the markets in 2012-2013. This essentially indicates that you can identify footprints of strong performers. The lion and bullish star stocks can become flyers and produce great returns when the overall sector or space performs.

Interestingly, about 32% of stocks of those winning stocks were positive in the next couple of years when the Nifty 500 index was flat and underperformed the Nifty 50.

This study indicates that:

- We must keep in mind stocks which shows early signs of outperformance and makes a move ahead of the sector. Top performers more often show early signs because their individual stories are bullish. In simple words, keep in mind lion and bullish star stocks.
- Buy them when the group or sector itself starts moving and outperforming.
- Look for the exit when a group or sector starts underperforming. Look for better opportunities that are available in the fresh outperforming sectors and indices.

I believe, the key to success in stock markets lies in identifying the market phase. If you are running a trading system, you can have a switch between different phases using the relative strength chart.

The ratio chart of Nifty 50 to mid-cap ratio chart can help decide index trading strategies. When the Nifty 50 index is outperforming the Nifty 500, then momentum trading strategies in the Nifty 50 index will prove profitable. When the ratio reverses, selling options and range bound strategies would prove more favourable.

So, even if you are not trading stocks–the study of relative strength will help you in deciding the index strategy.

By following this method, your portfolio will do better even during a sharp fall or a global market correction because Nifty will start underperforming against other asset classes in such a scenario. Your allocation would therefore shift to other asset classes or at least the exposure to equity would be reduced. Relative strength helps us in understanding the market theme, which space to look for and how to select stocks for trading or investment.

When a greater number of stocks are bullish or bearish producing flying or drowning patterns, it tells us about prevailing market sentiments. I strongly recommend the use of breadth indicators an integral part of your market study to understand overall market sentiment.

Apart from analysing which group is performing well, it would also help to identify the sectors and sub-sectors that are outperforming. This will help in fine-tuning the strategy and shortlisting the candidates.

I tweeted about increasing the allocation to mid-cap and small-cap stocks in February 2021. Here is the screenshot of that tweet.

Image 11.2: Screenshot of the tweet

The breakout strategies in the Nifty 50 index was performing well until then. In the next few months, the Nifty 50 index went into a consolidation, while the small and mid-cap stocks outperformed. The Nifty Index was confined to a broad range while the mid and small-cap index appreciated by about 20% in the next few months. Your performance would have been better had you increased your allocation to the small mid-cap stocks instead of index strategies during this period.

Knowing when to increase allocation to a particular segment, or market type can be identified using the relative strength analysis. Price analysis is helpful to decide how to trade a particular asset class while relative strength analysis helps in deciding what to trade.

Another interesting aspect is that the breadth was stable even when the market corrected amid negative news. Increasing bullish participation is a strong bullish sign. The market was not reacting significantly to bearish news and the participation of the stocks were rising. The mid cap, small cap ratio charts were also bullish. All these factors suggested that the underlying sentiment was bullish.

There are many approaches to decide how to trade. What is more important is to decide what to trade. Relative strength charts can help you in this context.

Selection of Denominator

We have discussed that the trend of the denominator is an important aspect of relative strength analysis. For the large-cap stocks, the Nifty 50 index would be a logical choice to be used as the denominator or as the benchmark. Even for derivative traders, the Nifty 50 index would be the logical choice for the denominator.

Being a broad market index, Nifty 50 can be the denominator and any stock, index or sector can be plotted as the numerator. The group or sector that a stock belongs to, can also be used as a denominator.

For mid cap and small caps, the denominator should be Nifty 500 or the mid-cap or small-cap index they belong to. Mid-small 400 indexes can also be a logical choice for the denominator.

So, you have two types of denominators–the nifty 50 Index and the Group or Sector index.

Decide your universe and denominator and stick to it. Normally, there will not be a major difference when you select Nifty 500 or Nifty 50. But here is a trick, if Nifty 500 is outperforming Nifty 50, it would mean Nifty 450 stocks (Nifty 500 minus Nifty 50) are doing well because Nifty 50 stocks are also part of Nifty 500 stocks. When that is happening, the denominator should be Nifty 500 for mid caps and small cap stocks. You will get the candidates that are outperforming the Nifty 500, which is outperforming the Nifty 50 index.

The bottom line is, plot the relative strength chart of the group or sector versus the Nifty 50 and then study the relative strength of individual stocks about the group. Let us discuss this in detail.

Sector analysis

Sector analysis is an important aspect of market analysis. Sector rotation is always at work, and it is important to analyze how different stocks and sectors perform in different stages of the market. We discussed in the first chapter that stocks and sectors tend to show early signs of strength before the strong trends of outperformance become apparent. Usually, there will be bullish star or lion patterns before they become flyers.

We should know about the leader of a particular market leg. They continue to perform and keep providing affordable trading opportunities. Traders keep looking for other sectors which are correcting in the assumption that the risk is low because they are already correcting. What turns out is, they keep falling more. The stocks and sectors that are outperforming would however keep rising. The short-term correction in these stocks is an opportunity to participate in bigger trends.

Always remember, irrespective of the market being bullish or bearish, there will always be sectors or groups which would be stronger and in favour. Some sectors will perform relatively well even during a bear market. A classic example was the FMCG sector during 2011–2012. The Pharma sector is another such example in 2020. All the stocks from the sector were performing and they did well for several months.

A sharp fall triggered by a global or macro reason is an exception to what we discussed above. In such a scenario, moving to a safer asset class such as gold or bonds would be a better strategy. Relative strength analysis of asset classes helps in identifying such shifts early on. When you are focusing on equities, then the analysis of sectors and groups plays an important role.

Leading stocks and sectors might seem expensive, but the risk is low in buying them. Laggards may appear affordable, but they are riskier. Similarly, the weak stocks are the best candidates to short when the equity market is underperforming.

Another aspect of sector rotation is that there is a rotation that happens in the short and medium-term time frames. The strong sectors go through a period of consolidation or correction while the other sectors would perform in the interim. A broad understanding of this rotation concept can help in filtering the sectors further. Reversal patterns in sectors that are weak in the medium term but rising in short term can be a good opportunity to initiate short trades.

Over a period, I have realised that knowing how sectors and groups performing, and who are leaders or the laggard of the space plays a particularly important role in short-term or medium-term trading or investment as well.

I remember a popular story in this context.

A car owner could not find solutions to fix the car which refused to start owing to engine failure. Despite the efforts of several experts, there was no solution. Experts tried many solutions and also replaced parts, but all attempts failed. Finally, the owner sought the help of an old and experienced mechanic. After studying the car, the old man pulled out a small hammer from his toolbox and tapped something and the car engine was back in action.

How to tap the hammer is not important, where to tap is the key and it requires skill and experience.

Price analysis teaches us how to buy or how to build trading systems, but what to buy and which universe to track, or which type of strategy to adopt is a more critical aspect.

If we find early signs of strength in the sector or sub-sector, it provides a heads-up about which sectors or stocks to focus. Here are a few anecdotal examples.

The IT rally of 2016–2017, the mid-cap IT rally of 2019, Pharma in 2020, Sugar, Fertilizer, Agriculture and Metals in 2021 are classic examples. The story or the reason for these sectors to perform better would be apparent only subsequently. You may for example recall the ethanol story that fuelled sugar stocks or the pandemic related concerns for Pharma. It would always be wonderful to identify such triggers in advance, but confirmation from price is essential. Ultimately, it is the price that determines our returns.

Most of the time we get to know about the cause when a rally in a sector is already underway. Such stocks can still outperform. I studied these sectors and their behaviour on different timeframes to learn how we can identify those traits earlier. Tracking the stocks hitting a 52-week high in the sector can be a logical point to start but this can turn out to be a late signal in many cases. There are ways to identify these signals earlier.

Now that you have learned about breadth, think about what will happen when the entire sector or group starts moving up? The first indicator that will capture this turnaround in sentiment would be the breadth of the sector. The stocks from such sectors would start performing well. It is important in this context to identify the appropriate breadth indicator to use.

If the 52-week high or 200-day moving average is used as a breadth indicator, then the signals could be delayed. We need a momentum-based breadth indicator to get a heads up. I find the X%-P&F indicator or DT% or Renko bullish brick%

to be useful indicators in this context. They capture stocks that are turning into a bullish swing.

When the entire space is moving, the stocks from the group would typically form an important low and turn around. Most of the stocks would perform well and the sector's breadth would also improve. If you analyze the breadth indicator of each sector daily, you will get to know the sector or sub-sector recording strong bullish numbers in the breadth indicator. It can be temporarily in the overbought zone, but it suggests strength. You should then analyze the charts of that sector to identify opportunities.

When the sector corrects, or if there is a pullback, look for trading or investment opportunity in those sectors. Look around any favourable development relating to the sector. If such developments, the subsequent move can then be more significant.

If the sector again records top breadth numbers after the pullback, that is evidence that the move is here to stay. When the sector breadth is bullish, check the relative strength of the sector with the broad market and other averages. The combination of an outperforming sector with a bullish breadth is a typical trait of the sector being in favour.

So, keep looking for sectors, sub-sectors and groups that are witnessing improvement in the swing breadth indicator. That is where you get to know about the next big story of the market. Keep in mind the BRS principles that we have discussed earlier for sector analysis. Strong relative strength sectors with strong breadth numbers are the sectors that are in a strong momentum. Correction or consolidation in them is an opportunity to participate in the broader trend.

The averages that we use for sector analysis are the sector indices defined by the exchanges. Certain sectors are not part of the exchange index. For example, sugar, fertilizer, chemicals, agriculture stocks etc.

There are two ways to deal with such sectors or sub-sectors:

1. I recommend creating a weighted average index of the group of stocks and making it a benchmark for relative strength comparison. We can create our universe of those stocks and calculate their weighted average index for the relative strength analysis of those sectors with the rest of the universe.

2. Another option is to keep the Nifty 500 universe as a benchmark in such stocks and compare them with their larger universe.

When you identify the sector or group that is outperforming, look for the top-performing stocks in that sector. Generally, the top performers in the earlier part of the movie would end up as the leaders and remain top performers. Though the other stocks would also start participating at a later date, the rise in such late movers might be mostly short-lived.

Typically, when the sector is already leading and buzzing around, most of the rallies in the stocks are already behind us. Of course, they may remain strong, and we should look for continuation or pullback opportunities in such stocks.

Let us discuss early signs to keep an eye on.

Early signs
- Strong momentum in stocks.
- Bullish breadth even on down days.
- Ratio charts of multiple stocks in the sector are bullish.
- Stocks making higher bottoms.
- More lions and bullish stars in space.

Stock Selection Approach
When we compare stocks in a sector, the typical approach would be to study the business and competitive strengths and weaknesses. Other factors to consider could include profit margins, valuation, market share and management quality. Along with that, another important factor to consider would be the performance of the stock price in relation to the benchmark and the sector index. If the whole sector is performing well, the quality stocks will deliver better returns.

It should be apparent by now that the combination of relative strength and breadth analysis can aid price analysis. So, how do we select stocks for trading? Either we select it using some price analysis system and then check the ratio chart for confirmation. Or, we can shortlist stocks using relative strength chart analysis, and then seek confirmation from the price chart.

The former approach is known as a bottom-up approach and the latter is the top-down approach. Let us discuss these two approaches.

Top-down approach
We can compare the performance of sector averages against the broader market index to assess its relative performance. Below is a chart.

Below is Nifty Metal Index to Nifty 50 daily ratio chart plotted with a 200-day moving average.

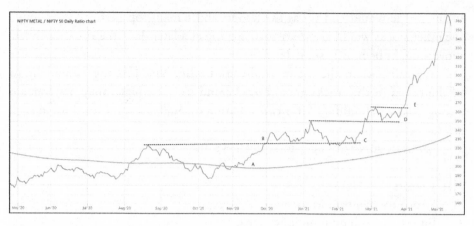

Figure 11.16: Nifty Metal Index to Nifty 50 Daily Ratio chart plotted with 200-day moving average

The metal index ratio chart crossed above its 200-day moving average at point A during November 2020. The ratio completed a breakout at B and retested the breakout level at C. The pattern and the indicator were bullish suggesting that the metal index is a strong outperformer against Nifty. There were continuation breakout patterns at D and E when the sector was in a strong outperforming zone.

Featured below is the Tata Steel to Nifty Metal index daily ratio chart plotted with a 200-day moving average.

Figure 11.17: Tata Steel to Nifty metal index daily ratio chart plotted with a 200-day moving average

Tata Steel to Nifty metal index chart moved above the 200-day average line at A indicating that Tata Steel is outperforming the space in that leg. A bullish inverted head and shoulders pattern breakout was completed at B while the price was above the average line. There were continuation trend lines and pattern breakouts at points C and D while the price was holding above the average line.

The metal sector was outperforming Nifty and Tata Steel was outperforming the metal index. If you were aware of this, you should focus on trading bullish patterns in the price chart of Tata Steel. I reiterate that the relative strength chart analysis can improve your chances of success in the price analysis.

The trend in the denominator–Nifty 50 was also bullish during this period. That means the metal index was a flyer and Tata Steel was a flyer in the metal index. Favourable breadth when the sector is outperforming provides confirmation. Breadth zone can help in deciding on allocation and trade strategies.

Here is a checklist of steps or factors that we considered:

- A broad market index is bullish (analysis of the denominator).
- Identified a sector displaying relative strength.
- Identified the stock displaying relative strength versus the sector.
- Check if breadth is favourable
- Planning trades on the price chart of the stock.

With this approach, we have designed the top-down process to select the stocks. Below is an image.

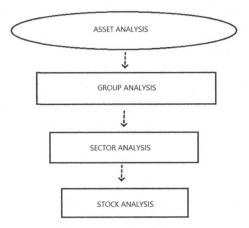

Image 11.3: Top-down approach

Let us articulate the process in greater detail. Here is a flow chart of the process.

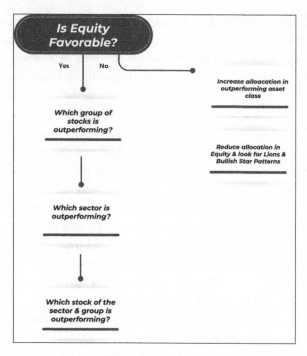

Image 11.4: Top-down approach flow chart

If the equity asset class is outperforming, then we need to identify if the large-cap, or mid-caps or small-caps are participating and outperforming. Within these categories, we should identify which sectors are leaders are more favoured. The price analysis of stocks in that sector would tell us how and when to trade those stocks. If Equity as an asset class is not performing, we need to trade price breakouts of the other outperforming assets. And the equity allocation must be reduced during such times. We have already seen examples of asset classes delivering better returns even during equity bear markets.

With this approach, the idea is to identify outperforming stock of the outperforming sector and the index.

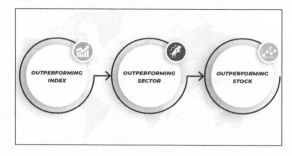

Image 11.5: Outperformer of outperformer

Bullish patterns in the relative strength chart indicate outperformance while bearish patterns indicate underperformance. A top-down approach begins with the study of the relative strength chart of the sectors vis-à-vis the broader market index. The patterns on the sector ratio charts would provide information about the performance of the sector versus the benchmark. This helps you identify strong sectors.

The next step is to identify strong stocks from the outperforming sectors. This is achieved by studying the relative strength charts of the stocks from the outperforming sector(s) in relation to the sector index. Trading the price breakout patterns in the leaders can prove more rewarding. Similarly, underperforming stocks can also be identified using such a top-down approach.

When a stock moves, it could be due to stock-specific fundamental developments. But, when an entire set of stocks are moving, there would be a bigger development at the sector level. When there is a positive development at the micro and macro level, that is when a stock gets into an accelerated uptrend and the price chart would tell us what to do thereafter.

Sector performance analysis gives an idea of sectors that are outperforming and underperforming across various time horizons.

A top-down approach is a logical approach to identify stocks for trading or investment. We are identifying a leader amongst the leading universe. This approach is used in the fundamental analysis of the stocks as well. One of the interesting ways to perform sector analysis is to listen to the budget speech and track government spending. Those are the sectors where you should look for good companies to invest. Once you identify such sectors, you can look for companies that are market leaders and have better free cash flows, less debt and better return on equity (ROE).

With relative strength, we are identifying stocks using the price action. If a sector is outperforming the broader market index, it is a bullish sector for some reasons known or unknown. It would be wonderful if we can identify fundamental developments supporting the outperformance. But, it is okay even if we are unable to identify any significant fundamental development supporting the outperformance. If the stock is outperforming its peers in an outperforming sector, there obviously must be some logical reasons behind it. In a favourable environment, stocks with high valuations continue to perform better and the market is not according to such premium valuation to these stocks without a reason. It is just that we may not be aware of those reasons in some instances.

The top-down approach is recommended to identify stocks to building a portfolio. Once strong stocks have been identified, it is then a question of patiently waiting for continuation patterns or buy signals to be triggered in the individual stock price charts. Nifty 500 or Nifty mid-cap indices can also be used as the denominator for this purpose.

A stock selected from a strongly performing sector is likely to perform better than stock from a weak sector.

Similarly, a stock from an underperforming sector is likely to fall more and is a better bet for shorting as compared to the one from a strong or a stable sector. While one would want to build a portfolio consisting of stocks that are outperforming the markets, and it is equally important to keep away from the underperformers. Relative strength is the best approach to identify outperformers and underperformers.

There are numerous price-based trading strategies that one can adopt. But it is essential to keep in mind better risk-reward trade opportunities while identifying the trades. Look for better chances of success by studying charts.

The following components in your trading system will improve your odds of success:

- Outperforming stocks
- Strong momentum
- Breakout or pullback pattern
- Proper risk management.

Recent swing high or low can be an important reference area to use as a stop loss in trading. In P&F charts, the double top buy or the double-bottom sell are objective patterns. The length of retracement can help identify the risk in advance.

Below is an example of swing breakout on the candlestick chart and how you can find the recent swing low for the stop-loss.

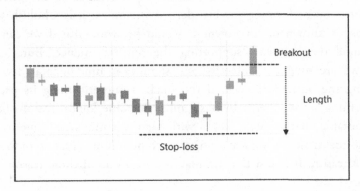

Image 11.6: Swing breakout pattern and stop-loss at swing low

You can calculate the distance between entry price and stop-loss and consider taking trades only if the risk is affordable. That way, you improve the risk-reward ratio of your overall trades.

I have studied many tools for stop-loss and risk management over the years and realised that swing high and lows are simple yet highly effective approaches for stop loss placement.

Below is a P&F chart that can make this job easier.

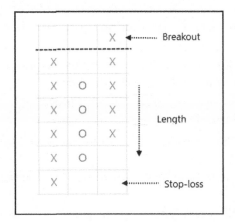

Image 11.7: Stop-loss calculation for double top buy pattern

You know the price at which the double-bottom sell will be triggered. This sell trigger level would be the logical stop loss level. What is more interesting in the P&F chart is that you can calculate the number of boxes for stop-loss. For example, in the above case, the stop-loss will be six boxes away from the current price. See the image shown below.

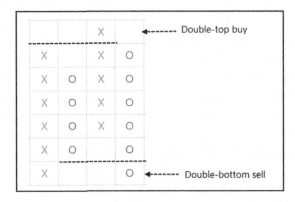

Image 11.8: Stop-loss of double top buy gets triggered

If it is a 0.25% chart, your stop-loss would be roughly 1.5% away from the entry price. If this risk is within your tolerable limits, you can build this condition in the scanner to identify candidates that offer opportunities with a predefined risk. You can focus on the stocks offering entry with a maximum risk of six boxes, or any other parameter that you deem fit. This way, you can filter out the stocks with an affordable stop-loss while scanning itself.

The anchor column follows through the pattern in outperforming stocks can be an interesting combination. We can plan trades on the price chart with affordable risk when there is a continuation pattern in leading stocks from the leading sectors.

We can use matrix tables, charts or one of the various methods we discussed in the book for relative strength and breadth analysis.

Try to make this top-down stock selection process more objective. Here are some pointers to achieve this.

Let us use a simple moving average indicator to define the trend. A simple set of filters could be:

- Nifty should be trading above its 50-period average to suggest that the market trend is bullish.
- The Sector to Nifty ratio line should be above its 50-period average line and rising to suggest outperformance.
- The stock to sector ratio line is above the 50-period average line and rising to suggest that the stock is outperforming the sector index.
- The stock price chart is above its 50-period average line to confirm that the stock is in an uptrend.

Any stock meeting the above criteria can be traded based on price breakout pattern or retracement. The use of moving averages makes this process more objective. Other indicators may also be used instead of moving the average in the above equation. You can also use a different moving average length instead of 50.

A relative strength chart can be plotted against the benchmark index or the sector index. Normally, if a stock is bullish versus the sector, it will invariably be bullish against the benchmark index as well if it is a continuation pattern.

When the price or the ratio line is above the moving average and if the ratio or price is falling, it can represent a temporary period of underperformance and could be an opportunity to participate in the broader trend with an affordable risk. Think of the Eagle pattern in this context.

Something similar may be considered in Point & Figure charts as well. Here are some conditions to consider:

- The Nifty price chart is above the 10-column moving average.

- Sector to Nifty RS chart is above the 10-column moving average.
- Stock to Sector RS chart is above the 10-column moving average.
- The stock price chart is above the 10-column moving average.

Plan a trade with a stop-loss below the previous column low or the double bottom sell level on the price chart. Other P&F patterns and methods that we have discussed earlier, can also help improve results. The advantage of the P&F charts is that they are noiseless, time-independent and provide objective price patterns to identify and trade.

To make things more objective and easier to comprehend, I have designed a method of scoring and ranking based on the P&F chart. You can use the Top-Down Approach scanner in the TradePoint software which makes this process of scoring and ranking very objective.

In the Top-Down Approach scanner, the software calculates the score based on the price chart and RS chart. Here is the logic for calculating the scores.

When the price is above the moving average, the trend is bullish. There are four possible price patterns while the price is above the moving average.
- Double-top buy pattern = Very bullish scenario; Score assigned is 3
- Colum of 'X' but not a double-top buy pattern = Bullish scenario; Score assigned is 2
- Double-bottom sell pattern = Bullish trend but a bearish pattern; Score assigned is -1
- Column of 'O' but not a double-bottom sell pattern = Bullish retracement; Score 1

Similarly, here are the pattern possibilities when the price it is trading below the moving average.
- Double-bottom sell pattern = Very bearish; Score assigned is -3
- Column of 'O' but not a double-bottom sell pattern = Bearish; Score assigned is -2
- Double-top buy pattern = Bearish trend but bullish pattern; Score assigned is 1
- Colum of 'X' but not a double-top buy pattern = Bearish retracement; Score assigned is -1

The moving average is used as a trend filter to assign scores for the top-down approach. The unique feature of this scanner is that we can select a sector or a group as the numerator and compare the performance with two denominators. Let us call them denominator 1 and denominator 2. The two denominators would typically be the sector index and the broad benchmark such as the Nifty 50 index.

We will calculate the above scores on these three charts:

1. Price chart of stock
2. The ratio chart of the stock divided by sector index and
3. The sector index is divided by the market index.

We can calculate the total score and can sort the candidates based on the total scores to rank them logically.

The top-down approach can also be identified using the pullback or reversal method. Eagle pattern knowledge is useful here. If a sector is strong but the correction is temporary and you anticipate reversal, identify the stocks from the sector showing the signs of outperformance if the sector resumes an uptrend.

The PMOX Indicator can help identify the Eagle pattern candidates. Typically, the PMOX indicator will turn to an oversold zone when it is an eagle pattern.

When the PMOX indicator sector relative strength chart is in the oversold zone, look for buying opportunities in that sector. When the PMOX indicator is in the overbought zone, look for shorting opportunities in that sector.

Below is a daily 0.25% x 3 P&F RS chart of Nifty IT index to Nifty 50 index along with a10-column moving average and 10,3 PMOX indicator.

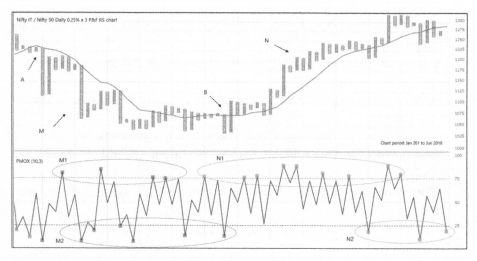

Figure 11.18: Daily 0.25% x 3 P&F RS chart of Nifty IT index to Nifty 50 index along with 10-column moving average and 10,3 PMOX indicator

In the above chart, the IT index slipped below moving average at A in January 2017 and underperformed Nifty during the period M. This index recovered and moved above the moving average at B in November 2017 and outperformed the Nifty during period N.

The red dots in circle M1 captures instances of overbought reading in the PMOX indicator that provided bearish pullback opportunities in IT stocks. Circle M2 captures instances when the index entered a strong bearish momentum zone. The green dots in circle N1 indicates the instances when the IT index was in a strong outperformance mode. Green dots in circle N2 shows an oversold zone that gave bullish pullback opportunities to buy the IT stocks.

You can also use the tools such as the fusion matrix, ultimate matrix, ratio trend matrix or the RS indicator scanner to filter stocks.

For example, once you identify the outperforming sectors, you can use the ultimate matrix to find the stocks outperforming within the sector. Resort to price analysis in the stocks that are at the top slot for identifying trading opportunities.

Finding Leaders

When a sector is going through a temporary phase of underperformance, the stocks outperforming the sector and having a healthy score during such period can turn out to be outperformers when the sector resumes its outperformance.

When the sector is trading above the average line but if the price flips to a column 'O', it may be the case of a temporary pullback. If the PMOX indicator is also in the oversold zone, then run the ultimate matrix or any other method of ranking to identify the stock where a lion RS pattern or a bullish star RS pattern is completed. These stocks can outperform the market if the sector underperformance turns out to be a temporary phenomenon.

This is a vital and useful observation that can help you immensely in identifying the stocks and sectors to trade. A strong and outperforming sector, which has a favourable breadth during a rally also goes through temporary corrections during the trending phase. Those corrections would typically be temporary. I have observed that in each of those sub-bullish trends, the leaders might be different.

Take a look at the image below for more clarity.

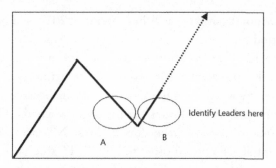

Image 11.9: Correction at A, reversal at B

The sector is in a strong bullish uptrend. When it corrects at A or reverses at B, look for stocks outperforming the sector. They often turn out to be the leaders of the next leg.

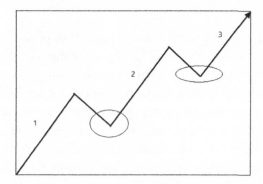

Image 11.10: Corrections during a strong trend

Many stocks will outperform in the sector during its favourable period. Stock rotation would often happen during such times. There will be different legs of the rally, and there can be different outperformers in each leg of the rally. It is fine to find an outperformer and remain invested throughout the rally, but if we can identify the stocks before each leg, it can help us from a short-term trading and investment perspective as well. That could be a highly effective method of stock selection.

Let us consider an example here. The IT Index appreciated by about 30% from January to mid-October 2018. The IT index stocks such as COFORGE, MINDTREE, LTI & TCS gained more than 50% during this period while others such as MPHASIS, TECHM and INFY gained by about 35% during the period.

Featured below is a daily ratio chart of the Nifty IT Index to Nifty 50 along with 100- period AMA.

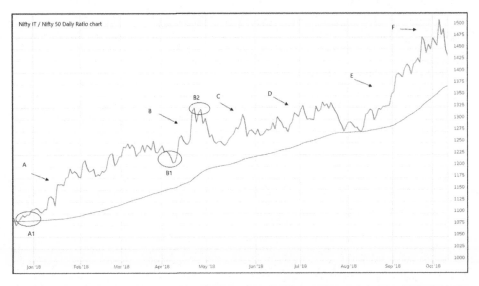

Figure 11.19: Daily ratio chart of Nifty IT Index to Nifty 50 along with 100- period AMA

The ratio moved above the moving average in late 2017 and stayed about the moving average, suggesting strong outperformance of the IT index. The rally is segmented into a few parts.

Mindtree, COFORGE & TECHM were leaders during this outperformance cycle.

MINDTREE gained around 30% during A in January 2018. It appreciated by more than 15% in December 2017 at circle A1 even before the IT index crossed over above the moving average. This indicated that MINDTREE was already an outperformer, and hence was the lion stock of the index. You can easily visualise how bullish the ratio chart of MINDTREE to NIFTY IT index would have been in December 2017 itself. IT sector was correcting during B1 but MINDTREE was still outperforming. It appreciated by 30% during B.

In segment B, COFORGE and MINDTREE were the top performers. MPHASIS did well in segment C. During D, TCS & LTI performed better. During E, Wipro & HCL TECH were the top performers from the IT space. Interestingly, Nifty was down by about 10% during F while the IT index was almost flat. IT was an outperforming sector and investing in that sector would have yielded better returns when the benchmark Nifty 50 index fell by around 10%.

Most of the time, there are such footprints or clues about the leaders of the sector. Often the bullish stars and lions morph into the flyers category. In the same way, the bearish star and cats can end up as drowning patterns.

Below is a daily ratio chart of the Nifty Pharma Index to Nifty 50 along with 100- period AMA.

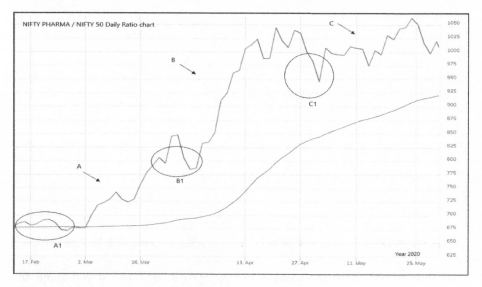

Figure 11.20: Daily ratio chart of Nifty Pharma index to Nifty 50 along with 100- period AMA

The above chart captures the uptrend in the Pharma index from March to May 2020. During this period, the Nifty index lost close to 20% while the Pharma index appreciated by more than 26%. Most of the stocks of the Pharma index performed well during this period. Stocks such as CIPLA, AUROPHARMA were up by more than 40% and others such as LUPIN, CADILAHC, DRREDDY, SUNPHARMA gained more than 25%.

I have divided the uptrend in chart 11.20 into three parts. In part A in the above chart, Nifty Pharma was outperforming against the Nifty index. The Nifty was falling but the Pharma index was relatively flat, resulting in a strong rising ratio line. The pharma index was a bullish lion or a bullish star candidate during most of this segment. The ratio chart moved above the moving average in late February 2020 at A1.

The most rewarding phase was during Phase B. The Pharma index was up by more than 38% during this phase. Pharma stocks such as AUROPHARMA gained about 78%, CIPLA 53%, LUPIN 45%, DRREDDY 40% and BIOCON gained 26% during this period. AUROPHARMA, BIOCON and DRREDDY were bullish during the circle B1 period. LUPIN was down by around 13% during that period but it turned out to be a significant performer during B.

Pharma index was up by around 3% during C but the Nifty index was down by more than 8%. All Pharma stocks were negative during the correction in circle C1 except AUROPHARMA. Naturally, AUROPHARMA to Nifty Pharma chart was bullish at that time. In the subsequent rally during C, it was not surprising to note that AUROPHARMA was the top-performing stock, and it was up by more than 16% even while the Pharma index was flat.

I have numerous examples to highlight how leaders keep changing during a strong sector trend. We typically end up buying those that outperformed in the previous leg but something else turns out to be the winner. You can also use the PMOX indicator in this context. It is an effective indicator to study pullbacks and identify the leaders when PMOX reaches the oversold or overbought zone.

We discussed a few bullish examples. The same logic applies to bearish patterns as well.

Top-down and eagle

Strong leaders can undergo a temporary phase of underperformance. This does not mean that the uptrend is over. The stock rotation leads to a temporary phase of underperformance where weak players exit the stock during this pullback. Subsequently, the prior uptrend resumes, and the leaders continue to reassert themselves.

The BRS principles that we have discussed are also applicable to sectors. When you identify a sector using relative strength analysis, the analysis of breadth can help you understand the state of the trend and time the entries accordingly.

Table 11.1: BRS principles

Breadth	Relative Strength	BRS Trend
Overbought	Bullish	Strong Bullish Momentum / Exhaustion
Above Mid level	Bullish	Strong Bullish
Below Mid level	Bullish	Bullish & Pullback / Caution
Oversold	Bullish	Bullish & Oversold
Oversold	Bearish	Strong Bearish Momentum / Exhaustion
Below Mid level	Bearish	Strong Bearish
Above Mid level	Bearish	Bearish & Pullback / Caution
Overbought	Bearish	Bearish & Overbought

When a sector is bullish, but correcting in the short-term, it is an opportunity to participate in the uptrend. When the breadth chart is oversold in such sectors, it provides an entry opportunity with an attractive risk reward. When a sector is bearish and the breadth is overbought, it offers an affordable trade opportunity to initiate short trades.

When you identify a stock through a top-down approach in the medium-term and the stock is correcting in the short-term, it would provide a trade opportunity with an affordable risk. For example, consider a scenario where an index, the sector, and the ratio chart are trading above their 200-day moving average. But if the stock price chart corrects to the 50-day moving average, you can consider long trades using the recent swing low as a stop loss. The trade may be considered after some signs of bullishness is apparent in the price chart.

Let us consider another example where the index, sector and RS charts are trading above moving average while the price chart is in a column 'O' in the short-term. Look for a column reversal to 'X' and buy with a stop-loss below the recent column of 'O'.

This is an example of a bullish eagle pattern in stocks identified using a top-down approach.

Lion of the sector

Sectors go through a rotation even during bull markets. Leading sectors of the bull market would also correct or go through a short-term cycle of underperformance and consolidation. When a sector is underperforming, the stocks that are outperforming the sector during such times are lions of the sector. There must be something inherently bullish about those stocks. And these stocks can deliver significant returns when the sector turns bullish.

This is particularly useful when a sector is not going through a severe fall in price. In this scenario, the underperformance is just a technical correction and the stocks that perform well during this phase are the interesting candidates to focus on. Price breakouts in them are worth trading.

Here is another scenario. Suppose the market and the sector ratio are above their long-term moving average, but the sector is below its short-term moving average. In this scenario, when the stock to sector ratio crosses above the moving average, it would be a buying opportunity if the initial risk is affordable.

Let us visualise the same scenario in P&F charts. The index and sector RS charts are positioned above the moving average. The sector RS is in a column of 'O'. The stock to sector ratio is in a column of 'X' or triggering a double-top buy with an affordable risk.

Given below is a daily candlestick chart of the Nifty metal index with the high-low momentum index.

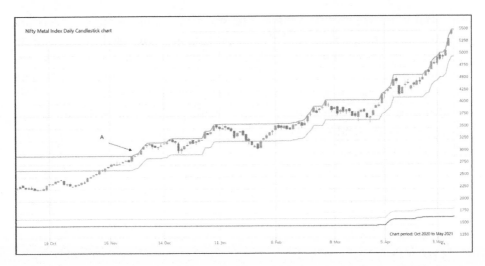

Figure 11.21: Daily candlestick chart of Nifty Metal index with High-Low Momentum index

The Nifty Metal index registered a new 250-day high in November 2020 at point A. It remained within the upper bullish momentum band thereafter indicating a strong momentum in the sector.

Featured below is a daily ratio chart of SAIL to Nifty metal index plotted along with a 50-day average line and a 20-day RSI line.

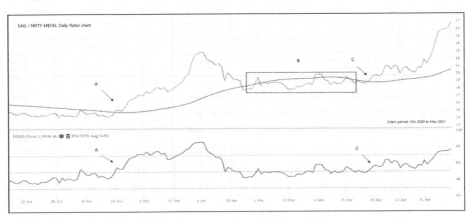

Figure 11.22: SAIL to Nifty 50 index daily ratio chart plotted along with a 50-day average line and a 20-day RSI line

SAIL moved above the moving average line at point A. The stock price was above the 200-day average already. The RSI in the above chart too moved above 50 at A. After the initial outperformance until point A, the stock corrected even though the metal index was outperforming. The stock was amongst initial leaders but went through a temporary period of underperformance followed by consolidation at B. But stock resumed its outperformance and the ratio chart moved above the moving average and the RSI too moved above 50 at C, in late Match 2021. This was followed by another rally resulting in a strong outperformance.

Below is a daily ratio chart of SAIL to Nifty 50 Index plotted along with a 50-day average line and a 20-day RSI line.

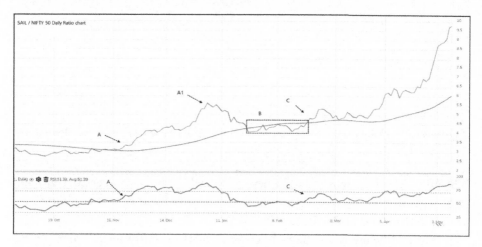

Figure 11.23: SAIL to Nifty 50 index daily ratio chart plotted along with a 50-day average line and a 20-day RSI line

SAIL was outperforming Nifty and Metal index between A to A1 in the above chart. There was a brief period of consolidation at B. The stock resumed its outperformance versus Nifty at C in February 2021 even though it was underperforming the metal index. This means the stock was doing well but other metal stocks were outperforming. Soon the stock regained its momentum and outperformance.

SAIL was an example of outperforming and leading stock of the sector going through a temporary period of correction.

Below is a daily 0.25% x 3 Point & Figure chart of SAIL during this period.

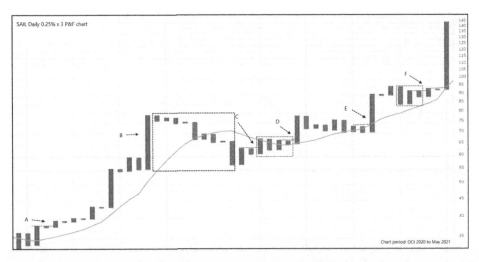

Figure 11.24: Daily 0.25% x 3 Point & Figure chart of SAIL during this period

Point A is a double-top buy signal with affordable risk above moving average during November 2020 when the sector was outperforming Nifty and SAIL was outperforming the metal sector.

This was a perfect scenario of a Flying Sector -> Flying Stock -> Swing breakout with an affordable entry.

There was no double-bottom sell pattern until the anchor column at B. C is anchor column follow-through pattern that was in February 2021 when stock resumed its outperformance versus Nifty. The anchor column follow-through here is an objective pattern that clearly showed that the stock has completed the consolidation and is set to move again. Point D is a four-column triangle breakout pattern above the moving average line with an affordable risk.

Pattern E is another anchor column follow-through pattern above average line in March 2021 when the stock resumed its outperformance against the Metal index. Pattern F is a continuation triangle breakout with an affordable risk-reward with the price trading above the average line. It was followed by a strong uptrend and outperformance. During the consolidation breakout at F, the Nifty was bullish, the metal sector was outperforming against Nifty, and the stock was outperforming against the sector. More importantly, there was an objective pattern to initiate trades with a very affordable risk.

This is a classic case study of the concepts that we discussed for a top-down approach.

Flyers and KNKN

How about if I tell you that I studied the chart of Jindal Steel and bought Tata Steel instead. It might sound strange, but this has happened to me many times.

Stocks in the above examples were from the metal sector. When you see stocks are moving from the sector and triggering price breakouts, choose to trade the stock which is an outperformer. If I see a breakout in Jindal Steel, and if I know that Tata Steel has been mostly a winner of the rally, I would like to check the chart of Tata Steel as well. If the price pattern in Tata Steel is also bullish, I would prefer to trade Tata Steel instead of JSW Steel. This is just an example.

The message here is to not get influenced by names and focus on principles. I saw cement stocks moving, and Ramco Cements was doing well. I checked other cement stocks but ended up buying Grasim. Why? Because Grasim was outperforming and displayed relative strength. If cement does well, Grasim will do better. Similarly, metals were doing well but I noticed reversal and weakness in stocks which were only for that day. Hence, I looked at metal stocks and identified that Jindal Steel is a relatively weak performer on that day in that space. I saw a reversal pattern in that stock also and shorted that because it was an underperformer of that sector.

This approach can do wonders in your stock picking. Identifying stocks based on strength and weakness. Looking at one stock, and trading another based on sector and stock RS is a logical approach. I call this concept KNKN–*Kahin pe Nigahe Kahin pe Nishana.* This means you look at something but aim for something else.

If you are using the 200-day moving average as a trend filter and if the price crosses its 200-day average line, then check if it is outperforming the benchmark and the peer group. You might probably find better stocks in the same group. For example, if you notice Maruti moving above the 200-day average then check the charts of other Auto stocks. If say Tata Motors is outperforming against the Auto index and showing more strength, then buy it. You were looking at stock 'A', but you ended up buying 'B' because 'B' was a flyer or had a better relative strength pattern.

How do you know who is a leader? The simple answer is to study the relative strength charts regularly. It will help you identify the leading stocks of that leg or the flyers of the rally.

You must have done this in trading or heard about it. If the stock of one sector is bullish, look to buying another stock as well. For example, if HINDPETRO has done well, then BPCL is also expected to do well. This approach may sound logical in most instances, especially when the overall sector is in a strong outperformance cycle. But, what would make an overall difference is the individual company-specific factors that would help a stock become a top performer from the sector. Even fundamentally weak stocks could move up during sector outperformance. But this will not be sustained and the weaker ones would deliver inferior returns. If a sector performs but the stock does not contribute enough or underperforms, it is a case of a cat pattern or a bearish star pattern. These stocks will underperform significantly when the sector goes through a correction or consolidation.

The bottom line is, if you have a view or opinion on a sector or index, buy the flyer of the rally or the leader of that leg.

Till now we have been discussing the top-down approach. Let us now shift our focus to the bottom-up approach.

Bottom-up approach

In the bottom-up approach, the first step is to analyze the stock, then looking at the sector and the overall market trend thereafter. Some well-managed companies have good management, business prospects and a compelling fundamental story.

Such stocks would continue to perform irrespective of the market or sector trend. If there is a strong fundamental conviction in the stock, there is no need to look at market trends or averages. That's about stock analysis and would not qualify as a bottom-up approach.

You can use screeners and shortlist stocks that suit your criteria based either on price analysis or any other kind of analysis. If the number of stocks qualifying the screener criteria is more, you can filter them based on relative strength analysis. Your stock selection would improve dramatically if you can identify the ones that are market or sector leaders and if the sector is also an outperformer.

Instead of picking a stock expecting it to do better than the market, it would be logical to invest in stocks that are outperforming the markets. Price is the reality and 'IS' (price) is more powerful than 'CAN' (assumptions) in the markets.

In the above process, even if the price pattern is bullish, but not outperforming the index, we will ignore such candidates. If you are still left with a huge list of stocks, check how the sector to which the stock belongs is performing. This can help filter the list further.

When a stock is moving irrespective of the sector, the individual story is bullish. It is the lion of the group it belongs to. If the group also moves, the stock will do much better. If the group does not move, the move of the stock depends entirely on the stock-specific factors.

If a stock is registering a new high or if there is a significant price breakout, or there is a growth in earnings and top line, it is a stock to look for from a trading and investment perspective. If you notice a similar behaviour in other stocks from the same group or sector, then there must be something favourable happening at the sector or industry level as well.

This can help in also exploring peer group stocks and analyze related sectors. This is a bottom-up approach. The positive kicker for your portfolio is that the sector is also performing well which will contribute to the rise in the stock, and you have also invested in the leader of the space.

Bullish consolidation and bearish consolidation

The horizontal pattern or range-bound price action in the price chart is a typical pattern of consolidation. It can be a box pattern or can come across as a triangular converging pattern of varying width. We do not know about the direction of the breakout unless it happens. We can consider this consolidation as an accumulation pattern if there is an upside breakout. The consolidation would be considered as a distribution pattern if there is a bearish breakout.

There is a shortcut or a trick to guess the direction of the breakout. Check the relative performance during price consolidation. If the ratio chart is bullish during the price consolidation and if the stock is not underperforming the index, the likely direction of the breakout would be bullish. The logic here is that the stock is displaying signs of strength when the index or sector is witnessing a correction. As the stock is not underperforming during the consolidation, it would be logical to expect a bullish breakout post the consolidation pattern.

A similar logic applies to the underperforming stocks. In such cases, the breakout direction is likely to be to the downside.

Strategy Indices

There are some strategy indices developed by the National Stock Exchange of India based on investment strategies and models they have designed. These are very useful and effective when we perform relative strength and use the breadth analysis tools in these indices.

Nifty Alpha 50, Nifty Quality 30 of Nifty 100 and Nifty 200 indices are examples of such types of indices available and regularly updated by NSE. For example, Nifty Alpha 50 aims to measure the performance of securities listed on NSE with high Alphas. It tracks the performance of 50 stocks with high Alphas in the last year. Weights of stocks in the index are assigned based on alpha values. Security with the highest alpha in the index is assigned the highest weight.

People use this index for benchmarking portfolios, launching index funds, structured products, and ETFs etc. We can plot such types of indices against Nifty to track their relative performance.

Below is Nifty Alpha 50 / Nifty 50 daily ratio chart.

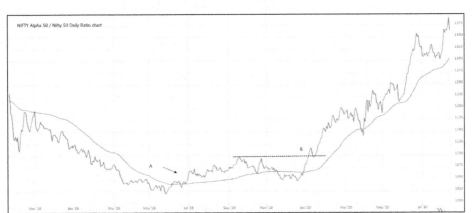

Figure 11.25: Nifty Alpha 50 / Nifty daily ratio chart with a 100-period AMA

Alpha 50 index started outperforming at point A. There was a pattern breakout at point B above the average line during January 2020. The alpha index went up by about 50% in the year 2020 while Nifty was up by around 14%.

When we see the strategy index outperforming, we need can find the leading candidates in the index making it outperform and look for trade opportunities in them. The tools and techniques we discussed in sector analysis are also applicable to these strategy indices.

Asset classes, sectors, indices, and stocks go through multiple cycles. By tracking the trend of the sectors, index, and market, we can reduce the pain during the non-favourable phase of a stock or sector and the group it belongs to. Ignoring all these and just sticking to a price-based system and accepting the drawdowns during bad phases is also a viable strategy. But I strongly believe that relative strength and breadth analysis can improve the profitability of price-based trading systems.

Let us discuss another interesting feature in the TradePoint software which will be helpful in this context.

D – Sectors

We discussed sector performance. Below are important tools that we need to keep in mind regarding sector trends:

- Price trend and pattern
- The trend in relative performance against a broader market index such as the Nifty 50
- Performance versus other sectors

- Momentum and exhaustion–Oversold or overbought
- The breadth of the sectors–the behaviour of stocks in the sector

Using a ranking system based on the above criteria, we have created a tool called D-Sector in TradePoint software. This feature provides an overview of this information on a single screen.

If the price trend and relative strength trend are bullish, the instrument is bullish. We can get this information from the fusion matrix. Using the ultimate matrix, we can also ascertain if the instrument is bullish versus the other instruments. The PMOX indicator will indicate if the stock is in a momentum phase or if there is a pullback opportunity. All breadth related concepts that were discussed in the earlier chapter would provide information about the trend of stocks in the sector and whether the breadth indicator is overbought, oversold, neutral or in strong momentum.

Here is a screenshot of the D-sectors feature available in the TradePoint web version.

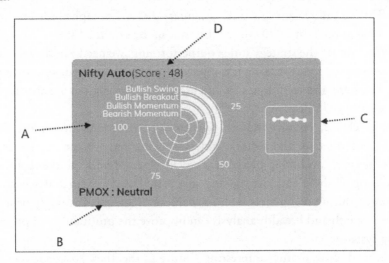

Image 11.11: D-Sectors calculation

The information relating to the breadth is captured under A in the above image. It indicates the number of stocks that are in a bullish swing, the number of stocks where a bullish breakout is triggered, the number of stocks in a bullish momentum and the number of stocks in bearish momentum.

The information about the PMOX indicator is captured at B. It indicates whether the PMOX Indicator is in bullish momentum, Neutral, Overbought or Oversold zone.

Point C indicates the trend score over the last few sessions.

Point D is a cumulative score based on the trend of price, relative strength and performance compared to other sectors.

You can view the above information in the short-term, medium-term, and long-term time frames. The screen provides all relevant information about the sector in a single screen.

The sectors are ranked, sorted, and displayed in a heatmap format. This helps to analyze the trend, breadth, and relative performance of all sectors.

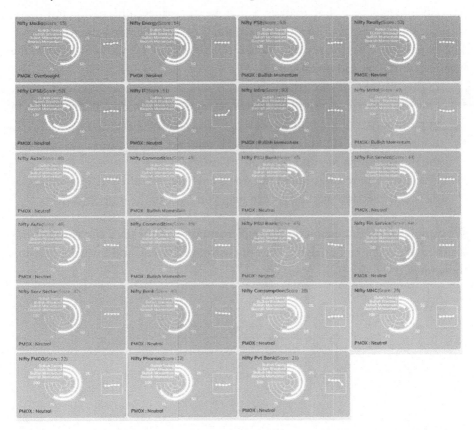

Image 11.12: D-Sectors report

The method and indicators discussed earlier help to objectively identify the outperforming stocks, and sectors. The concepts discussed thus far apply to all timeframes. I have explained many concepts to identify stocks on the buy-side. The reverse logic or approach holds good for identifying and trading bearish stocks.

I have extensively used the moving average as a trend filter but feel free to experiment with any other indicator. It is essential to focus on the concepts and the principles and not the method. You can use any trading system, indicator, or pattern instead of moving average to objectively identify and define the trend as bullish or bearish. You can also define a higher low pattern as a bullish pattern and a lower high pattern as a sign of bearishness. The key is to make it as objective as possible. You can frame rules for trading price charts and use also include the ratio chart analysis discussed in this book to fine-tune your stock selection. The best advantage of technical analysis is that we can achieve objectivity and frame rules for our trading and investment activities. Avoid predicting the price action and focus instead on the process. This is one of the key aspects of success in the business of trading and investment.

In this chapter, we discussed:

- How to analyze different asset classes and markets and make them an important part of the process of our trading and investment.
- RS Switch helps you know how to treat the asset class or the sector based on the trend and the method that you are using.
- It is important to understand the sector analysis and different approaches for the stock selection method. It can help you stick to the outperformers.

We completed the discussion on the implementation of the tools and the methods for the asset and sector analysis. Let's discuss more trading and investment using these tools.

Chapter 12

TRADING AND INVESTMENT

. . . .

We have discussed the study and the importance of relative strength. The inclusion of relative strength analysis in your routine will be useful from a trading and investment perspective. Here are a few aspects where relative strength study will be helpful.

- Market, sector and stock selection.
- Understanding the strength of the trend and the market phase to decide the appropriate strategy.
- It complements price analysis.
- Divergence in price and relative strength is a crucial lead indicator.
- Ranking the stocks based on performance and ratio trends.

Breadth indicators will capture information about the participation of the stocks from the sector and the broader market and will ensure that you do not get complacent during strong trends. Breadth extreme zones are extremely helpful tools during sideways or range-bound market conditions. Oversold breadth when the market or sector is in an uptrend and overbought when the market or sector is in a downtrend offers a trading opportunity with an affordable risk.

You can trade based on the ratio chart by engaging in pair trading that we discussed in the earlier chapter. But you cannot place a stop-loss in the system in that case, and you must track the ratio chart to figure out when to exit. More importantly, the price and relative strength analysis complement each other.

Let us discuss some important aspects related to trading and investing using relative strength and breadth in this chapter.

Trading Systems

One important aspect that I learned all these years is that there is no alternative to a process-oriented approach for consistent success in trading or investment. Mindless speculation, baseless trading and exorbitant use of leverage are the common reasons why people lose money. The biggest issue in the market is that there are no rules to trade. Executing a trade is just a thought away. It is essential to gain control over this aspect.

If the focus is on the process, money can be made in the markets. On the other hand, if the focus is on money or the outcome, you might end up losing what you have.

I have stressed enough in both my previous books on the importance of objectivity and a process-oriented approach to trading. This is one of the primary reasons why I love noiseless charts. I have tried to bring objectivity in relative strength and breadth charts as well. Topics covered until now including scoring the occurrences, deciding the zones, and naming the patterns are intended to achieve objectivity. Having a ratio and relative strength chart along with indicators allows us to define rules and design systems using relative strength charts.

We typically create trading systems using the price chart. There are very few who include relative strength and breadth charts as a part of their trading systems. If you integrate breadth and relative strength study in your strategy, it will result in a sharp improvement in your trading edge.

Relative strength patterns, indicators, breadth charts and price patterns can help one create a trading system using a combination of price and relative strength charts.

Remember, if there is a breakout in price, and the relative strength chart is bullish—the breakout is strong. If the price is at support, and the relative strength chart is bullish—the support is strong. If there is a bearish breakout in price, and the relative strength chart is also weak—the downside breakout is strong. If the price is at resistance, and the relative strength chart is bearish—the resistance is significant.

Price analysis can complement relative strength analysis and can vice versa. The net impact would be reduced drawdown. In fact, RS study can help reduce the drawdown of price systems, and price analysis can reduce the drawdown of RS based strategy.

Investing

The concepts that we have discussed thus far apply to all timeframes and all types of trading or investing. Investing for the long-term in blue-chip companies is a different approach. Unless you are buying and willing to pass it on to your grandchildren, you are indulging in trading in some form or the other. You could either be a short-term, medium-term, or long-term trader. We may call it either investing or trading.

People often want to invest their money for a certain period like a year or beyond. But, if you want to withdraw profits or need that money after a certain period, you are essentially indulging in trading. You can call it long-term trading.

The world markets and their underlying dynamics have undergone a big change over the past several years. Information is easily and almost immediately available now. Price moves that used to take several years are happening now in a matter of a few weeks or months. The moves that you would not even get in several years, seems to transpire within days and month during strong trending phase. Identify trends and be prepared to shift your investments across assets. The active investment approach has immense potential to produce significant returns.

It is difficult in today's highly regulated environment to manipulate prices beyond a point. You must remember to stay away from those "manipulated" stocks or instruments when you follow price and relative-strength-oriented strategies.

If you are serious about trading, you must have objectively defined rules for entry and exit. When I talk about processes or rules, it must include clear and objective rules for entry, exit, position sizing and capital allocation. Your core method can be subjective, objective, technical analysis, fundamental analysis, quant, or anything else. But without a clear thought process and well-defined plan for different outcomes, the successful investment would be difficult.

Trading methods keeps evolving as we learn new concepts, but the core principles should be in place for a trader or investor. The core principle should encompass aspects that suit one's trading or investment style, temperament, and belief system. It is essential to ensure that trading strategy evolves around these core principles.

We have covered various aspects relating to the relative strength and breadth analysis. Numerous tools were discussed to study relative strength and breadth. A simple example of core rules of a system trading could be trading the continuation patterns in the outperforming stocks using the top-down approach.

The strategy adopted to identify these stocks may be different, but this principle has stood the test of time for me, and it is very much an integral part of my belief system.

As an investor, it is important to understand the trend of asset classes and identify where the funds are flowing. If the equity market is outperforming, then you will do better by increasing the allocation in favourable groups and sectors in the equity market. When the tide turns against equities, then move your money from equities to fixed-income assets or gold. Allocation to asset class and sectors should be decided as per the relative strength analysis.

Relative strength is a leading indicator. Every stock that becomes a multi-bagger from an investment perspective would appear in RS studies beforehand.

All concepts that we have discussed, are applicable for higher timeframe trading or investment as well as short term trading. Use a higher time frame chart such as a weekly or monthly chart if you want to stay in a trade for a longer period. You may also increase the box value in P&F charts to study bigger time frames.

Portfolio building

The relative strength patterns that we have discussed can be defined by simply applying tools like the 200-period moving average in price and ratio charts. A 250-day high-low momentum index or 3% P&F breadth indicators can be followed for breadth analysis. Stocks trading above the 200-day RS Indicator can be added to the list. Use the 10-column moving average in the P&F chart as the exit criteria if you wish to participate in the trend and ride the winners.

You can design a portfolio based on relative strength rules. For example, you can rank the stocks based on the RS indicator and invest in the top eight or 12 stocks in Nifty 50. An indicator period of 120 days or 250 days is recommended. You can adjust the portfolio monthly for entries. Exit the stock if it falls below the zero line. This way, you remain invested in relatively strong stocks. Refer to the points we discussed in Chapter 8 for investing based on ranking. There are many such types of possibilities of rebalancing tricks in a portfolio based on relative strength analysis tools we have discussed in the book.

A simple rule of thumb is, do not to remain long in stock when its cumulative score drops below zero in the fusion matrix. The general question while building a portfolio is that how to shortlist the stocks when multiple stocks qualify based on your study. If you are a running price-based system, then using a relative strength analysis can help you weed out candidates. If multiple stocks qualify even after the relative strength filter, the best answer is First-in, First-out or FIFO. Focus on the strong stocks that emerge as winners from the important market bottom. The top candidates from this list tend to remain strong performers.

The concept of relative strength analysis makes us focus on winners which is essential to generate alpha or outperform the markets. It may advance on the back of a few winners, and we should not end up getting stuck finding value and investing in stocks that are doing nothing.

When there is a bull market, many stocks perform simultaneously. It's a problem of plenty from an investment perspective.

Identifying the outliers and winning stocks is possible using relative strength analysis. It helps in-stock selection strategy and helps make a better decision. The performance of bullish trading systems can improve if the allocation is reduced in bearish relative strength instruments.

Remember this basic and cardinal rule: Avoid buying in bear markets. When the markets are falling, keep in mind the lions and stars. Buy them when the market stabilises and shows signs of strength. The strategy in bear markets should be to sell on weakness and not buying the strength. Remember that in a bullish trend, supports are more important than resistances and in bear markets, resistances are more important than supports.

Investing in outperforming stocks and sectors work well if it turns out to be a bullish year for the equity market. If the stock market reverses, the strong stocks can underperform drastically. It is therefore important to focus on exits. Let us discuss more exits.

Exits

Even stocks in strong trends go through short-term underperformance. When a stock is in a bearish RS trend against the index and the sector, then the money is flowing out from the stock and moving to other stocks of the group or maybe even other sectors. This is where one needs to be cautious and look for exit options to seek better investment opportunities.

Overbought breadth in a higher timeframe is an indication of exhaustion. Overbought conditions in multiple timeframes is an important signal to take note of. I discussed the concepts of breadth zones. They can also help in planning exits.

If the trend is strong and the market breadth is neutral, you should ride the trades and stay in the move. If the breadth is moving towards exhaustion and if there is a bearish star kind of a pattern in the stock or sector that you are holding, you can then tweak your exit strategy and decide to book profits or adopt an aggressive exit approach.

The RS and ratio chart turning negative or not being in sync with the price can be a good reason to exit an instrument and shift to a better performer. If you use a ranking model, any stock going below the mid-level in the ranking hierarchy should not be a part of the portfolio. For example, stocks underperforming on multiple timeframes will invariably have a score of zero or a negative value in the matrix table. Such stocks should be excluded from the portfolio.

If the price is bullish but the RS is turning bearish, then shift to the better performing instrument. This also makes you book profits which is an essential part of utilizing your capital. Riding bigger trends is easier said than done. Pyramiding in winning stocks must be your goal. To begin with, you may consider taking profits and re-entering on continuation patterns.

As a rule of thumb, reduce allocation to the portfolio when the equity market starts underperforming other asset classes. If the underperformance continues, it could signal a major reversal, and you should look to drastically cut your exposure to the equity asset class and switch to those assets which are either trending or less risky assets.

On many occasions, you might have regrets about having exited a stock too early. Exiting too early to shift to something else is a big mistake. You can earn more by sticking to the same stock instead. Remain invested in the stocks that are in an uptrend. When you are tempted to book profit, ask yourself what will you do with that money? You will look to invest in some other stock. If so, why not remain invested in something that is already performing well. Treat the existing profitable trade as a continuation pattern trade in your books and ride the same stock. You may have fresh stop-loss. It is all in the mind.

Life in markets is not simple. Searching for the perfect entry-exit methods or the search for a holy grail never ends. If you are a trader, there will be instances where your stop loss will be triggered, or the price might move up even further after your exit or maybe you missed participating in stocks that you had identified as winners. All these are part of the business.

Accepting that these factors do happen is essential to be a successful trader or investor. Most professional and experienced traders take these events in their stride and move on. The critical difference between a rookie investor and an experienced one is that the latter group understand the above factors and focus on important aspects such as managing risk, not chasing the trades, and avoiding revenge trading.

The advantage of retail traders and investors is that they can buy or sell instantly. Unlike large funds, they do not have to plan the accumulation or distribution of their holdings. They can place a stop-loss and manage risk effectively. The large funds are a bit constrained in this regard owing to the scale at which they operate.

It is crucial to understand which events are more relevant for the market. People track and draw a comparison between events such as past state elections and RBI policy. I have never seen the result of a state election or such other things impacting the market unless there is an impending Lok Sabha or central election. Unless there is a big surprise, the markets would not react significantly to the RBI policy or state election results. Instead, the retailers will be over-cautious, and many would fall for the Hedge-trap or take hedge that is driven by an unwarranted fear of minor events.

Markets typically react to the news that would impact the GDP and earnings, and other major government policy decisions. If the markets are not reacting to bearish news, it is then a bullish sign. Similarly, markets not reacting to bullish news has bearish implications.

Hedge Trap

If you consider a hedge due to an upcoming event or driven by worries about overnight risk, then such hedges might not prove beneficial for most of the time. Unless you have backtested or if hedging is part of your system rules, hedging a position due to the fear of carrying overnight positions will not result in profits. Remember the hedge also has a cost and it will affect the profitability of your trading system. Over time, you will realise that those fear-based hedging resulted in increased costs of the system and led to underperformance.

Another point is, if you are shorting weak stocks in the bull market, you are trading with the trend. Those stocks are inversely proportionate to the market, they will continue to behave the same. A hedging strategy requires a different approach.

Remember, bearish setups, which are exactly opposite to bullish setups, does not necessarily work in strong bullish trends. During a reversal, most of the strong stocks would also correct. The bearish star stocks are better candidates for trading reversals and or hedging.

Position sizing

Position sizing is also an important aspect of trading and investment.

When you trade or invest in the stock and wish to increase the position size, you have two options to achieve this.
*   Add to your holdings when the price falls after your previous entry. (Averaging)
*   Add to your quantity when the price rises and confirms the strength in the trend. (Pyramiding)

When you are trading based on any system, there will be a profitable phase and a drawdown phase where the system does not perform well.

Broadly, there are two ways of position sizing while trading a system— Martingale and Anti-Martingale.

The Martingale system was introduced by French mathematician Paul Pierre Levy in the 18th century. According to the Martingale system, you should double the position size when your last trade was a losing trade. You should reduce the position to half when your last trade was a winning trade.

This approach is based on the premise that a system will not have a losing period forever. The losing streak will be followed by a winning trade. Increased size of the winning trade will help recover the losses incurred during the drawdown period.

The exact opposite of the Martingale approach is the Anti-Martingale strategy.

In the Anti-Martingale system, think about increasing the position size when you had a winning trade and reduce it when you had a losing trade.

It operates on the premise that when a system is in a favourable phase, you should trade with more quantity to take advantage of the positive phase of the trading system. You should trade with less quantity when your trading system is going through a drawdown or losing phase.

People use either of these strategies or their variations while deciding on position sizing. There are pros and cons of both strategies. It also depends on the nature of the strategy and what suits your approach. But having a logical rule-based approach to position sizing can help improve the overall returns. Implement RS based position sizing. Increase exposure in outperforming markets, sectors, and stocks. Use relative strength patterns for deciding allocation in stocks.

Beyond a point, finetuning a system is difficult. It is the position sizing engine that will help improve the portfolio returns. When you are trading a system, you must not stop when it is in the midst of a drawdown phase. The pain endured during the drawdown phase can be reduced by using appropriate position sizing strategies. Reducing the positions during unfavourable phases and increasing during the favourable phase should be a broad goal. Relative strength study and breadth analysis can be helpful in this regard.

Volume

Many traders also use volume as confirmation. If you are in this camp, then a rising volume could be used as an additional filter to shortlist candidates which are bullish in the price and ratio charts. Typically, higher volume on advancing days and lower volume on corrective days are considered a bullish volume pattern. Strong volume during falling days and low volume during advancing days is a classic signature of a bearish environment. The bullish volume pattern in outperformers is more bullish and the bearish volume pattern in underperformers is more bearish.

Let us take a brief look at Mutual Funds. The steady growth in the investor base in India has resulted in a strong rise in the assets under the management of the mutual fund industry.

Mutual Fund

The daily NAV (Net Asset Value) of Mutual Fund schemes is widely available in the public domain. The NAV is calculated using the total value of the stocks held by the fund. We can use the daily NAV value to draw the line chart of any mutual fund scheme. This chart will capture the performance of the Mutual Fund in a chart format. If we can plot the chart, we can also use other tools associated with technical analysis in the NAV charts as well.

We cannot plot a candlestick chart of mutual fund schemes since we get only one price as NAV which is the closing price of the day. We do not get the open, high, and low data for mutual fund NAVs and hence it is not feasible to plot candlestick or bar charts. We can however plot a ratio chart by dividing the NAV by the Nifty index or any other instrument.

Featured below is a daily ratio chart of the NAV of ICICI Pru Technology Fund (G) divided by the Nifty index.

Figure 12.1: Daily ratio chart of the NAV of ICICI Pru Technology Fund (G) divided by the Nifty index

The green line in the above chart is a 200-period moving average. A rising ratio line suggests that the fund is outperforming Nifty while a falling ratio line suggests that the fund is underperforming versus Nifty. The ratio line crossed above the above moving average line at point A in May 2020 after recording a series of higher lows patterns. There was a horizontal resistance breakout at point B that happened above the moving average line. Another continuation breakout was triggered at C.

As we plot P&F or other noiseless charts by using a single price, we can therefore plot a P&F chart of mutual fund NAVs.

Take a look at the chart of HDFC mid-cap Opportunities fund (G) to Nifty Index in the P&F format plotted. The 20-column moving average and a 20-period XO zone are also plotted in the chart.

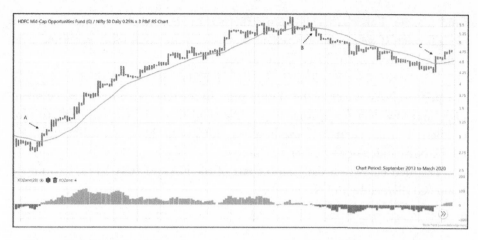

Figure 12.2: Daily HDFC mid-cap opportunities fun (G) to Nifty Index 0.25% x 3
P&F chart with the 20-column moving average and a 20-period XO zone

The ratio moved above the moving average at point A in September 2013
indicating outperformance. The XO-Zone also turned bullish. The ratio turned
bearish at point B during May 2018. It again turned bullish during February
2020 when a bullish anchor column was printed.

Notice that the above chart covers price action of about six and a half years.
Keeping track of NAV charts and RS studies based on them can help identify
favourable sectors and the relevant mutual funds' schemes to invest in. One can
also analyze Debt, Hybrid, ETF, Global, small-cap, mid-cap, multi-cap, sector-
specific, thematic funds to understand which space is moving and which mutual
fund scheme is performing better.

The most common technique of ranking or assessing the funds is based
on their past performance, management, fund house and fund manager's track
record, AUM size and the nature of the stocks held in the fund portfolio. The
NAV analysis will reflect the cumulative impact of all these factors and will also
help identify if the fund is outperforming the benchmark index or not. We can
rank the mutual fund schemes based on NAV and the relative performance of the
fund. We can rank MFs using the tools that we studied earlier such as the fusion
matrix, ultimate matrix, ratio trend matrix, relative strength scanner or the ratio
rank scanner.

Below is an example of funds in the Pharma sector sorted based on the multi-
timeframe ultimate matrix.

Table 12.1: Pharma sector multi-timeframe ultimate matrix

Scrip	LCP	Score-0.25%	Score-1%	Score-3%	▼ Total
ICICI Pru Pharma Healthcare & Diagnostics (P.H.D) Fund-(G)	20.33	8	7	5	20
Mirae Asset Healthcare Fund-Reg(G)	21.92	8	6	6	20
Nippon India Pharma Fund(B)	297.24	4	8	6	18
Nippon India Pharma Fund(G)	297.24	4	8	6	18
SBI Healthcare Opp Fund-Reg(G)	228.35	5	5	1	11
Tata India Pharma & Healthcare Fund-Reg(G)	16.92	4	3	0	7
UTI Healthcare Fund-Reg(G)	161.56	0	5	2	7
DSP Healthcare Fund-Reg(G)	21.48	4	0	2	6
Aditya Birla SL Pharma & Healthcare Fund-Reg(G)	18.63	3	2	0	5
IDBI Healthcare Fund-Reg(G)	18.82	3	1	0	4

The relative strength analysis of the mutual fund can be an extremely helpful tool from an investment perspective.

Types of sessions

I have worked as a dealer and placed orders for clients during the initial years of my career in the stock market. I have spent considerable time in tape reading. I did not know much about charts then, but I practised screen reading or tape reading.

I am trying to channelize my thought process and my experience in the hope of converting it into a process-oriented objective approach.

For example, when I look at the ticker tape, I like to watch the stocks which display strengths or weaknesses. But the key question is what do I mean by strength or weakness? By strength, I refer to the stocks that are not falling much when the market is weak. Such stocks quickly reverse when the market turns around. Trading price patterns in such stocks prove rewarding.

When the market is on an uptrend, stocks typically move up along with the market. When the market falls or consolidates, a few stocks would fall less or even continue to rise. When the market recovers, these stocks would typically perform even better. A pick-up in trading volume during this period can be a nice confirmatory signal.

While the index is rising, if a stock is unable to cross its important resistance, then that resistance is a significant level to watch. The key is to avoid pre-empting. Always take trades based on your system rules. Similarly, when the index is falling, but the stock has not broken the prior support level, it may be considered a strong support level. You must have realised by now that the former is a bearish scenario that refers to bearish star pattern candidates, and the latter a bullish star pattern.

To define the above observations, the rising ratio chart is bullish, falling ratio chart is bearish. The lion, cat and star pattern candidates are interesting ones to focus on. The concepts and simple patterns that you have learned in this book are extremely powerful and are a result of years of study and experience. In simple words, look for lions when markets are falling and cats when markets are rising. These would offer interesting trade opportunities if the market reverses.

For short-term trading, you need to track the markets regularly. Daily or weekly session trends are more relevant to you. You need to take advantage of strong trends in the lower timeframe. Being aware of the trend of the market, leading, and lagging sectors, the leading and lagging stocks, breadth position will help you immensely in selecting stocks and also in deciding the appropriate strategy.

When you study the markets after the session or the day is completed, there are some important things you can observe from it. The type of session and behaviour of the market can help you understand the market phase and choose your strategy.

There are some important aspects to consider while studying the behaviour of the past session:
- What was the market trend?
- Was there a trend continuation, sideways move, or a reversal?
- What is your view on the market for short-term and medium-term?
- Which sectors showed strengths and weaknesses?
- Which group and stocks outperformed and underperformed?
- Which relative strength pattern you will look for before you decide on price analysis?
- What was the breadth status?

Broadly, any trading session may be categorized into the four types listed below:
- Bullish
- Bearish
- Range-bound
- Volatile

The session in question could be the just concluded day, week or even a month. We have discussed that even during strong uptrends, the sector and stock rotation happens. Different stocks and sectors take the lead in different legs of the trend. That changes the nature of the session even when it was bullish. The bullish session does not always mean that all stocks performed well, or strong stocks and sectors did well.

Broadly, listed below are the various types in which we can categorize a session.

- When strong stocks rise, and weak stocks fall = Continuation session
- When strong stocks rise = Bullish continuation session
- When weak stocks fall = Bearish continuation session
- When strong stocks reverse and falls = Bearish reversal session
- When weak stocks reverse and rise = Bearish reversal session
- When consolidating stocks turn up= Bullish pullback session
- When consolidating stocks fall = Bearish pullback session
- When everything is falling = Waterfall
- When everything is rising = Rocket

The price range of sessions may vary. If it is a huge move, the session trend is strong. It can be a different type of day for a few groups and sectors but largely we can judge the type of day for the market as a whole.

I try to judge this when I read the screen every day. We need to know if a sector or group is the flavour of the market on that day, week, and month. This judgement helps in deciding the strategy for the following sessions. For example, if we see that it is a reversal session, we should stay away even from winners in that session and wait for the dust to settle.

If it was a continuation session, we should focus on winning stocks and the stocks that are in a strong momentum. Trying to find some other stocks instead of what are already performing well will be waste of time and effort. Better returns can be generated by trading stocks that are already in momentum. If it is a pullback session, it can be a field day for traders. It is an opportunity to find outperforming stocks that are in consolidation or correction. If such stocks trigger a bullish breakout in the pullback session, or if the underperforming stocks breach their supports and generate fresh bearish breakouts, such stocks will perform well in that session.

When it is either a waterfall or a rocket type of market, then do not try to be a superhero and just go with the flow. Identifying market types may seem like hindsight analysis but with consistent observation, your judgement improves, and you get the idea early in the day about the type of session that may be in store. This can be an extremely helpful strategy for short-term traders. How to treat relatively strong and weak stocks based on the day type can be a game-changing strategy. One more important observation in this context, when many instruments are strongly bullish or bearish at a time, then just trade the index.

You can also use real-time relative strength scanners to identify outperforming and underperforming stocks in that session. You can run this scanner using Nifty as the denominator and also use a moving average or any other indicator for shortlisting candidates. You can also run scanners for the patterns that we have discussed on relative strength P&F charts to identify interesting candidates to trade. The fusion matrix in real-time is also an extremely useful tool in this context.

You can also have a list of bullish candidates and bearish candidates ready for the next day based on the fusion matrix study of price and relative strength scores. A remarkably interesting table on the lower timeframe is the ratio trend matrix. One can study the RS pattern of the stocks over the last 15-20 bars on a 5 or 15-minute timeframe. This feature helps identify the patterns and objectively assign scores. Open Interest breadth is another useful indicator for short-term and derivatives trading. You can run a scanner using any other study that we have discussed in the book in real-time to facilitate better short-term trading decisions.

If you are a day trader or a very short-term trader, divide the trading session into three parts. In the first part of the day, look for stocks and sectors that are outperforming. In the middle part of the day, look for candidates who are sustaining the strength or weakness. Look for follow-through action in the third part of the session.

You can perform these studies in a single session or over a week or even a chosen phase of the market. During strong trends and continuation sessions, focus on the flyers and strong performers. During pullback, sessions focus on the lions, cats or identify the leaders that we discussed in the previous chapter. There will be phases where even the strong stocks will reverse, and a trading reversal formation will be more rewarding during such times. When you are trading reversal, try to identify the weak stocks in the strong sector or strong stocks in the weak sector. These stocks would offer trades with an affordable risk during such times.

Keep track of the leaders and laggards of the current leg from a trading perspective. Remember, KNKN pattern. When you see a stock that is rising, find the leader from the universe from the sector. Price at support or patterns offering an affordable trade opportunity in the price chart in the outperforming sectors is an effective trading strategy. This applies to all timeframes.

Patterns
Which patterns to look for in a relative strength chart is an important aspect of the strategy.

When markets are bullish and it is a bullish continuation session, you should look for flyers. You may have numerous instances where the stocks would have a massive uptrend without your participation in it. Every trader would have their share of such candidates. This is because it is exceedingly difficult to participate in them. Even if you do participate, you will be tempted to book profit early, or panic exit on a small counter-trend move.

It is difficult to participate in such stocks without the awareness of the relative strength concept and conviction. At times, you trade stocks that are not participating and ignore those already bullish. The bullish stocks continue to perform and the ones you traded may not do much. Keep track of the stocks that display strength during the correction. Such stocks would be the big winners when the market rebounds. This approach of identifying leaders in each leg is also relevant in lower timeframe trading too.

Let us dissect this and discuss the process.

The first thing that you must do is identify the trend in the Nifty index or the broader market index in:

- Short-term
- Medium-term and
- Long-term

Tools to assess the market trends include:

- Price analysis
- Relative strength with other asset classes
- Breadth

If the market or denominator was bullish, you will broadly confront one of these three patterns in stocks and sectors.

- Flying: Bullish continuation
- Cat: Bearish reversal
- Bearish star: Sign of bearishness

If the market or denominator was bearish, you will broadly confront one of these three patterns in stocks and sectors.

- Drowning: Bearish continuation
- Lion: Bullish reversal
- Bullish Star: Sign of bullishness

Once you are aware of the trend of the market, you can segregate the stocks and sectors based on the above patterns.

You must have a broad assessment of the market condition. Here are some pointers in this regard.

- What is your trading horizon? Is it short-term, medium-term or long-term?
- Have a view and assess the trend in the bigger timeframe, based on your trading horizon.

If you are looking for a short-term positional view, your view for the medium-term matters. If you are looking for a medium-term positional view, your view for the long-term matters.

Below are the patterns you should look for based on your view or market assessment:

- If the market was down or sideways, and you think the medium-term trend is not bearish: Look for lion, eagle and bullish star candidates.
- If the market was down or sideways, and you think the medium-term trend is also bearish: Look for drowning and bearish star candidates.
- If the market was up or sideways, and you think the medium-term trend is not bullish: Look for cat, bearish eagle, and bearish star candidates.
- If the market was up or sideways, and you think the medium-term trend is also bullish: Look for flying and lion candidates.

The above approach can assist you to decide the strategy. Keep in mind the BRS principles while studying the market and the RS patterns. The above pointers apply to all relative strength tools, studies, and breadth indicators that we have discussed in the book. You should try to arrive at your market assessment objectively based on the price, RS chart and breadth studies. Ratio chart with moving average, relative strength indicator, double-top buy, double-bottom sell the pattern or other P&F patterns are a few tools that may be used to make the market assessment very objective.

These concepts are applicable for short-term, medium-term as well as long-term trading. Choose your timeframe and use the same principles.

Trading Options

The technique that we have discussed can also be implemented in options trading as well. A simple approach could be to form a view on the underlying and then trade in the relevant options contract.

The portal Opstra.definedge.com has a wonderful set of tools to build and study various options strategies.

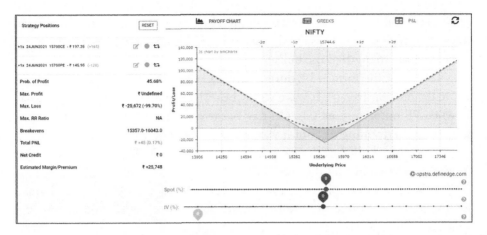

Image 12.1: Options strategy pay-off chart

We can also plot Call Option Premium to Put Option premium ratio chart. Think, what will the rising ratio indicate in that case?

Below is a chart of 15700 CE divided by 15700 PE on a five-minute timeframe plotted with a 200-period moving average.

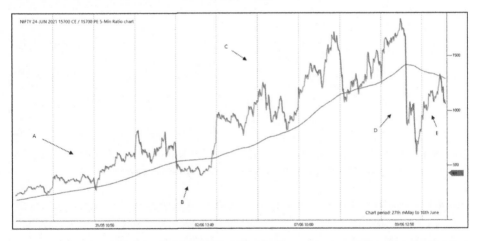

Figure 12.3: 15700 CE divided by 15700 PE on a five-minute timeframe plotted with a 200-period moving average

The vertical lines on the chart are intraday-separating lines. You can observe the trend of each session. At A, the CE was outperforming PE. The increase in the call option premium was more than the put options premium. The trend was bullish, and the momentum was strong. The CE or call option premium was underperforming the PE or put option premium at B. But the scenario changed towards the end of the session with the ratio chart rising above its moving average indicating the strength of the bulls.

The CE outperformed PE during period C when the ratio was rising and was above the moving average. It was a strong bearish session in the second half of day D when PE outperformed CE. On day E, there was a retracement session when CE was outperforming PE, but it was below the moving average.

You can track At-the-Money or Out of the Money Option liquid strike prices to plot the chart and read the behaviour.

Below is an example of a 1% x 3 P&F RS chart of 15500 CE divided by 15500 PE on a one-minute timeframe plotted with a 10-column moving average.

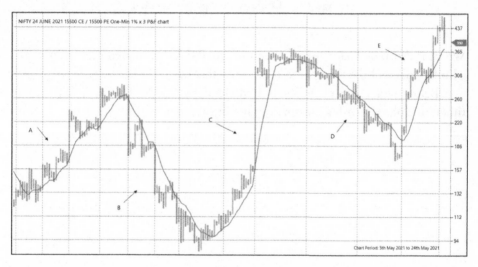

Figure 12.5: 1% x 3 P&F RS chart of 15500 CE divided by 15500 PE on a one-minute timeframe plotted with a 10-column moving average

CE was outperforming PE during A, C and D. PE was outperforming CE at B and C. You can also observe the patterns that we discussed earlier. It can help decide the trend and plan the strategy accordingly.

Periods A and C show a strong uptrend because CE is rising and PE is falling, and CE is outperforming. Period B and D are strong downtrends in the index because CE is falling and PE is rising, and PE is outperforming. Hence, the above chart shows the strength in the trend of underlying. The P&F patterns like turtle breakout and anchor column follow-through can prove highly effective on these charts.

Open Interest is another useful tool in Options. It tells us about the long or short built-up in the contract. We can divide the open interest of Puts by the Open interest of Calls. It is known as PCR or the Put-call-ratio. A PCR indicates that the open interest in PE is increasing and falling PCR suggests that Open interest in PE is reducing. There are many ways to read that indicator.

How about dividing the open interest of multiple strike prices instead of one and calculate the weightage dynamically? We call it Total Open Interest or TOI.

Below is a TOI chart of multiple-strike prices from 15700 CE and PE plotted in a 15-minute timeframe.

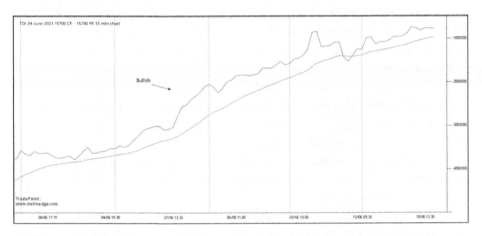

Figure 12.6: TOI chart of multiple-strike prices from 15700 CE and PE plotted in a 15-minute timeframe

Greenline is the TOI line and the orange line is the 20-period moving average line. You can keep the morning ATM strike price as the middle price of the chart and plot it to study the trend of the session. It shows multiple open interest and price trends in a single line. A rising TOI line is bullish, and a falling TOI line is bearish.

In this chapter:

- We tried to touch upon important aspects of the trading and investment using RS and breadth analysis.
- Session analysis, Mutual Fund and Options were also discussed.

The concepts and tools that we have discussed apply to any instrument. Focus on the principles and think about the possibilities. These lesser explored methods can help you define an edge in your methods and systems and help you outperform the markets.

Finally

Each chapter in the book offers numerous ideas to trade or invest using relative strength and breadth analysis. Numerous indicators that may be used in relative strength studies were also discussed. Even trading price patterns in top-performing stocks is a simple form of relative strength-based trading. But a structured approach using the ratio and relative strength methods are more important for better performance in the long run. Many successful traders and analysts have repeatedly talked about relative strength analysis but unless it is systematised and made rule-based, the real benefits may not fructify.

I have tried to touch all important aspects related to the relative strength and breadth analysis keeping in mind the practical aspects of trading and investment. It is a wonderful concept, there are many ways to deal with the concepts that are discussed in this book.

I have discussed a few principles related to relative strength and breadth in the book. Remain consistent with the tool or method that you opt for.

The top-down approach is what you can begin with for practising the subject. Plot the charts and study whether equities are the favoured asset class or if some other asset class is performing better. If the equity market is outperforming, then identify the groups and sectors that are performing better. Shortlist the candidates from outperforming sectors or groups.

If you are tracking any stock, or instrument that is bullish or bearish based on any study, then check the performance and price pattern for the sector or group. Also, check the performance of the peer group stocks. Then look for RS patterns that we have discussed in prior chapters. This applies right from short-term trading to lower timeframe and higher timeframe trading/investment. Relative strength is a leading indicator. Strong market leaders tend to show a strong relative strength pattern before the big move begins.

Identifying the theme or flavour of the market is an extremely important aspect for successful trading and investment. Understanding the sentiments, trends and where funds are moving are the other key aspects. Identify if the equity as an asset is in favour. If there are strong trends in other asset classes—you will do better by investing in those assets. If the equity market is doing good, try to identify where the money is flowing into? Is it the large caps, mid-caps, small caps? And ask yourself which sectors are performing better?

No trend remains forever in the market. There is a season for everything, and funds will shift, and sectors and stocks will rotate. That is how life and market works—nothing is permanent. When you spot a trend and tweak your strategy what may happen is that the market trend changes immediately thereafter. That is why many traders keep feeling that *Main jo karta hun uska ulta hi hota hai*!

There is a saying in Dalal Street–when you feel that you have the key, the market changes the lock.

Many people fail to understand the rotation concept even after having spent several years in the market. Phases change as per instruments and timeframes. There are times when end-of-the-day or higher timeframe strategies work well. They go sideways, and the trending move appears in the lower timeframe when momentum index strategies work better. When money moves from large-cap to others–the selling option works well in large caps. There are times when only large-cap moves. There are times when the index performs well, but your portfolio may not. Momentum trading strategies in the index should be the strategy to follow then. There would be times when the index does nothing or is range-bound but stocks may be buzzing. Trading the breakouts in the stocks would be a profitable strategy then.

That is why we say that there are good and bad phases of every price trading strategy that we follow. We can stick to that strategy, accept the drawdown, and take advantage when the favourable phase occurs. We can however try to identify these adverse phases by using relative strength and breadth charts and thereby improve the overall profitability.

Most people are comfortable in buying what is available cheap. They are in essence buying the drowning stocks. Hence the market may recover but their portfolios might not. People stick to weak stocks and book profit quickly in stocks that are doing well. It is exactly the opposite of what should be done. Investing in stocks that appear cheap and /or falling can prove expensive from a portfolio performance perspective.

We have seen that high PE stocks continue to do well in a bullish environment. There is a reason why the market is paying a high premium to such stocks. Most people are worried about buying stocks that are in an established trend. They instead look for an opportunity when the stocks correct.

There is a natural tendency for many traders and investors to look for a trend when the price is in a consolidation. When the strong trend gets underway, they feel that the price is too expensive to get involved. When there is a steep and established trend, there is this thought or fear of a bubble and they look for a reversal. This is a vicious cycle and prevents many from participating in strong trends.

If these people find someone's strategy working, they will immediately fall for it. But they would not be able to sit through or tolerate even a small drawdown. They keep switching strategies during difficult times and in the process, they end up trading the bad phases of multiple strategies. Markets are the same for everyone. Some behave irresponsibly or illogically and blame the market for their losses. Others make the best use of them and build a great future.

All successful traders have repeatedly attributed their success to the following factors:

- Manage risk.
- Avoid leverage.
- Get rid of weak stocks.
- Ride strong stocks.

Under positioning or dealing with a relatively small position size is better initially. You may increase the position size when you gain more experience. These simple things, if followed correctly, will not let your account be wiped out. These are the basics and extremely important things. If you do not get the basics right, nothing can help your cause.

But somehow, holding on to the profits is the toughest psychological aspect while holding on to losing trade is much easier. You need a reorientation in thinking to develop the right mindset and to get rid of the bad habits.

Talk to yourself and meditate regularly. Observe, ask questions and do not jump to conclusions. I have learned that understanding the problem without trying to jump to a conclusion is the most important skill to find permanent solutions. The repeated observations will help you develop conviction on several things.

Let me share an interesting anecdote in this context. I explained the concept of market breadth in a workshop. It was well-received. After the event, a person came to me and told me that the breadth chart concept was excellent, and he has lots of takeaways from the presentation. I was glad to hear that and thought that I had done a good job. Then he asked, "Can I get to see the breadth chart of a particular stock?" I then realised that I had done a terrible job with my presentation!

I failed to explain or drive home the point that you cannot plot the breadth chart for a stock. It is always plotted on a universe of stocks. The point is, please spend time understanding the concept. Our education system has taken enough tests of our memory. Let us now learn to think and understand the concepts. This will help you come up with your methods.

Don't try to replicate anyone's method, you will not be able to borrow the conviction required to follow it. You give me the world's best system on the five-minute candlestick chart, I will show you how to ruin it. Is there a problem with the system? No, it is just that I do not have the right mindset for trading it.

If you give me the best system based on Fibonacci numbers, I will not be able to trade it successfully. The problem is that I do not believe in the relevance of those numbers in the market context. Maybe, I am ignorant. But there is no point in blaming other methods just because you do not have confidence or conviction.

I keep observing these useless arguments people engage in social media or elsewhere about which system is better or which indicator is the best. They try to prove their methods are superior and disrespect others in the process. Tearing apart others' work does not prove your intelligence.

The basic premise of the argument is baseless. If I do not understand something, then it is my issue. Maybe I might not have spent enough time understanding it. I will typically focus on the merits of things that I understand and trust. The day you understand that there is nothing called the best system in the market, your journey to successful trading and investment will take a big leap thereafter.

The data and methods discussed in this book can help you to understand the importance of sentiment analysis. Your journey in this field starts from here. Once you go deep in understanding these concepts, study them more, observe in real-time and practice them, your understanding of the subject, and belief will improve. As Van Tharp says, we do not trade the market, we trade our belief systems. Extraordinary performance needs extraordinary efforts and extraordinary discipline.

It is essential to remain focused. Becoming a professional trader or investor is also a process. Learn the principles of everything that you come across. When you meet an experienced trader, ask the right questions. Do not ask for his views on the market, it will not help you. Ask him how he manages trades when it is going against him or how he handles the bad phase of his systems or methods.

Relative strength and breadth analysis are the tools to outperform the market. You need to outperform other traders in terms of efforts, practice, and discipline. The market will reward a disciplined approach.

Run from people who use words like "guarantee" or claim that they make money every other day. Have rational expectations and the market will always surprise you. Have a long-term approach, even for short-term trading. Indiscipline can bring short-term success but would do more harm in the long run.

The ideas and concepts discussed in the book are mostly my work but credit goes to the Definedge development team that code my thoughts into a computer program. The TradePoint software is the flagship product of Definedge solutions and has all the tools and concepts that are discussed in this book.

If these ideas inspire you, it would be a dream come true for me personally. If this book helps you develop conviction in the subject, I will consider it as an accomplished task. If there is a Holy Grail in the market, it is your conviction in your method and approach.

Life and the market are no different from the battle of Kurukshetra in Mahabharata. Try to be Krishna and Arjuna in your life and in that of others too.

Be Krishna and do not let yourself wander. Be Arjuna by becoming a disciple with an unwavering focus!

You are welcome to write to me with queries or feedback.
My email id is prashant.shah@definedge.com
– Prashant Shah

BIBLIOGRAPHY

Aby, Carroll D. J. Point & Figure Charting: The Complete Guide. Grinville, SC: Traders Press Inc., 1996.

Bollinger, John. Bollinger on Bollinger Bands, New York, NY: McGraw-Hill, 2002.

Bulkowski, Thomas N. Encyclopaedia of Chart Patterns. New York, NY: John Wiley & Sos, Inc., 2000.

Carney, Scott M. Harmonic Trading, Volume One: Profiting from the Natural Order of the Financial Markets. FT Press; 1 edition (April 22, 2010)

Covel, Michael W. The Complete TurtleTrader. HarperCollins e-books (2009).

Dorsey, Thomas J. Point & Figure charting: The Essential Applications for Forecasting and Tracking Market Prices. Hoboken, New Jersey: John Wiley & Sons, Inc., 2007

Douglas, Mark. Trading in the Zone. Prentice-Hall Press, 2001.

Du Plessis, Jeremy, The Definitive Guide to Point and Figure: A comprehensive Guide to the Theory and Practical Use of the Point and Figure Charting Method, Petersfield: Harriman House Publishing, 2006.

Edwards, R., and J. Magee. Technical Analysis of Stock Trends, 8th ed., 2003. 1948 edition revised by W. H. C. Bassetti, St. Lucie Press, Boca Raton, FL.

Elder, Alexander. Trading for Living. New York, NY: John Wiley & Sons, Inc., 1993.

Faith, Curtis. Way of the Turtle: The Secret Methods that Turned Ordinary People into Legendary Traders. McGraw-Hill Education, 2007.

Kaufman, Perry J. Trading Systems and Methods, 3rd ed. New York, NY: John Wiley & Sons, Inc., 1998.

Kirkpatrick, Charles D., and Dahlquist, Julie R. The Complete Resource for Financial Market Technicians. New Jersey: Pearson Education, Inc., 2007

Minervini, Mark. Trade Like a Stock Market Wizard: How to Achieve Super Performance in Stocks in Any Market. McGraw-Hill Education, 2013.

Minervini, Mark. Think & Trade Like a Champion: The Secrets, Rules & Blunt Truths of a Stock Market Wizard, Access Publishing Group, LLC (2017).

Morris, George, L. The Complete Guide to Market Breadth Indicators: How to Analyze and Evaluate Market Direction and Strength, Gregory L. Morris; Second Edition (2015).

Murphy, John J., Intermarket Analysis, New Jersey: John Wiley & Sons, Inc., 2004.

Nison, Steve, Japanese Candlestick Charting Techniques, New York, NY: New York Institute of Finance, 2001.

O'Neil, William J.; O'Neil, William J. How to Make Money in Stocks: A Winning System in Good Times and Bad, Fourth Edition. McGraw-Hill Education, 4th Edition, 2009.

Pring, Martin J., Technical Analysis Explained: The Successful Investor's Guide to Spotting Investment Trends and Turning Points, McGraw-Hill, 2002.

Schwager, Jack D. Market Wizards. New York, NY: New York Institute of Finance, 1989.

Taleb, Nassim. Fooled by Randomness. Penguin, 2007.

Tharp, Van K. Trade Your Way to Financial Freedom. McGraw-Hill Education; 2nd edition., 2006.

Tharp, Van K. Definitive Guide to Position Sizing Strategies. The Van Tharp Institute, 2nd edition, 2013.

Wheelan, Alexander, Study Helps in Point and Figure Technique, Morgan Rogers and Roberts, New York, 1954 and Traders Press, Greenville, 1990.

Wilder, J. Welles Jr. New Concepts in Technical Trading Systems. Greensboro, SC: Trend Research, 1978.

Zieg, Kermit C., Point & Figure Commodity & Stock Trading Techniques, Traders Press, Greenville, 1997.

Made in the USA
Las Vegas, NV
10 December 2023

82474058R00208